Getting Along in
Family Business

Getting Along in Family Business

The Relationship
Intelligence Handbook

Edwin A. Hoover, Ph.D., CMC, and
Colette Lombard Hoover, M.S.

Routledge
New York and London

Published in 1999 by
Routledge
29 West 35th Street
New York, NY 10001

Published in Great Britain by
Routledge
11 New Fetter Lane
London EC4P 4EE

Printed in the United States of America on acid-free paper.
Designed and typeset by The Whole Works® New York City.

Library of Congress Cataloging-in-Publication Data

Hoover, Edwin A.
        Getting along in family business: the relationship intelligence handbook /
by Edwin A. Hoover and Colette Lombard Hoover.
                p.   cm.
        ISBN 0-415-92189-9
        1. Family-owned business enterprises-Management. 2. Interpersonal relations.
I. Hoover, Colette Lombard. II. Title.
HD62.25.H66   1999   98-37329
658'.045——dc21   CIP

How many things a family can be—
a nest of tenderness,
a jail for the heart,
a nursery of souls.

Families name us and define us,
give us strength, give us grief.

All our lives we struggle to embrace
or escape their influence.

They are magnets
that both hold us close and drive
us away.

George Howe Colt
Life, April 1991

Contents

Acknowledgments

In the process of writing *Getting Along in Family Business: The Relationship Intelligence Handbook*, we have learned four things about being authors:

- You are not so much a creator as a recorder and synthesizer of the many insights and experiences you have gained through your relationships with others.

- It is a wonderful and profoundly personal opportunity to contribute something about which you feel passionate.

- The arduous journey from concept to finished product is only possible because of the support, guidance, and understanding provided by business associates, family, friends, and your publisher.

- The most difficult period of writing a book is when you are between fifty and eighty percent done. Like in mountain climbing and arriving at the halfway or three-quarters point—it's too late to turn back, but you seriously wonder if you will reach your destination on time!

There are a great many people who have contributed directly and indirectly to the practical ideas and stories contained in these pages as well as to our success as a family business. We are humbled by, and deeply grateful for, the lifelong journey of learning and growing that our parents and siblings have shared with us. We are especially grateful to Ed's mom and Colette's dad. Lida Hoover was our constant cheerleader during the grueling start-up years of our business. Among many things, she provided child care, home-cooked meals, and assistance with direct mail when we needed it most. Michael Lombard, a family business founder himself, has been a business mentor, embodying so many of the sustaining values at the core of our own family business partnership and encouraging us by his fatherly interest and support.

Being copreneurs and coauthors has been shared with our immediate family, especially by our daughter Kathy. At the age of six riding in the back seat of the car, having been unable to break into her parents' front-seat conversation about "the business," Kathy reminded us of just how easy it is to ignore our most precious relationships when she finally shouted, "Hey, am I invisible or what?!" She continues to keep us focused on what is important in life. And to Merle and Barbara Jordan, our extended family and Kathy's godparents, we are grateful for their ongoing celebration of marriage and family with us. As Ed's dissertation advisor—and his first instructor in marriage and family—Merle's encouragement and editorial wisdom throughout the writing of this book gave us courage during that fifty to eighty percent completion time.

We could not have taken the book from concept to finished product without support from our publisher, Routledge. Our publishing director, Melissa Rosati, was a great collaborator and source of energy.

It was difficult to stay on top of the details of running a business for several months while writing this book. During this time it was the talent and loyalty of our staff that held everything together. A big thank you to each of them: to Linda Melnyczuk who could probably recite the book by heart after typing so many revisions; to Rita Spearman who copied, collated, and sent drafts back and forth; and to Cheryl Falardeau, our practice manager, who saw to it that clients were served by keeping us headed in the right direction.

Last, but not least, we are deeply indebted to our family business clients who have unknowingly been our partners in the writing of this book. We hope that they feel very much a part of *Getting Along in Family Business*. Without all we have experienced and learned from them, this book could never have been written.

Those who know us well, know how much we believe that our work with family businesses is a personal calling. For this special ministry, for the chance to serve others in such meaningful ways, and for the enrichment it brings to our lives, we are truly grateful to God, source of all that is good in life.

Foreword

When people meet, something new is created. When they get along they experience understanding, mutual respect, and regard; they feel safe and trusting in their relationship. This makes it possible for us to solve problems, work together harmoniously, and manage our differences in a constructive manner. Yet, day in and day out, we live our lives as if who we are and what we do and achieve are the products solely of our own handiwork. This can be especially evident in a family business where most everything hinges on how well family members get along and yet the emphasis is most often on what family employees get done.

Take a moment to write about your day yesterday—How did you live out your various roles and responsibilities? More likely than not, most of you will make a list of activities accomplished and meetings attended. For example, your morning may look like this:

- 7:30 a.m. Meeting with customer—getting new contract
- 9:00 a.m. Meeting with executive team—approved new equipment
- 10:00 a.m. Meeting with supervisors—resolving bottlenecks
- 11:15 a.m. Returned phone calls, answered correspondence, etc.

This would be an accurate description of the activities and meetings that involved your time. But do you notice what's missing? There is no mention of the relationships with all of the people who were involved with you in the activities of the day—family members, customers, employees, and friends. Even though the success or failure of your daily activities very likely depends upon your relationships, you will realize that you actually didn't give much thought to the quality of your most important relationships nor consciously take time to nurture them. The one exception might be a run-in with someone—an incident like this may have stopped you long enough to attend to what's going on in that relationship.

The truth of the matter is that it isn't the activities of the day, the way you spend your time, alone that lead to success. It is more like the old truth found in John Donne's meditation XVII, "No man is an island entire of itself, every man is a piece of the continent, a part of the main." The experience of success, or lack of it, is wrapped around relationships that are important to us. It is the quality of our relationships—those moments of interaction—that make activities energizing or draining, meaningful or meaningless. In contrast, reviewing your morning from a relationship perspective, it might look like this:

- 7:30 a.m. I started my day with Bob Smith of ABC, Inc. He was straightforward with his company's discontent with our delivery schedule and prices. I worked hard at understanding where we went wrong and what his needs were. We negotiated a win-win agreement that deals with delivery time and costs.

- 9:00 a.m. My meeting with Alice and Allen about the new equipment started out rough. Seems like family issues always have a way of creeping into business matters, but we kept moving forward and really did a good job listening to each others' perspectives. We made a good decision together.

- 10:00 a.m. Later I was able to engage the shop supervisors in a process for resolving the bottlenecks causing the late deliveries. They were very open to suggestions—mine and each other's. Because of this great team work, a plan was developed to resolve slow delivery problems and to follow up with a customer satisfaction survey. In all perspectives it was a satisfying and successful morning.

The former way of thinking about your day is focused on activities accomplished, the latter on the relationships that made it all possible. The point here is not to fill your calendar up with the details of looking at your day from a relationship perspective, but rather to make you more aware of how much thought you put into, or fail to put into, the relationships that have an impact upon who you are and what you accomplish.

Getting Along In Family Business: The Relationship Intelligence Handbook is a practical guide for business-owning families and their professional advisors. What is it that makes it possible for some families in business to work together successfully for more than a hundred years and for others to end up in litigation in an unsuccessful attempt to pass the business on to the second generation? You will be able to answer this and other questions about relationships by working your way through this book. It is our purpose to take the mystery out of what getting along in family business is all about. Basically, *getting along* is a relationship phenomenon. It is not something you do by yourself, but rather it is how effectively you interact with others.

We have created a special name to describe all the elements that go into getting along. We call it Relationship Intelligence, or RQ for short. RQ refers to the whole range of interpersonal behaviors that reflect the capacity of individuals to establish and maintain significant social, family, and work relationships. RQ is the measure of ability within a family business to:

- manage individual differences and conflicts effectively;
- engage in mutually rewarding contacts;
- preserve open and productive communication;
- adapt flexibly to changes;
- preserve a complete sense of self while being fully part of the relationship; and
- be able to create an abiding sense of trust, optimism, and respect in the relationship.

From our experience of over a decade of working closely with family businesses of all sizes and types, the Relationship Intelligence, or RQ, model has evolved as our way of understanding and strengthening the most crucial aspect of family business success—the family relationships. RQ is an integrative approach that draws together many important elements from the theories, practices, and perspectives of family, developmental, and group psychology; organizational development, business management, mediation, change management, and even human motivation. To our knowledge this is the first such integrative and comprehensive approach that addresses the two most important distinguishing characteristics of family businesses—the complexity and protracted history of their relationships.

ONE + ONE = THREE

A relationship between two people consists of three elements: two individuals plus a new creation, which is unique to them together. This is a difficult idea to grasp because it is so intangible. Let's try to make it somewhat more tangible. A baby is a cocreation of a man and a woman. In their baby, we can see each parent's individual contribution; the blue eyes like dad's, the hair that is dark and full like mom's. Yet, the individual contributions of each parent are joined into a new creation. This baby has a smile more radiant and a nose more beautiful than either parent. As she grows, the raw material of both parents is obvious in her developing temperament. She is sentimental like her mother and stubborn like her father. But again, the new creation that she is shows through, and she is more outgoing and carefree than either of her parents.

Steven Covey has written about this reality in both *The Seven Habits of Highly Effective People*,[1] and *The Seven Habits of Highly Effective Families*.[2] Covey has made a great contribution to helping us understand this difficult concept, which he calls "synergy." Synergy is the experience of one plus one equaling three in a relationship. For example, the authors do a lot of team consulting together. This means we have to "tie our minds together" about what the problem or goal is, what the best solution would be, and how best to accomplish it. Over the years through active listening, which creates mutual respect and regard, we have discovered that the best solution was not mine nor my business partner's, but ours. Real creativity has emerged as an option neither of us considered alone, but rather it is the third option we discovered together.

This is the experience of synergy. . . the whole is greater than the sum of its parts—a new part in and of itself. Synergy can only be created in a relationship characterized by trust, optimism, and respect. Every relationship you have throughout life has a life of its own that is more than the simple combination of you and the other person as individuals.

Our best work with business-owning families is when we can get them to look at things in a new way, which later we will discuss as changing their *Relationship Paradigm*; their beliefs and prejudices about the way things are. In doing this and by learning to communicate in an open and productive manner, we find that what at first seems impossible to change is most often more possible than first believed. The following brief story will demonstrate this point:

> A second generation business owner in his early sixties called for help. "I'm stumped," he said. "Look at this, I have developed two estate plans with two different attorneys which address how to pass the business on to our children." Hearing his frustration, we asked, "So, what's the problem?" "Well, my sons don't like either plan and now my wife won't talk to me. She thinks I'm not being fair."

Through a series of questions and careful listening the three of us discovered the real problem. Bill, the business owner, worked with his attorney in a closet. Not literally in a closet . . . but he never took time to talk with his wife or his sons about their goals, expectations, and desires. His paradigm was that estate and succession planning was something that he had the responsibility to do alone. We worked with him, his spouse, and his sons to increase their RQ, thus enhancing their ability to get along, to share openly, and to look for options no one individual had thought of. This eventually brought a win-win solution. In this particular situation, business ownership was split with each son taking ownership of one of the two locations. They needed to work out a number of partnering covenants, policies, and procedures, especially since both sons wanted to continue business under the family name. The family name was not only a legacy each was proud of, but gave the business a distinct image, history, and marketing advantage. Not until they each understood the needs and expectations of the others were they ready to work with their attorneys to draw up the necessary legal documents.

This story demonstrates how central relationships are, especially when we relate to others in multiple roles in a family business. For example, my dad may also be my boss or supervisor and my siblings may be my business partners and co-owners of the family enterprise. These multiple relationships with family members increase the complexity of dealing with expectations . . . which sometimes conflict with one another. Our happiness, health, and productivity depend upon how well we develop the skills and abilities necessary to keep our relationships in alignment. Managing these relationships becomes the very foundation of our success. We will be discussing specific ways to assess the effectiveness of your relationships and what to do to enhance your family's RQ in the chapters ahead.

OVERVIEW

The book is organized into three sections. Chapters 1 through 4 answer questions as to why relationships are as important as they are in family business, how RQ offers an important new way of understanding them, and ways to improve relationships through the application of the principles and practices of Relationship Intelligence. Chapters 5 and 6 discuss methods for assessing RQ in family business, determining what next steps and resources are needed to develop stronger RQ, and developing the necessary management, family, and ownership structures to support the development. Chapters 7 through 10 focus on four specific areas of family business relationship management that are closely related to the development of RQ and the successful operation of a family business: philosophy of ownership, ethical dilemmas, leadership, and working with advisors/consultants. To provide an overview of the terrain that we will cover in the ten chapters of *Getting Along in Family Business: The Relationship Intelligence Handbook,* here are highlights of each one.

Chapter 1, **The Business of Relationships**, presents the fact that relationships are the language of family business and discusses several common false assumptions about this fact. Congruency within the relationships is a primary measure of health for a family business. The most important question is not the one frequently asked as to whether yours is a family-first or a business-first family business, but whether yours is a relationship-first family business. The solutions to the vast majority of problems and the opportunities for improvement are to be found, first and foremost, within the web of relationships from which every family business is built.

Chapter 2, **Understanding Relationship Intelligence**, discusses RQ as a type of intelligence that goes beyond intellectual intelligence (IQ) and the more recent notion of emotional intelligence (EQ) developed by Daniel Goleman.[3] Relationship Intelligence is not intelligence about relationships but rather the intelligence of relationships. It is the *shared creation* of the members of the family business group, and the level of RQ is specific to every relationship just as IQ and EQ are specific to every individual. The two interdependent dimensions of RQ are *relationship paradigm* and *relationship skill*, and the RQ Matrix provides specifics as to how they interact.

Chapter 3, **When Family and Business Meet: The Relationship Intelligence Challenge**, provides further details as to why and how

RQ has special meaning to family businesses. Family businesses are distinguished from nonfamily businesses in two important ways: first, they are comprised of a complex network of family relationships, and second, those relationships have a history that reaches back not only to childhood but also across generations. The former reflects the fact that every family business is made up of the three domains of family, business, and ownership among which there are different and conflicting measures of success. The reality is that in family businesses *there are constant compromises being made* among the domains, and there is a constant need to adjust to changes occurring within those relationships. The ultimate goal is to strive for the best possible alignment among them. But this is always a moving target, and RQ is the essential ingredient in hitting it. The positive message of RQ is that relationship dynamics are never cast in stone and can always be improved with the right understanding and effort.

Chapter 4, **Improving Relationship Intelligence,** discusses the four principles of RQ and, in detail, the important tools and methods for improving RQ in the family business by building a more positive relationship paradigm and a higher level of relationship skill. One of the greatest barriers to higher RQ is the lack of motivation on the part of family members. Understanding and increasing motivation, along with keeping expectations and commitments fresh and viable, are essential to improving RQ. LSi's Relationship Roadmap, the guide for relationship renewal, and LSi's Paradigm Kaleidoscope, the lens through which to view and redefine beliefs and prejudices about relationships, are explained and illustrated. Several specific and proven tools for improving RQ are also discussed, including Partnering Covenants, communication that creates understanding and builds self-esteem, and issue (versus problem) management.

Chapter 5, **Assessing Your RQ,** tells you how to evaluate your family business in terms of your level of RQ and what you need to do to improve it. Inquiry-based evaluation is discussed as one method for evaluating RQ on the basis of questions about, and observations of, the relationships in the family business. In addition, the RQ Questionnaire is a paper-and-pencil evaluation that provides a quantitative assessment of your level of RQ. Used together, the two methods provide the most reliable evaluation. Advisors/consultants can use the inquiry-based method when the RQ Questionnaire cannot be completed. Implications of your assessment for where and how to improve RQ are presented.

Chapter 6, **The Architecture of Family Business**, provides a detailed discussion of the important organizational structures needed to achieve optimum alignment between family, business, and ownership. The theory behind the structures is presented and specific suggestions and models are offered for establishing a Family Forum, Board of Directors, and Shareholders' Council. The primary organizational and planning tasks of each structure are also presented in detail with actual illustrations from family businesses doing them. Given the fact that family businesses are increasingly being led by co-CEOs, special consideration is given to the Office of the President as a way of organizing at the CEO level.

Chapter 7, **Promoting RQ through Stewardship**, discusses the single most important factor behind successful multigenerational family businesses: their perspective on the meaning of ownership. Every family business that has made it beyond the third generation has developed their version of ownership as a responsibility of stewardship rather than as a privilege of proprietorship. Ownership accountability is directly related to this as well. The chapter presents The Six Principles of Stewardship and how to use them to evaluate your family's ownership perspective.

Chapter 8, **Ethical Dilemmas in the Family Business**, covers one of the most frequent sources of conflict in family business. No, it isn't when one person is right and the other is wrong, it is when both are right but their positions are incompatible or mutually exclusive. Although we know how to deal with right-versus-wrong situations—gather evidence to defend our position and prove the other position wrong—we don't know how to deal with right versus right issues. Much conflict in family business grows out of right versus right issues being turned into right versus wrong because we don't know how to deal with them otherwise.

Chapter 9, **Leadership in the Family Business**, focuses on the unique challenges and opportunities of leadership in the family business. Just being a good leader is not enough when it comes to leading a family company. The primary challenges that uniquely face leadership in the family business—for example, reinforcing alignment among the three relationship domains of the family, management, and owners—are presented. The characteristics of effective family business leadership are discussed, including the three styles of leadership: push, pull, and centered. Tools for developing centered family business leadership are presented.

Chapter 10, **RQ and Working with Family Businesses**, applies the principles and practices of RQ to the relationship between advisors/consultants and family businesses. Too often, families in business and their advisors think of the relationship as one in which the advisor/ consultant does something for, rather than with, the family business. Regardless of how knowledgeable and skilled the advisor/consultant is and how desperate the family business is for assistance, the success of their work together depends upon the level of RQ in the family business advisory relationship. RQ is likewise the key ingredient in the success of collaborative relationships among advisors/consultants working together with a family business. A new model of interprofessional collaboration is presented. Tools and methods for enhancing RQ in both the family business advisory relationship and in interprofessional collaboration are discussed.

Each chapter of *Getting Along in Family Business: The Relationship Intelligence Handbook* contains questions for reflection (QFRs) for use by the reader and by the family together in thinking about and discussing the key elements presented. For advisors/consultants and students the QFRs allow you the opportunity to "get inside the heads" of families in business and think about RQ in the ways we suggest they do. In addition, we suggest that advisors/consultants use the QFR's to think about their family business clients, how RQ could help them understand their work in new ways, and how it could enhance the effectiveness of their family business advisory relationships.

IS THIS BOOK FOR YOU?

This book is a practical relationship guide for business-owning families and professional advisors/consultants who work with them. We hope it will spark discussion for family meetings and be used as an essential tool in developing advisory relationships. It can also provide an excellent resource to family business management programs offered through many universities today. Our goal is to present, in user-friendly terms, understanding, tools, and methods families in business can effectively use for:

- managing differences, conflicts, and false agreement;
- clarifying and renegotiating expectations and commitments;
- improving communication, respect, trust, and problem-solving methods;
- understanding change and improving flexibility;
- remapping family relationship paradigms;
- creating the organizational structures and management mechanisms to support success in a family business; and
- working effectively with advisors and consultants.

Likewise, the success of professionals who work with family businesses depends upon the level of RQ they develop with their clients. It is essential that they understand the special relationship challenges that business-owning families face. Attorneys, accountants, insurance agents, bankers, and others also must understand the complexity of the family business and find ways to blend technical advising with relationship management. Brilliant technical solutions in estate planning—as we saw in the story above—are wasted when the professional gets trapped in family dynamics and conflicts among the family, business, and ownership expectations and concerns.

We have included guidelines for working with advisors and a model for advisors brave enough to work out interprofessional collaboration. Since very little has been written on interprofessional collaboration, we believe this will enhance the quality of advisory relationships for the business-owning family and the advisors themselves.

So if *getting along in family business* and understanding how to help yourself or others do just that is important to you, we invite you to follow along chapter by chapter. As stated before, our purpose is to take the mystery out of what getting along in family business really means. This will be accomplished by helping you to understand what makes and breaks relationships and by presenting practical tools and methods for creating excellent family business relationships, whether that be with family, advisors, employees—really anyone important to you. Enjoy your journey through *Getting Along in Family Business: The Relationship Intelligence Handbook*. We welcome hearing your comments about how these ideas help you as a family business raise the level of your family's RQ, as an advisor improve your family business advisory relationships, and as a student in understanding this wonderful and rich subject. We also encourage and invite your questions and ideas for further application.

Edwin A. Hoover
Colette Lombard Hoover

Notes
1. Stephen R. Covey. *The Seven Habits of Highly Effective People*. New York: Simon & Schuster, 1989.
2. Stephen R. Covey. *The Seven Habits of Highly Effective Families*. New York: Golden Books, 1997.
3. Daniel Goleman. *Emotional Intelligence*. New York: Bantam Books, 1995.

1 The Business of Relationships

INTRODUCTION

Above all else, family business is the business of relationships. Ask a family employee, a professional advisor to family businesses, even a casual reader of the *Wall Street Journal*, and there will be consensus that the biggest factor in the success or failure of a family business is the relationships between family members. The intensity that this reality creates is demonstrated by the following story:

> Two attorneys who had been working for some time to resolve a very difficult family business problem and had run out of ideas, sat down to discuss what to do next. One of them said, "As I see it there are really only two alternative solutions; one is logical and rational, and the other would be a miracle. The logical, rational solution is that an angel will suddenly appear from heaven, float down and sprinkle angel dust over this family and make the problems all go away. . . .The miracle would be that these people could just sit down for more than five minutes and talk to each other like civil human beings!!"

Yes, relationships are at the heart of family business. When things go well it's an awesome opportunity, but when there are problems it is just simply awful. There is little middle ground in family business, and everything is at stake: personal well-being, family life, financial security, and even standing in the community. While family business successors or new founders are more prepared today with the business and management knowledge they need to deal with a competitive global marketplace, the need for relationship knowledge and skill is often ignored. Most people simply "wing it" when it comes to managing relationships. They rely on what they learned from family and others when growing up. Every time we see a par-

1

ent slap a child and tell him to quit hitting his brother, we see one more negative lesson in relationship skill training.

The greatest threat to the long-term survival and success of any family business has less to do with what's going on outside with customers, competitors and technology, than it does with what's going on inside with relationships among the key players, especially among family members. Is the very idea of "family business" an oxymoron? Some people would argue that it is. Comparing it to other terms like "government service" and "giant shrimp," they say that the two words "family" and "business" are contradictory and mutually exclusive. They argue that business relationships and family relationships are each complicated enough by themselves, and impossible when put together. Thus, the commonly heard admonition, "Don't ever go into business with relatives!" While we do not agree with these sentiments, we can certainly understand how others have drawn this conclusion. Life and relationships for those within a business-owning family are indeed more complex and challenging. The business is like another family member that has immense and often unrecognized impact on the family's expectations, prejudices, patterns of interactions, values, lifestyle, and worldview.

The interdependence of family and business is what makes a family business different. A big city is different from a rural hamlet, piloting an airplane is different from piloting a ship, and parenting a teenager is different from parenting a toddler. A family in business is different from one that isn't. A business owned by a family is different from one that is publicly owned. We're not talking about better or worse, good or bad, just different. That difference lies in the fact that every family business joins two very different kinds of organizations: a family and a business. This is a combination that creates something bigger than either the family or business alone can account for. The joining of a family and business produces a new reality, the family business, a combination that incorporates each. Together in the family business, both the family and business travel a journey that either one alone would never experience.

DEFINING THE DIFFERENCE: WHAT IS A FAMILY BUSINESS?

What really defines a business as a family business? This seems like a simple enough question, but the answer is not obvious to everyone, as the following brief scenario demonstrates. Many years ago we received a call from a young man who sounded desperate. He began the conversation by saying he worked in a family business and felt he and his father needed help in succession planning. He went on to say that he had been passing our newsletters on to his father with no response and wondered if we would initiate a call to his father in the hope that a meeting could be set up. While not our usual practice, we agreed to make the call to his father, but only to inquire if he had been receiving our newsletter and had found it useful. Later that day one of us made the call and found the father in his office. "Mr. Jones, I believe you have been receiving our newsletters, and I am calling to see if you find the information useful." We knew that Mr. Jones's reply was not what his son would want to hear. "Yes, I have seen it. Somebody, I'm not sure who, has been putting them on my desk . . . but you know we're not a family business." There was only one question left to ask: "Don't you have other family members in the company?" To which Mr. Jones said, "I do. My son works here, but he *just* works here. If it got out that I thought we were a family business, my employees would all leave!"

Experiences like this have sometimes led us to say that a family business is like beauty, it's all in the eye of the beholder. Over the years we have also said that a family business is a business that is owned and managed by members of one or more families. The first definition is too vague and the second does not adequately deal with the second- or third-generation family businesses now owned by one family member. Some second- and third-generation businesses consider themselves "family businesses" because of the family's continuing pride and emotional attachment even when only one family member is involved. These businesses may still anticipate other family members' involvement in future years.

A good definition of anything should reflect the characteristics that make it different from everything else. With this in mind, that which differentiates family businesses from all others is the unavoidable blending of the dynamics of both the business and the family. Therefore, the definition we have settled on is one that fully takes into account the reality that successful family business is synonymous with successful relationships:

> A family business is any business in which business and family relationships have a significant impact on each other.

It is the interdependency of family and business dynamics that offers the litmus test of whether a business is a "family business." Our definition points to the key dynamic present in every family business: family members are economically dependent upon one another, and the business is linked strategically to the quality of family relationships. It also incorporates a range of situations from multigenerational family firms with hundreds of family owners to single generation husband and wife, sibling, and cousin family businesses with only a handful of owners.

For some of you, family business is a fact of life, meaning you have a business enterprise in which multiple family members are directly involved. You didn't start out with a plan to create a family business, it just happened. For others, family business is a fact of choice, meaning you are the owner/manager of a company and dream of the day when children or other family members will join you. Whether you are a family business as a fact of life, or a fact of choice, *Getting Along in Family Business: The Relationship Intelligence Handbook* is your guide to making it work.

FALSE ASSUMPTIONS

Because family businesses present a set of unique complexities, a number of false assumptions can easily get imbedded in how a business-owning family view themselves and interpret the challenges they face. These false assumptions are detrimental to business-owning families who need to be encouraged to work with the complexities, instead of denying their significance.

False Assumption #1
All we need to do is learn how to communicate better.
••

In a conversation with the daughter of a family agricultural business she said, "My parents don't see any need for outside help. They think we should just sit down and talk to one another. We did that last December—there were hugs and 'I'm sorry,' but the problem is still there. We're stepping on each other's toes and everyone runs this business like it's their own." Learning how to communicate has become a catch-all phrase that purports to solve all relationship ills in family business. It usually follows on the heels of people complaining about not knowing what's going on, or people avoiding each other, or people withholding information to protect power and control. We see communication breakdowns most frequently as a symptom of something else that has gone awry in the relationship.

Don't get us wrong, we are firm believers in the importance of learning how to communicate. Being a skilled communicator doesn't just happen. Communication is a fundamental tool in all good relationships. However, the rush to diagnose relationship breakdowns simply as a lack of communication can lead to solutions that are temporary at best and can lead to further demoralization when they don't work.

False Assumption #2
The biggest problem around here is the clash of egos!
••

How often have we heard, "Dad will never retire. This business is a big ego trip for him," or "My children don't want to *work* for success, but are always clambering to take individual credit for the good that's accomplished." All healthy and productive people have strong egos, they like themselves, value their abilities, and take pride in their accomplishments. That's the way it should be. The job of every parent is to develop children with healthy egos, right? Why then are personal egos such a problem in family business? Wouldn't it seem that a collection of strong egos would foster a strong company? What the term "clash of egos" usually refers to is an unnecessary and destructive competitive relationship characterized by the belief that when one person wins, another will lose. The assumption is that there is not enough recognition or opportunity for everyone to share in. The truth is that clash of egos is hardly ever the real problem. The real problem is that trust, respect, and optimism in the relationship have broken down. Competition and win-lose battles are misguided attempts to resolve a problem by individual force when the only lasting solution requires everybody's participation.

False Assumption #3
The answer/solution is simple. We just need to
really care about each other.
••

While caring about each other is an essential ingredient to getting along, it does not displace the inevitable tension and friction that develop when family members work together. Family members have been known to say to each other, "I care about you, I just don't like you very much!" All too often, families in business place an impossible burden on family love, loyalty, and caring. They believe it is like a huge reservoir of good will that will always be there to draw on. Positive and caring family relationships are a necessary but not sufficient cause for family business success. Caring creates the motivation to deal with the complexities of running a business, but it doesn't provide the solutions. Likewise, family relationships must be maintained, but are far too often taken for granted and left unattended until they fracture under the pressure of dealing with business problems.

False Assumption #4
Who's to blame?
• • • • • • • • • • • • • • • • •

The reason "Who's to blame?" is a false assumption is that it is never possible to find the first cause in any relationship event. Cause and effect are mutually reinforcing when it comes to relationships. Your brother yelled at you in the office because you decided not to deliver the report you promised. You made that decision because your brother told you that if you didn't sign the buy-sell agreement your minority ownership would be worthless in the future. Your brother precipitated the showdown over the buy-sell agreement because you announced at the board meeting that you were giving all your shares to your son who is a street musician in San Francisco . . . and so on. Where did the problem start, what caused this ongoing series of confrontations, who is to blame? No one will ever know because the truth is that in relationships every effect becomes another cause producing another effect. It is a circular, not a linear process as we learned in school. The assumption that someone is to blame, is the originator of a problem, will always result in either a false accusation or a biased solution. Solving relationship problems means beginning with the understanding that everyone involved is both a recipient and a perpetrator. If there is cause to blame—it must be shared. You've heard the old saying, "If you're not part of the solution, then you're part of the problem."

False Assumption #5
Everything's going fine, we never
have conflict.
• •

Lack of conflict is not a sign that everything is well; it is just as often an indication that people have gotten numb to its effects. It's similar to dropping a frog in a pan of hot water. Everyone knows that the poor frog will jump frantically doing everything possible to escape. But what happens if you put the same frog in a pan of water at room temperature and then gradually turn up the heat? That same frog, being the cold blooded creature it is, will gradually adjust to the increasing temperature and make no effort to escape. That frog will literally cook to death in the water making no attempt to escape. Substitute conflict in your family business with the water in the frog's pan. Drop an outsider into it and the poor individual will jump and scream and do everything to escape. But put family members together and gradually turn up the intensity of conflict over time, and they will get used to it until it destroys them.

False Assumption #6
We'll never be able to work well together,
we're just too different.
●●●

How many times have we heard this one? "That's just the way I am, you'll have to accept me, I can't change." Differences between us is not a condition that inevitably produces relationship disharmony; it is a normal element in relationships that potentially can produce every form of creativity. As one man said of his brother with whom he had been in business, "We were as different as night and day: I was always seeing the light at the end of the tunnel and he was always blowing it out!" Blaming the breakdown of family relationships on the differences between people is like blaming gray hair on getting old. If you don't manage aging well, then gray hair is an enemy; but if you do, it is a sign of maturity and wisdom. If you don't manage interpersonal differences well, they pull you apart; but if you do, they give you leverage and perspective you otherwise wouldn't have.

False Assumption #7
We can't worry about getting along, we've
got to focus on the bottom line.
●●●

The corollary to this false assumption is another one: As long as the bottom line is O.K., we have nothing to worry about. Remember the frog in False Assumption #5? It's back! The fallacy in this assumption is that there are no hard costs associated with the breakdown in relationships, nor definitive gains to be gotten when people are getting along. The following scenario should dispel this myth. It isn't unusual, when conflict is intense, to find key family executives consuming an hour every day fighting, cooling off, dealing with noncooperation, avoiding each other, and commiserating with other employees about what an idiot "so and so" is. That's conservatively five hours a week or 12.5 percent of productive work time available. When each of three people cost the business $200,000 a year in salary and benefits, this translates into a direct cost of $75,000 ($600,000 x 12.5%) in lost productivity just for these three people. Of course, the total cost to productivity is even greater, by at least twice, or $150,000, because of the distracting and negative spillover onto other managers and employees. Family relationships are a monumental bottom line issue in family business both directly and in opportunity costs. Yet how much time and money do we spend on repairing or renewing our relationships with family?

False Assumption #8

As long as we keep family matters and business issues totally separate, we will never have problems.

• •

For businesses that have been burned by family dynamics and for families that have been wrenched by business battles, there is no more sincere plea than to keep the two separate and distinct. But the truth is that separating family matters from business issues in a family business is like unscrambling eggs.

Some years ago, a client called and said he needed a third opinion. His mother had some business assets—pieces of valuable artwork—in her home. He wanted to make sure these were "earmarked" in her will to be returned to the business upon her death. Wishing that he could separate family and business, he already received two opinions about how to handle the situation. His partner said, "This is a business issue, have your lawyer write up an agreement and deliver it to your mother to sign." His wife said, "No way . . . she's your mother. At least go and talk to her first—this is a family not a business matter." So he said, "What do you think—is this a family or a business matter?" Our response was, "*Yes*." Yes, it was a family and a business matter, and that needs to be considered when deciding how to deal with it. The fact of the economic interdependence that ties family members and business so tightly together cannot be avoided. The negative side of this reality is that there are inevitable compromises that must be made to accommodate the differing and competing needs of family and business. The positive side is that business-owning families have access to opportunities not available to their nonbusiness counterparts. Businesses owned by families benefit from a legacy and devotion not available to their nonfamily counterparts. Keeping family and business *totally* separate is not only an impossibility but also it misses the fact that when combined correctly family and business can be a powerful and positive mixture.

QFRs Questions for Reflection

- Which of the eight false assumptions applies to your family business?
- How are false assumptions affecting the way you handle relationships? Think of specific situations that illustrate your answer.
- Do different generations have different false assumptions?

How might this affect the relationship between the generations?

• What is the likelihood that your false assumptions will
  change? What will it take to change them?

IT ALL COMES BACK TO THE RELATIONSHIPS

Every one of the false assumptions we have presented is based on
two fundamental facts that govern relationships. The first is that
whenever we build and participate in a relationship, something new
and unique is created. The second is that when we get along in our
relationships, that is, when we experience enjoyment and reciproci-
ty in achieving mutually beneficial goals, we are blessed by success
together. Every relationship has a life of its own. It is a new creation,
meaning it is more than the simple combination of you and the other
person as individuals. You have experienced this new creation in
those relationships where you can say, "None of us could have done
this alone." Many family businesses were successfully built by two
partners and failed when one of them left or died because the success of the business was an outgrowth of the new creation of their
relationship. This is the central truth about relationships in family
business, the all-encompassing reality that your family business will
rise or fall based on how you handle your relationships.

STRIVING FOR RELATIONSHIP CONGRUENCY

The two key elements for which congruency is most essential are the
same two ingredients present in every relationship: attitude and aptitude. Simply defined, relationship congruency means that these two
elements fit well and easily together in mutually beneficial ways. On
the other hand, relationship incongruency means that the key elements in the relationship conflict and compete with one another in
ways that are mutually detrimental. Relationship incongruency is
the source of a vast array of difficulties and conflict in business relationships. Let's take a closer look at attitude and aptitude as the two
key ingredients that create quality in our relationships.

Attitude consists of the feelings, intentions, and aspirations
that are present in a relationship. Attitude provides the motivation
and passion in a relationship, and it must be consistent with the
long-term goals of the relationship. Take marriage for example. In a
successful marriage, an attitude based on love, lifelong commitment,
willingness to give and take, and the desire to grow old together is

consistent with the goal of a lifelong marriage commitment. There is congruency between the attitude and the long-term goal. A significant reversal of this attitude into indifference, conditional commitment, and self-centeredness creates incongruity with the goal of a lifelong marriage commitment and parallels similar patterns in family business.

The second ingredient that determines the quality of a relationship is aptitude. Aptitude consists of the relationship skills and abilities that are present in the relationship. These must be congruent with the tasks, functions, and responsibilities that take place in the relationship. Take the parent-child relationship for example. In every successful parent-child relationship the parents' ability to communicate, create safety, plan for the future, maintain appropriate accountability, and establish age-appropriate boundaries is consistent with a relationship designed to develop a happy, healthy, independent, and successful child. A significant deficit in these relationship skills and abilities will make it difficult to fulfill these tasks, functions, and responsibilities.

Incongruency in aptitude typically occurs when the nature of the relationship changes, making obsolete the relationship abilities that used to work. Continuing with the parent-child analogy, when the child becomes a teenager, the particular parenting skills and abilities that worked previously must be changed. Attempting to parent a fifteen-year-old the same way you did a five-year-old simply does not work.

Congruency problems anywhere within the relationship interactions can curtail and completely sidetrack the final results. Congruency within relationships must be monitored, evaluated, and corrected every step of the way. Every minor incongruency will inevitably mushroom into a major relationship breakdown. You can count on it.

QFRs

- Where do you think there is congruency and incongruency of attitude (among the feelings, intentions, desires, and the long-term goals) in your family business? (Be specific.)

- Where do you think there is congruency and incongruency of aptitude (among tasks, functions, responsibilities, skills, and abilities) in your family business? (Be specific.)

RELATIONSHIP-FIRST FAMILY BUSINESS

"Is yours a family-first, or a business-first, family business?" This is a question often posed to business-owning families in seminars and workshops. The question is meant to challenge participants to think about whether they put family concerns above business or business concerns above family in operating their businesses. It is a useful exercise that can help focus on core principles and guidelines a family business operates by. On the other hand, the dichotomy of family-first versus business-first is much too black and white. To label a family business as one or the other fails to take into account how both business and family change over time.

More important, to suggest that a family in business must choose between being either a family-first or a business-first family business is an unnecessarily forced dichotomy. If you say, "Of course we love each other and our family relationships are the most important relationships in the world," then you must conclude, "I guess we must be a family-first family business." Or, if you say, "We have to run this business like a business, we can't put family above the well-being of the company," then you must conclude, "I guess we must be a business-first family business." In either situation you may be left with an unwanted and uncomfortable impression that the other side of the dichotomy doesn't matter. To be stuck in one side or the other, or to have these as the only options is not healthy in the long-term.

There is a third choice that is relationship based and firmly rooted in our definition of family business. Every family business needs to be a "relationship-first" family business. At first, this seems a lot like "family-first" but it is actually very different when you recall what we have been saying about relationships. Remember that a family business is a living entity that joins together the dynamics of both family and business. This brings to life a new creation, as we discussed earlier. Something new is created when a family and a business are in a long-term, interdependent relationship. *A new relationship is created where the boundaries of family and business intermingle. This is what makes a business-owning family different.* Business-owning families know the difference. They see it at conventions and trade shows where family business people migrate toward one another. As one of our clients said many years ago, "At trade shows we family business people always wind up together by the end of the week . . . we understand each other, we don't have to draw pictures." A relationship-first family business is one in which there is a deep sensitivity and understanding of the fact that decisions are often a compromise between family and business. There also is a great appreciation that both the family and the business are more than either would be by itself.

BUSINESS VS. RELATIONSHIPS

In the world of family business, relationship issues are often pitted against business issues in a way that is unfortunate. In terms that are neither complimentary nor understanding, it is not uncommon to have relationship issues in family business referred to as the "Kleenex box issues," and the "touchy-feelie issues." For some, these descriptions belie a discomfort with sensitive, emotional, and psychological relationship problems. For others, the descriptions represent a disparagement of such problems as if those that suffer them lack maturity or sophistication. But for others who are more enlightened and tolerant the descriptions simply imply that relationship issues are different from, and inherently more difficult to deal with, than the so-called "hard," "practical," and "quantifiable" issues of business operations. We refer to relationship issues as the "soft issues" to distinguish them from technical problems or solutions.

It is often said that "accounting is the language of business," an adage to which many MBAs, accountants, and other business professionals, not to mention family business owners, subscribe. This principle often occupies center stage when it comes to how a business is viewed and what skills are considered essential to its ongoing success. This statement contains an element of truth that is not to be underestimated. An important way to measure success and failure in business is with the scorecard of revenues, expenses, and profit.

Approached from this perspective alone however, next generation successors and current generation owners and managers are told that the most basic set of tools they must master are knowing how to read financial statements and how to understand key financial ratios related to performance. This is an important perspective, but it is not the most important when it comes to long-term success and survival in family business. Accounting or numbers are a scorecard, nothing more or less until they are vested with meaning and purpose. When numbers become attached to the fulfillment of a vision or the experience of a defeat, the satisfaction of accomplishment or the dismay of failure, then they mean something. This is when numbers leap off the page and create energy, motivation, and enjoyment, or their opposites.

THE LANGUAGE OF FAMILY BUSINESS

Relationships are the language of family business. This is a universal truth in the world of family business. Whether the family business is a tool and die shop in Chicago, a bank in Brussels, a newspaper conglomerate in Dusseldorf, a leather and perfume company in Paris, or a spice manufacturer in Tokyo; this principle is at the heart of their success or failure.

One of the oldest family business stories with which we are familiar is close to two thousand years old. It is the parable of the prodigal son from the Bible. The story is first and foremost about love and forgiveness, but it is also a story about relationships and how difficult they become when individual self-interest wins out over common interest. It is a story about reconciliation and the importance of remembering that relationships form the big picture into which everything else ultimately will have to fit. Everyone in family business is intimately familiar with the presence and power of divisive self-interest and the necessity of common interest. In every family business the big picture is formed by the relationships into which the business fits, not vice versa.

FAMILY BUSINESS—"THE TIE THAT BINDS"

Unique to family businesses is the fact that relationships are built around both family and economic interdependence. This interdependence is at the heart of family business. We call it the "tie that binds" because it not only joins people together, it sets up major constraints to their freedom to exit. Even for a financially successful and profitable family business, this interdependence can result in much misery, unhappiness, and conflict. We often hear professional advisors to family businesses: attorneys, accountants, bankers, insurance agents, and others say, "It's such a shame, they should be celebrating what they have, but all they do is fight like cats and dogs. . . . They're all such nice people individually, I don't get it. It will all be lost if this keeps up!"

Yes financial performance and consistent monetary success are necessary to business. After all, no margin – no mission. But it is only a necessary, not a sufficient formula to ultimate success in any family business. *Relationships are the language of family business*: the court battle among the family members who control Koch Industries (based in Wichita, Kansas) is a case in point. Koch Industries, founded by Frederick Koch, Sr. during the late 1920s is today the second largest privately held business in the United States with revenues of $35 billion. The four current generation Koch brothers became embroiled in a costly and destructive court battle over money and control. The judge in the case issued the opinion that "The case is obviously driven by family spite and is undeterred by general financial considerations."[1] The article concludes, "Whatever the outcome at trial, it seems unlikely the Koch brothers' long divorce will become final. In October, William is bringing another lawsuit against Koch Industries in federal court . . . seeking $1 billion over allegations that the company steals oil from Indians. . . . The proving ground might have changed since the Koch brothers pounded on each other as boys, often instigated, William says, by Charles, but the sibling rivalry remains unsettled."

Though the magnitude of the financial issues may be nowhere near what it is for the Koch family, and the interpersonal rancor nowhere near as vicious, such unfortunate situations can be found throughout the world of family business.

Family business problems generally don't arise out of the blue overnight. They begin as a glimmering awareness that things aren't quite right. Business discussions increasingly have a tense edge to them. Sidebar conversations become more frequent. People start looking over their shoulders more and feeling less tolerant of ideas that affect them. Things are not as they used to be, but nobody talks about it nor takes the time to explore and clarify just how changes have affected what they can expect of each other. Change piles on top of change, misunderstanding on top of misunderstanding, partial resolution on top of partial resolution. No one intends for things to get bad. People hold back from bringing issues up in order to keep the peace, but it doesn't work. In fact the more the problems are avoided, the greater they become, not immediately but over time. The need to find solutions to the relationship struggles that infect family businesses is so universal and so prevalent that it could easily be the number one need of family enterprise.

THE SOLUTIONS ARE IN OUR RELATIONSHIPS

We frequently deal with clients that are experiencing a severe breakdown of relationships. The level of stress and anxiety is high and the volume of finger pointing and blame unbearable. In these situations, somebody will almost inevitably raise with us the question of whether another person is one brick short of a load, the culprit, the fly in the ointment. Our response is almost always the same. While mental illness and substance abuse are diseases that affect families in business, just as they do all families, the problem this family is having is not because of mental illness or substance abuse in most cases. It is because there are some major deficiencies in the relationships among people, and these will always make somebody, if not everybody, look (and probably feel) a little crazy.

It is easy to fix blame on an individual, but it never helps in finding a solution to the problem. We once worked with a father and son who had become locked in mortal combat over the father's sale of the business to the son. When they came to see us, the father was convinced that the problem was his greedy, self-entitled, and arrogant son, who had been a problem kid since the age of sixteen. The son was convinced that the problem was his father, who was controlling, overdemanding, and simply couldn't face letting go of the business.

The interesting thing, though not at all uncommon in our experience, was that even though very angry with each other, both the father and the son told us separately how miserable they felt about the breakdown of their relationship. Both were especially grieved by how this was affecting the son's children, who hadn't seen their grandfather in over a year. In conversations between them they each came across in ways that certainly provided evidence for the other's indictments. The father appeared unyielding and the son uncaring. To focus on each of them and their individual contributions to this battle would have proved futile to getting them unstuck.

The problem became unlocked though, when we pointed out to them that they were struggling with a very fundamental relationship problem. It involved both of them, but was bigger than the two of them. It went like this: As the seller of the business, the father needed to make sure he never had to worry about financial security again. But it was his son who was putting up the cash to buy the business. Dad's need as the seller of a business was in direct conflict with his fatherly desire to see his son get the business he wanted at the best price possible. The son indeed wanted to get the business without having to mortgage away the next twenty years of his life and drain capital from the company. When he also took into consideration his twelve years of sweat equity in the business, it seemed reasonable that he should get it for less than the market value. His desire was legitimate as the buyer of a business, but it was in direct conflict with his family wish to see his father rewarded, to the maximum, for years of hard work and sacrifice.

Their conflict had its genesis in this very basic relationship dilemma. As family members, they had a relationship with very different rules and expectations compared to their business relationship as seller and buyer of a business. In addition, they did not have the communication skills or the problem-solving tools needed to get to the bottom and solve it. They came to realize that the real problem wasn't an evil force in the other person, but conflicting goals and expectations within each of them that were having a negative impact on the relationship. Based on this they were not only able to complete the sales transaction, but family relationships were restored as well.

Their attorneys and accountant attempted several times to work out a solution by adjusting the terms of the sale to appeal to the individual needs of the other side. One proposal was to quantify the son's contributions to the business. This could be accomplished by deducting that from the sales price in exchange for a windfall profit provision in the contract, which would pay the father extra if the business grew more than expected over the next ten years. It didn't fly. This and other similar efforts were unsuccessful because they hadn't addressed the underlying relationship problem. In and of themselves, these technical solutions may have worked, but only after relationship issues were addressed.

As we said earlier, the vast majority of family business problems come from a lack of alignment between attitude, aptitude, goals, and relationship skills. There is a parallel in the field of mental health related to the cause of mental and emotional distress. Here too, the focus of attention, up to forty years ago, was the individual. The causes and treatment of depression, stress, anxiety, and the more severe forms of mental disorder focused on the individual. Even marriage and family were often treated by trying to locate the "mentally ill" individuals and getting them better. The tide turned when some psychologists and psychiatrists began to wonder why schizophrenic individuals improved in the hospital, but became disorganized again when they returned to their families. Similarly, it was found that when the families of patients hospitalized for depression or anxiety received therapy for their family relationships, the patients needed substantially less medication after discharge from the hospital.

In the mid-1970s, writing to family therapists who were finding it difficult to get beyond the individualistic psychiatric and medical models of that time, Bernard Guerney, Jr. wrote that "most difficulties and inability to achieve relationship goals that are chronic and essentially interpersonal in nature stem from: (1) lack of appropriate knowledge, training, and prior experience; (2) prior experiences that have led to unrealistic expectations; and/or (3) behaviors that produce unintended effects on others."[2]

Guerney's ideas have had a significant impact on our work two decades later as we seek ways to offer and instill new confidence and hope with our family business clients. In the following excerpt from his book, note how Guerney establishes the importance of relationships to our well-being, and provides a positive and hopeful context for understanding them.

> . . . genetic and biochemical forces are not the major determining factors in the problems of the overwhelming majority of people who see themselves, or are seen by others, as requiring the services of mental health professionals. Always for this larger group . . . the role of interpersonal relations is central to the problem and to the solution.

> *Such a conclusion seems inescapable when we consider that relationships with other people are at the heart of everything we do and are virtually inseparable from all the stresses and anxieties of life.*

On numerous occasions with new family business clients the subject of mental illness on somebody's part comes up. Often it is brought up by one family member informing us that, in their estimation, another family member is "crazy." Yet, true mental illness is more the exception than the rule in our work. When relationship problems get resolved, the behaviors that looked so crazy diminish or disappear.

Notes
1. Elliot Blair Smith. "The Billionaires's Brawl." *USA Today*, April 8, 1998.
2. Bernard Guerney, Jr. *Relationship Enhancement*. San Francisco: Jossey-Bass, 1977, p. 20.
3. Ibid., 3–4 (emphasis added).

Understanding Relationship Intelligence

INTRODUCTION
● ● ● ● ● ● ● ● ● ● ● ● ● ● ●

Intelligence has historically been the word used to describe a person's intellectual ability. IQ, the measure of intellectual ability, was viewed as one of the strongest predictors of individual achievement and success. Actually, intelligence is an interesting word. We use it as if it is something we can see, touch, or hear. Yet intelligence is an abstract and hypothetical concept. Even though we all understand and experience it, intelligence represents something intangible. As individuals, we possess the ability to perceive and process inputs from our environment. We sort and analyze them and use the result in problem solving and planning. Our individual levels of ability to do these things vary from one person to the next. Here is a simplified definition of intelligence that draws on a number of different perspectives.

. . . intelligence refers to the whole class of cognitive behaviors which reflect an individual's capacity to solve problems with insight, to adapt to new situations, to think abstractly, and to profit from . . . experience.[1]

This definition was developed by psychologists as a way to talk about the abstract concept called *intelligence* and provide a means to compare individuals with one another in terms of intellectual ability.

In 1995 Daniel Goleman published *Emotional Intelligence*, the first major variation on the concept of intelligence. Goleman, a psychologist, sifted through research on how emotions are processed by the mind. He says that while IQ and emotional intelligence are independent competencies, it would be rare to find someone high in IQ but low in emotional intelligence. More importantly, Goleman says that emotional intelligence has more bearing on an individual's overall success and achievement in life than does their intellectual intelligence.

Goleman's concept of emotional intelligence soon became popularly known as EQ. In his original book (1997) he defines emotional intelligence like this:

> . . . abilities such as being able to motivate oneself and persist in the face of frustrations; to control impulse and delay gratification; to regulate one's moods and keep distress from swamping the ability to think; to empathize and to hope.[2]

Breaking open the understanding of intelligence to include emotional as well as intellectual capacity was a great contribution to our understanding of what makes people tick. The overall point that Goleman makes is that "when it comes to predicting people's success, brainpower as measured by IQ and standardized achievement tests may actually matter less than qualities of mind once thought of as 'character.' "[3] In other words Goleman recognized a relationship between the ability to exhibit personal integrity and character, calmness and stability in tense emotional situations, and feel true empathy for others, and the ability to get ahead and to be successful. The person with both high IQ and EQ is in a very strong position to rise above the crowd in problem solving and achievement.

Both IQ and EQ describe the capacity of individuals to succeed at individual pursuits. Both IQ and EQ contribute to, and lay the foundation for, stimulating and enjoyable interactions between people. Yet they do not fully explain how bright and emotionally developed individuals participate in both high functioning and nonfunctional relationships. This can be described by comparing the difference between playing tennis and playing football. The tennis player can take full credit for her victory, alone she faced and defeated her opponent. She perfected her backhand and forehand strokes. She mastered both offense and defense. She trained her legs and feet to move exactly as she wants them to move because she will depend on those legs for victory.

In contrast, the football player only takes credit for having made his contribution to the team's efforts, even if he kicked the winning field goal or stunned the crowd with a sixty-five-yard kick off return for a touchdown. In football victory is totally dependent upon the collective abilities of the individual players. Success depends upon their ability to create a joint effort that combines their individual strengths with collective strategy and common will. It is the brute strength of the linebacker, combined with the arm and aim of the quarterback, along with the agility of the cornerback that leads to victory, not any one element by itself. Now what we need is a new way to understand the very different kind of skill and ability required to succeed in activities that depend upon relationships and collaboration between people.

WHAT IS RELATIONSHIP INTELLIGENCE?

Relationship Intelligence or RQ, is different because it is a shared ability, created in concert with others through your interactions with them. This kind of intelligence resides within the interactions you have with other people and makes it possible for you to create and sustain satisfying and productive relationships. Though you participate in its creation, it belongs collectively to you and the others in your relationship. Individually you possess IQ and EQ, but alone you do not possess RQ. Relationship Intelligence is community property.

Why is it that in one group the relationships work so well that there is great success at getting things accomplished; yet in another, with equally bright and emotionally well-adjusted people, every encounter ends in frustration and conflict? Common sense tells us that there is something intangible yet very real within our relationships that causes some to succeed better than others.

The variations we experience from one relationship to another clearly have something to do with the collective ability and energy that is unique to each group we are in. We all have experienced this. Like IQ and EQ it is an intangible but very real and powerful reality, and it makes or breaks families and their businesses. In other words, Relationship Intelligence can only be observed and measured as it comes alive within a relationship.

By yourself, only the raw materials of your RQ exist in the form of your learned relationship skills and abilities. Let us illustrate. A person may be trustworthy or trusting, but trust only exists in a relationship. I may be respectful or respectable, but respect only occurs when a relationship forms. Two people may each be loving or lovable, but they will only know love through their loving interactions with others. In other words, you cannot clap with one hand; clapping takes two hands. Likewise, RQ exists within our interactions with another person or persons.

Much like Goleman helped us understand ourselves more fully and deeply through his work on emotional intelligence, we hope that our work on Relationship Intelligence will improve the success rate of your most important relationships, especially your relationships as a family in business.

Relationship Intelligence is not having intelligence about relationships, and how they work, but the intelligence of the relationship itself. From its broadest perspective, Relationship Intelligence, or RQ, refers to the whole range of interpersonal behaviors that reflect the capacity of a particular group of people, whether social, family, or work, to successfully reach the goals of the group in a harmonious and productive manner. Notice that the definition says that RQ applies to a "particular" group because, as an individual, I will experience different levels of RQ in relationships with different people. My brother and I may have great difficulty in negotiation, compromise, and conflict management, whereas my wife and I find those things fairly easy to accomplish. RQ is exclusively a relationship phenomenon, meaning that it can only be observed when people are in significant interaction with each other.

We sometimes use an exercise with our family business clients to help them see RQ in action. We call the exercise "Puzzle Pieces" because it involves each person completing a puzzle from pieces they, and others, have been given. It works like this. Each family member in the family business, let's say there are six, is given an envelope containing six geometric shaped pieces of paper. Their assignment is to put the pieces together in such a way that they end up with an $8^1/2$ x 11 inch sheet of paper. However, there is an added complication. While there are sufficient pieces, within all the envelopes, to make six $8^1/2$ x 11 inch sheets, no one person has the pieces they need to do so, but they aren't told this up front.

The rules are: (1) there is no talking; (2) no one can complete anyone else's puzzle; and (3) no one is finished until everyone is finished. They are simply told they have a puzzle to complete as quickly as possible. As they try to put their own puzzle pieces together they discover the pieces don't fit. Some will try to make them fit into a square, not a rectangle. Some agonize over analysis of the pieces and try to find the "trick" to making them fit. Someone usually says, "Hey, I have the wrong pieces," and someone else will say, "There's got to be a secret to this," as they get started. Eventually someone says, "I bet we all have pieces of each other's puzzles." We then tell them there is a fourth rule: (4) no one can take a piece from another person; it must be offered.

Clearly, the skills needed to complete this exercise go beyond IQ and EQ, although high levels of both are most helpful. Any one person can apply their very best analytical and problem-solving skills. They can remain calm and avoid the impulse to grab a piece from another person. However, they soon figure out that success will only be achieved if they collaborate. Together they must create a way to communicate effectively without words. They must compromise and be flexible about how to do their project. Each family member must find the balance between sitting back uninvolved and overtly taking charge. In other words they must, in the long run, rely on the collective wisdom and ability of the group, not on their individual abilities or wisdom to complete the task. In fact, too much emphasis on bright and assertive individuals actually makes the task more difficult. This simulated group task, like so many in real life, requires a different kind of reasoning and skill, it requires RQ.

This exercise is not just a game, it's real life in family business where the ingenuity and control of one person can undermine cooperation and collaboration between people upon which ultimate success depends. While this reality exists at every stage and in every generation of family business, the classic examples are associated with succession planning. The transition of ownership and management is a group effort. At least two, but more often, many people are involved in making this journey. To fully succeed everyone needs to move together across the threshold from one era to the next. Succession planning is the epitome of give and take. Giving something not wanted or taking something not offered derails the process just as in the puzzle pieces game. Those left behind are not merely unfortunate stragglers, they become resentful family members and disgruntled minority shareholders. Nevertheless, all too often one or two individuals, and their individual advisors, tackle the transition of ownership and management as a top-seeded tennis player rather than the quarterback of a championship football team.

TWO CORNERSTONES OF RQ

RQ is made up of two dimensions that exist in all relationships. The success or failure of any group activity, whether with two or twenty people, revolves around these two dimensions. They are the cornerstones of Relationship Intelligence. One of these consists of the skill and ability of the group to communicate, plan, solve problems, and build unity. The first cornerstone of RQ is the Relationship Skills represented by the collective ability and talent of the group to maximize their joint capability in dealing with problems and opportunities.

Relationship Intelligence, as we said before, exists only in a relationship. For example, I may be a flexible individual but find that in my marriage we cannot compromise, or I may be a great planner at work, but in my family we can never figure out what to do on the weekend without a fight. Relationship Skill is the ability we have to create and sustain a particular relationship in a satisfying and successful manner. Specific tools of Relationships Skill include managing differences, resolving conflicts, creating intimacy, having fun, solving problems, adapting to change, and carrying out joint tasks.

The second cornerstone of RQ is the Relationship Paradigm: the spirit, morale, and culture of the group. This determines such important relationship factors as the level of trust, hope, respect, confidence, and openness within the group. We call this the Relationship Paradigm dimension. Relationship Skill causes us to succeed or fail at getting things done, whereas the Relationship Paradigm causes us to experience the interactions with others, as succeeding or failing, as positive or fulfilling, as negative or frustrating.

Thomas Kuhn, in his book *The Structure of Scientific Revolutions*, discusses his discovery about scientists, known and respected for their great objectivity and reliance upon facts. He found that they typically distorted the reality of their observations as the facts were filtered through their own perceptions, biases, and beliefs: their paradigms. He even discovered that scientists manipulated the facts to make them fit their paradigms. This discovery of Kuhn's, further popularized by others such as futurist Joel Barker and author Stephen Covey, has great significance in our understanding of RQ.

Another way to think about paradigms is that they are our mental maps that determine how we view our world. They define not only what we see, but how we interpret it, because our paradigms also define the rules for being successful within that view. An individual paradigm, for example "thin is beautiful," determines whether we view ourselves as beautiful or ugly.

Similarly, relationships have paradigms within them that determine how those in the relationship view themselves. For individuals, our paradigms are mental maps or filters that determine how we perceive the world. The Relationship Paradigm within a particular relationship determines the ethos, culture, and style of that relationship. It creates filters within the relationship that determine how people in it view their connections with one another and how they behave toward one another. A Relationship Paradigm that is built on trust, optimism, and respect will create a very different relationship than one built on mistrust, pessimism, and disrespect. In either case the Relationship Paradigm provides the rules of the road for navigating with others.

We use an interesting exercise designed to help families in business identify and understand the Relationship Paradigm they live with. In this exercise we invite each person to choose a symbol to express how they view their family and to draw it on a piece of paper. Someone who draws a heart symbol obviously has a different perception from someone who draws a picture of a tank.

It's always the case that individuals draw different pictures because they each have their own perception about the spirit, culture, and ethos of their family. Sometimes those differences seem so great that we ask ourselves if these people are actually part of the same family. For example, someone draws a tree to express his view that as a family in business they are growing and branching out but have a common root; while someone else draws a unicorn to express her view that what they have is real and worldly, but also magical and illusive.

PARADIGMS AT WORK

Two people were traveling on a lonely country road on a winter day. A rock in the road punctured a rear tire. Pulling over, they opened the trunk, pulled out the spare tire and discovered there was no jack. One of the two said, "We can't change this tire without a jack, we'll just have to wait until someone comes along and can loan us theirs." His paradigm of changing a flat tire required the use of a jack. The other person had a different paradigm: to change the tire we must lift the car. A long wooden plank left by a farmer constructing a bridge lay next to the road. Acting on the second paradigm, they took the plank and built a fulcrum out of other pieces of wood nearby, lifted the car, and changed the tire. Each person had a different mental picture about the problem, and thus, different rules for solving it. One would have waited indefinitely for someone to come along with the jack, while the other got them on their way using a different solution.

There is always at least one common thread, if not several, that connects the different perceptions and forms the common paradigm. It's like the pieces of a puzzle: each has its own shape but fits with others to create the big picture. This becomes clear when we ask the "paradigm question" of each person: "How does your symbol determine what is possible and not possible in your family business?" We found that the tree and unicorn pieces, along with several others, tied together into a paradigm of strong and very restricting loyalty to the past, and a pervasive fear that some unexpected force could snatch it all away in the blink of an eye. There were some additional dimensions as well, but this one gave them a new under-standing about their conflicts and decision-making patterns. Plan-ning was also very difficult for this group. They avoided it at all costs because they were so torn between wanting the security it could provide, yet believing it would be a total waste of time. In the discussion of individual perceptions, every family in business can create a collage of symbols that provides new awareness about the Relationship Paradigm they share.

Relationship Paradigm determines how interactions in a relationship will turn out because they set expectations and rules for what can and cannot happen.

We once worked with a business-owning family that had a very distinct Relationship Paradigm within their family. For them it painted a picture of their family as doomed to fail no matter what, utterly unable to meet the needs of individual family members. Though they were totally unaware of this Relationship Paradigm, their behaviors consistently undermined their success. They related to each other defensively and selfishly, as if there was no good will among them.

Interestingly, in separate conversations each one denied ill will and affirmed a desire to avoid win-lose situations. But when they got together their Relationship Paradigm took over. Every time they got close to a positive solution, someone would sabotage it. They would then blame one another for trying to get everything for themselves. Their Relationship Paradigm gave them definitions of each other, filtered their experience of each other to fit their paradigm, and told them how to behave to be successful within the paradigm. It was destructive and predictable. The resolution of this situation was the hostile and bitter sale of the business in which family members turned the sale over to a business broker and their attorneys. They simply were unable to cooperate in any form. In the end no one was satisfied financially since the business brought only half of its previ-ous value because key nonfamily executives left due to the conflict and turmoil; and their family relationships were shattered. As we said earlier, everything is at stake in family business. This situation does not represent a positive outcome. It was simply the least nega-tive of alternatives. Developing Relationship Intelligence by gaining improved relationship skill and redefining a more positive Relationship Paradigm is the road to positive change. Sometimes, as in this sad example, it's too late because the will and desire to put in the hard work is simply not there. However, there are many more examples in which a new level of Relationship Intelligence brought new optimism and a bright future. The two cornerstones of Relationships Skill and Relationship Paradigm interact together in all of your relationships. A high level of Relationship Skill combined with a positive Relationship Paradigm leads to success. A low level of Relationship Skill combined with a negative Relationship Paradigm leads to failure. We will explain how this works.

QFRs

- Take time to have family members draw a symbol to describe your family business.
- Discuss how much each person's symbol determines what is possible and what is not possible in your family business.

BUILDING BLOCKS OF RELATIONSHIP SKILL

Now let us explore how Relationship Skill and Relationship Paradigm come to be. When we are born into this world we are pretty much blank slates although we come outfitted with a set of instincts and reflexes necessary for our survival. Our sucking reflex makes it possible for us to get nourishment, and our crying reflex alerts our caregivers to our discomfort or pain so they can make it go away. We begin very early to learn and develop skills for interacting with our environment. Our learning early in life forms the basis of our RQ. We begin the process of learning the skills we will rely on in our most important relationships. We begin painting the mental pictures not only of who we are in relation to important people, but how we should conduct ourselves with them. As children grow up, they develop the tools of Relationship Skill and create mental images of what good or bad relationships with others can be like. They are learning to play life's version of football, where their success depends on their ability to work with other people and create a result that is greater than their individual abilities alone.

Beginning early in our lives we start our lifelong learning of the tools of Relationship Skill. We learn through observation, corrective feedback, and practice. The person who grows up in an environment where people don't talk openly and freely, or who argue when they do talk, learns to keep quiet and avoid tense situations.

The person whose life experience has included disciplined and rewarding planning (for example, a disciplined plan for getting homework done), learns that planning ahead works and good things come from it. The person whose life experience has helped them in decision making (for example, taking into consideration how a decision will affect others and her relationships with them), learns important elements in the decision-making process and reinforces her confidence in using them.

Relationship Skill is a set of tools that are needed to build and maintain healthy and productive group relations. The specific Relationship Skill we find most important fall into five areas.

• •

1. The ability to establish genuine understanding and build trust through good communication.

2. The ability to bridge inevitable differences with others and to help them do the same, through respect for alternative ideas and approaches.

3. The ability to constructively manage conflicts and false agreements, with and between others, through flexibility and ongoing renegotiation of expectations.

4. The ability to plan and accept appropriate responsibility for the future through effective and confident management of change.

5. The ability to maintain a full and positive sense of personal worth, value, and confidence, while fully participating in close family and other intimate relationships.

• •

We know two business partners, each of whom owns 50% of their successful business. They went into business together because of their complementary business skills in sales and production. They also liked each other and were seen by everyone as trustworthy, hard-working, competent, entrepreneurial individuals. Over eighteen years they worked side by side, but made independent decisions in their respective areas of the business. In many ways it was as if there were two companies operating interdependently, but lacking cohesion and common direction.

As they approached retirement the differences between them, which were the source of their strength, became more and more a source of conflict and divisiveness. They fought over the time line for exiting the business. They began to argue over resentments, disappointments, and angers that went back many years but had never been discussed. They started to avoid each other, with one moving his office to another building. Meetings between them often resulted in yelling contests. Employees felt they had to choose between the two partners and declare their loyalty to one or the other. What happened?

While possessing the technical skills needed to build a business, this partnership lacked the Relationship Skill necessary to maintain and grow it. Being business partners requires a very high level of relationship ability to discuss issues and concerns openly, make joint decisions, solve problems together, negotiate and compromise on differences, and participate in shared planning and direction setting. In other words, success ultimately depends upon the Relationship Intelligence of that partner relationship.

Unfortunately, these essential skills were not present for these two men. It's likely that they grew up in families that were also deficient in relationship skills. Relationship Skill is often consistent over several generations, as it is passed from one generation to the next, unless there is an intentional effort to improve them by some or all of the family. They are transferred, not by genetic encoding, but through socialization and learning. Both of these men, as in many business partnerships, concentrated on the technical skills they had and were unaware of the ultimate impact of their lack of Relationship Skill.

ESTABLISHING GENUINE UNDERSTANDING . . .

We will be discussing specific ways to develop your skill in these five areas later in the book, but here's a glimpse at the important issues in each skill area. In the first area, generally called communication skills, we don't see the goal as teaching people how to talk. Talking and communication are two different things. In our experience, families in business often talk a great deal but communicate very little. The purpose of communication is the building of understanding and trust, and that is the goal of this skill area.

BRIDGING INEVITABLE DIFFERENCES . . .

Lack of skill in bridging differences with others is a problem that taps into self-esteem issues and lack of negotiation skills. When your self-esteem is under attack and you're feeling vulnerable, there is little desire to build a bridge; a fortress seems more important.

RENEGOTIATING EXPECTATIONS . . .

Conflict is more often due to confused and diverging expectations than to any other single factor. In family businesses, the flip side of conflict, false agreement, is more often a problem than conflict itself. False agreement, which typically grows out of a fear of conflict, happens when an apparent "yes" is really a "no." It usually results in failure of the assumed agreement and is a huge financial and relationship cost to many family businesses.

PLANNING AND MANAGING CHANGE . . .

Change is inevitable. It is also the nemesis of family businesses because they have to deal with change on two fronts at the same time: change in the business and in the family. Responsible planning for the future requires skilled leadership in any business, and in family businesses the leadership challenges are greater because family relationships and emotions overlay the needs of the business.

BEING YOURSELF WITH OTHERS . . .

One of the ongoing challenges of life for all of us is having the ability to sustain a full and healthy individual identity in the face of the pressure to conform and blend in with family and other close relationships. In the world of family systems psychology this is referred to as "self-differentiation."[4] One of the most common struggles within family business is keeping this balance between individuals and the group. In some situations there is so much "we" there is no room left for "I," whereas, in other situations there is so little sense of "we" that the "I's" have nothing that ties them together.

In the earlier example the partners excelled in producing and selling superior products. Their industry reputation was unsurpassed. However, they found early on that they could not compromise or negotiate a mutually agreeable conclusion when they differed. For example, when they could not agree on the size of a building to buy, they dealt with it by leaving the decision up to their plant manager. Repeated experiences like this caused them to avoid issues about which they knew they differed greatly.

Believe it or not, these five areas all revolve around sets of skills that can be learned and relearned. The last thing in the world that we like to hear someone say is, "That's just me, I can't do anything about it!" It's not "just you" that you can't deal with conflict, experience understanding, or provide significant leadership for the future. These are skill areas that can be developed, and that's the reason we're so optimistic about reformulating relationships that have been difficult for years.

THE CREATION OF RELATIONSHIP PARADIGMS

As life goes on, especially in those early years, not only do we learn the skills related to managing our relationships with others but we also develop a complex set of expectations and prejudices related to navigating those relationships. Again, by observation, corrective feedback, and practice we learn what works and doesn't work in our relationships with others. We carry these expectations and prejudices with us throughout our lives, modifying them as in response to new experiences. The particular combination of expectations and prejudices we have depends on how we deal with the three basic dilemmas that must be resolved in every relationship.

Dilemma #1: Trust versus Mistrust—"How much can I rely on others?"

Dilemma #2: Optimism versus Pessimism—"What can I expect of others?"

Dilemma #3: Respect versus Disrespect—"How much do we value and regard each other?"

In our relationships with one another, our individual expectations and prejudices get linked with those of others. Like the collage of symbols that grows out of the paradigm exercise we described earlier, a Relationship Paradigm is created from the individual expectations and prejudices of the individuals in the group. In fact, one of the major challenges in any relationship is figuring out how to handle the interlocking patterns of our individual expectations and prejudices. The pessimist is drawn to the optimist, the timid person is attracted to the outgoing, the enabler is drawn to the alcoholic, and the visionary is drawn to the practical.

We come into every relationship with preexisting expectations and prejudices about how it should work, whether it's the relationship with our spouse, a boss, a sibling or cousin, a used-car salesperson, a physician, or an employee. An example about marriage will illustrate what we are describing.

A young woman we know grew up in a financially struggling but very loving single-parent family. She learned to value what she called the "simple things," like Sunday evening popcorn and a game of cards and baking cookies for the neighbors. She was often ridiculed in school because she lacked the newest fashions and money to go places with other kids. She and a very caring young man fell in love during college. He came from a large and wealthy family, caring but formal and emotionally controlled. His family was prominent in the community and material possessions flowed freely. He learned to value what he called the "finer things" like social events at the country club and enjoyment of his small but prized collection of antique cars. Clearly, expectations and prejudices about important marriage matters, like how money is spent and leisure activities, were quite different.

After only a few months of marriage these two began to clash badly. She felt intimidated by his expectations and he felt constrained by hers. His prejudices caused him to appreciate but disparage her family while she admired yet was defensive with his. In spite of their differences they quickly created a Relationship Paradigm that could be put like this: "Family values of love and loyalty are essential in marriage, and differences between classes of people are hurtful, divisive, and insurmountable."

Based on their Relationship Paradigm they were caught between the mandate to be devoted and loving with each other in spite of the growing hurt and resentment over their differences, which became more accentuated. They acted in a superficially loving manner with family and friends but at home were increasingly distant and detached. They did not share activities that were fun and fulfilling, but they never discussed it, nor attempted to bridge the gap, because their Relationship Paradigm told them the differences could not be overcome. Family and friends had no idea of their growing unhappiness because though opposite, they seemed so connected. Unfortunately, the inevitable result of their Relationship Paradigm was their divorce, about which both felt guilty and ashamed, yet relieved. On the one hand it signaled their failure to be loving and devoted enough to keep the relationship together, and on the other hand it reinforced their Relationship Paradigm that interpersonal differences are indeed insurmountable. Why is it always somewhat reassuring to have our expectations and prejudices, our Relationship Paradigms proven to be true, even when it's painful and destructive? This was the case here.

Another example: Here's a story told about a first-year psychiatric intern discussing a particularly difficult patient at a staff meeting.

Joe, the patient, believed he was dead and no amount of psychiatric magic could convince him otherwise. The young intern, filled with great optimism and a touch of grandiosity, said, "I have an idea that I am sure will work. Let me talk to Joe." The next day the intern saw Joe sitting alone in the day room of the psychiatric ward and decided to fix Joe and get him out of there. He sat down and said, "Joe, I understand you think you're dead." "Yep, that's right," said Joe. Been dead for almost fifteen years now." "Well, Joe, do you believe that dead people bleed?" asked the intern. "Of course not," Joe said, "dead people don't bleed." The intern produced a pin from his pocket, asked to see Joe's finger and proceeded to prick it with the pin. Of course, a drop of blood appeared on the end of Joe's finger, to which Joe exclaimed with great surprise, "Well, my gosh, Doc, I guess dead people DO bleed!"

Relationship paradigms are the product of our expectations and prejudices about relating to others. These become our beliefs which, like Joe's, are very powerful and can even withstand massive evidence to the contrary. They are born out of the ups and downs of life experience and then shape future life experience to fit what we know and feel most comfortable dealing with. Relationship paradigms provide the pattern we use to design life and give us the rules for operating successfully within it.

SKILL + PARADIGM = RQ

RQ is the capacity of a particular group of people to successfully reach the goals of their group in a harmonious and productive manner. As we have been saying, it has two dimensions: Relationship Skill and Relationship Paradigm. As the fuel that powers relationships, these two dimensions interact to produce a particular group's level of RQ. How does this happen?

First, let's look at Relationship Skill. The level of Relationship Skill for any group ranges from low to high. A particular group's level of Relationship Skill indicates how well that group of people can solve problems, resolve their individual differences, manage conflicts, plan for the future, and create understanding through good communication. The following table illustrates typical characteristics at the low and high ends of the range related to several key tools of Relationship Skill.

RELATIONSHIP SKILL

Tools	Low	High
Communication	Creates misunderstanding	Creates understanding
Differences	Divisive	Source of strength
Problem Solving	Recurring and avoided	Evaluated and solved
Planning	No direction	Clear direction
Organization	Unclear roles/lack of accountability	Clear roles/ accountability

The most simple way to understand a family's level of Relationship Skill is through observation of how the group works together, whether planning a family reunion or on the job, coordinating duties and responsibilities. In one family group, for example, differences over when to celebrate a holiday together becomes a source of contention and argument, whereas in another it is negotiated and compromised to a mutually satisfactory conclusion. In another family business decisions are made on the basis of avoiding conflict, whereas in others they are made on the basis of the needs of the business.

QFRs

- Thinking about your family business do you think your Relationship Skill overall is high, moderate, or low?
- Are there some relationships (groups, departments, teams, etc.) that seem to have higher Relationship Skill than others? Why do you think this is so?
- What specific areas of Relationship Skill are most in need of improvement: problem solving, communication, planning, resolving differences and conflict, other?
- What do you think a low level of Relationship Skill is costing your family business? (Multiply the total salary and benefit cost to the company of those involved by your estimate of nonproductive time per week caused by conflict, standoffs, etc., as a percentage of the total work time available. For example $500,000 for four people times one hour per day of nonproductive work time (= 12.5% of 40 hours) is costing the company $62,500 on an annualized basis.)

Comparably, a group's Relationship Paradigm is on a range, not from low to high, but from negative to positive. Relationship Paradigm is somewhat more difficult to get a handle on for the simple reason that it is so intangible and exists mostly between the lines of the relationships people have with each other. It can, however, be inferred even with only a cursory knowledge of the group. In fact, it is often easier for an outsider to see a group's Relationship Paradigm than it is for the group members to see it themselves. The extent to which a group's Relationship Paradigm is positive or negative indicates the presence of trust or mistrust, optimism or pessimism, respect or disrespect, openness or secrecy, inclusion or rejection, within the group as participants deal with each other. The following table indicates some typical characteristics at the negative and positive ends of the range of Relationship Paradigm in relation to several important relationship qualities.

• •

RELATIONSHIP PARADIGM

Qualities	Negative	Positive
Trust	High mistrust	High trust
Confidence	Pessimism	Optimism
Respect	Disrespect	High regard
Sharing	Secrecy	Openness
Well-being	Deprivation	Abundance

• •

Even without knowing the specifics of the Relationship Paradigm in a family business, the extent to which it is positive or negative can be observed by looking at three things: time, money, and energy. People in relationships that have a positive Relationship Paradigm invest time, money, and energy in the relationship, whereas those with a negative Relationship Paradigm do not. An investment in time means finding shared activities and doing them. An investment of money means allocating expendable financial resources on things that are of benefit to the group or even to individuals within the group. An investment of energy means placing attention, interest and concern into the activities and needs of the group.

QFRs

- Thinking about your family business do you think your Relationship Paradigm is mostly positive or mostly negative?
- Write one paragraph describing how your family business operates today in terms of trust/mistrust, openness/secrecy, optimism/pessimism, and closeness/distance.
- Write another paragraph describing how you would ideally like your family business to operate using the same categories.
- What will happen to your family business, in five, ten, and twenty years, if the Relationship Paradigm stays the same as it is today?

The interaction between Relationship Skill and Relationship Paradigm can be diagrammed as follows. Through their interaction they constitute the Relationship Intelligence, the RQ, of the group.

RELATIONSHIP INTELLIGENCE MATRIX

POSITIVE

	LEVEL 3 MOD RQ	LEVEL 4 HI RQ	
RELATIONSHIP **PARADIGM** LOW			HIGH
	LEVEL1 NO RQ	LEVEL 2 LOW RQ	

NEGATIVE

RELATIONSHIP SKILL

As you can see, every relationship falls somewhere within one of the four quadrants, and thus one of the four levels of RQ, created by the intersection of the Relationship Paradigm and Relationship Skill dimensions. Relationships with a high level of Relationship Skill would be characterized by:

- successful management of individual differences;
- routine and enjoyable interaction;
- open and productive communication;
- ability to negotiate and compromise; and
- a strong balance of respect for individuals;
  with awareness of the group's strength.

Relationships that operate according to a positive Relationship Paradigm are characterized by:

- a high level of trust, good will, and caring for individuals and the group as a whole;
- a strong feeling of optimism and positive anticipation; and
- mutual respect.

CHARACTERISTICS OF RQ LEVELS

A relationship that possesses a high level of Relationship Skill and a positive Relationship Paradigm has a Level 4 Hi RQ. This relationship is extremely resilient and enjoyable. The relationship maintenance costs are very low because the skills needed to deal with the routine ups and downs of life as well as a positive Relationship Paradigm are both present. If this group is a family, it is characterized by strong family ties that bring the family together for activities without a sense of obligation or coercion. They share family-oriented tasks and responsibilities easily with no feeling by individuals that they are unwillingly sacrificing their own interests and needs for the sake of the whole. The family enjoys and celebrates their heritage and legacy with both gratitude and humor and seeks to pass it along to the children.

The family business with a Level 4 RQ is characterized by a high level of respect and trust bestowed not just by family members on one another but by nonfamily employees as well. Leadership is either delegated to one person with demonstrated ability or shared among several individuals in a coordinated and collegial style. Decision making is effective with information provided freely and accurately. Protocols for dealing with issues and concerns are clearly spelled out and practiced regularly. Optimism, characterized by hope and positive anticipation, would provide energy and motivation to tackle even the most difficult issues together. Roles and responsibilities are clearly defined based on the needs of the business and the abilities of the individuals involved, and there is a strong and unifying sense of accountability to one another, the business, and the family.

At the opposite end of the spectrum is the relationship at Level 1 Low RQ. It possesses a low level of Relationship Skill and a negative Relationship Paradigm. It is devoid of the characteristics of the Level 4 relationship. If it survives it will be a scene of constant interpersonal battles creating very high maintenance costs. RQ is virtually nonexistent except in some survival form. If this group is a family, it is characterized by no family cohesiveness, and family members avoid spending time with each other. Participation in events that typically bring families together such as holidays, birthdays, weddings, and funerals are experienced as unwanted and coercive obligations. There are no shared family-oriented tasks and responsibilities because individuals, or individual family units, have chosen to avoid such connections. If circumstances such as managing a family estate imposes a joint responsibility, there is a strong resentment about having to sacrifice individual interests and needs for involvements that benefit other family members. There are many negative stories about the family's heritage and legacy often involving secretive stories about neglect, abuse, failure. Parents do everything possible to protect and insulate their own children from being "infected" by the negative and debilitating influence of the family.

The family business with a Level 1 RQ is characterized by a virtual absence of respect and integrity. There is no trust or confidence either by family members or by nonfamily employees that the company is operating in a truthful and genuine manner. Leadership revolves around power and control and is coveted by the individual currently holding the reins. Authority is based on legal control, reinforced by statute rather than competence, confidence, and respect. Decision making resides in one person or a very small group. Information that typically is available to employees, managers, or shareholders is highly protected. An atmosphere of secretiveness breeds further distrust and suspicion. Pessimism, characterized by hopelessness and resignation, would stifle motivation and energy for improving relationships. Great confusion exists as to who makes important decisions and how, so that there are constant surprises to those not on the "inside." Roles and responsibilities are either rigidly defined in an exclusionary manner or in a manner that has nothing to do with the needs of the business or the abilities of the individuals involved. No one has a sense of accountability to one another, the business, or the family, so everyone is guarding their piece of the turf.

Of course, few family businesses exhibit Relationship Intelligence at these extremes, although they do exist, as most anyone familiar with family businesses will attest. Most family businesses have a level of Relationship Intelligence somewhere between the extremes with a mixture of the qualities and abilities that characterize Levels 1 and 4. In other words, most family businesses possess Relationship Intelligence somewhere in the range of Level 2 to Level 3. The good news is that there is always room for improvement. The bad news is that change isn't easy and requires the will and commitment to make it happen. This is especially the case if your family business suffers from a negative Relationship Paradigm. Changing the Relationship Paradigm in your family business is far more difficult than improving Relationship Skill, because it requires a fundamental redefinition of the culture, atmosphere, and ethos of the group.

Certainly, in some situations the group should not stay together: the road is too steep and the costs too great. This is the situation when the Relationship Paradigm is so negative and so entrenched that revising it is impossible. In such situations, you must find the quickest, least destructive, and most viable way to end the relationship. However, in difficult relationships that have a moderate to positive Relationship Paradigm, yet which suffer from a low Relationship Skill, there are tremendous opportunities for improvement, fulfillment, and reward.

Notes
1. M. Maloney and M. Ward. *Psychological Assessment*. New York: Oxford University Press, 1976, p. 175.
2. Daniel Goleman. *Emotional Intelligence*. New York: Bantam, 1977, p. 34.
3. Nancy Gibbs. "The EQ Factor." *Time*. October 2, 1995, p. 62.
4. Michael Kerr. "Family Systems Theory and Therapy." In *Handbook of Family Therapy*, ed. A. Gurman and D. Kniskern. New York: Brunner/Mazel, 1981.

When Family and Business Meet
The Relationship Intelligence Challenge

INTRODUCTION

The types of relationships that must be managed by and among family members who work together are always measured geometrically, not arithmetically. For example, in a typical family of four there are a total of seven different relationship types, or combinations, shared by a mother, father, daughter, and son.

- Husband and wife
- Mother and father
- Mother and son
- Mother and daughter
- Father and son
- Father and daughter
- Sister and brother

If this family is in business together, you add to this the relationships of employer and employee, co-workers and owners. The number of relationship types, or combinations, doubles to fourteen. You can add the following list to the one above:

- Co-owners (husband and wife)
- Co-executives (husband and wife)
- Father/employer and son/employee
- Father/employer and daughter/employee
- Mother/employer and son/employee
- Mother/employer and daughter/employee
- Co-workers (sister and brother)

The complexity and complication of these multiple relationships grows out of the fact that each has its own rules for success and expectations about fulfillment. Success for a husband and wife is not measured in the same way as success for business partners.

41

Expectations about what is fulfilling in the relationship between parent and child is very different than in the relationship between employer and employee. The list goes on and on.

QFRs

- List the ways in which your family and your business are different from other families and businesses because you are a family business.
- What are the advantages and disadvantages of the complexity of relationships that exist in your situation?
- How would you respond if someone said to you, "Don't ever go into business with your relatives." What rationale would you give for your answer?
- What ideas are you beginning to develop about what could be done in your family business to decrease the negative consequences of the complexity of relationships?

There are two primary reasons why Relationship Intelligence (RQ) is especially critical to the success and survival of the family business. The first is the reality that there is a longer and more intense relationship history among the key players in a family business than there is in other forms of business. The second is that when it comes to relationships, family businesses are more complex and complicated than their nonfamily business counterparts. Let's look at both of these in depth.

RESPECTING THE HISTORY

The relationship history in a family business is longer than in any other form of business. In family business beyond the first generation the relationship history goes all the way back to the birth of its current CEO and the early childhood experiences of its family management team. In what other kind of business do you have employees say, "I remember her when she was five years old and sat on her dad's lap behind his desk. Now she's the CEO!"? In what other kind of business do you find a group of senior managers with vivid memories of fighting over who got the couch or who mom favored? Where in the world of business are there owners of multimillion dollar corporations who say, "I never bought a single share of stock from my parents and I don't intend to make my children buy it from me either, if they want it I will give it to them"? Nowhere do you find these and thousands of other relationship history examples, except among family businesses. In the world of business, managing such a long and entrenched relationship history differentiates family business from all the rest. Those that manage their relationship history well are differentiated from those who do not by the level of RQ they possess.

Of all the ways that the protracted relationship history affects a family business, the most important is the impact it has on the two dimensions of Relationship Intelligence: Relationship Skill and Relationship Paradigm.

Years of interactions between family members carve deep ruts in the ways they relate to one another. As we discussed in chapter 2, it is in these repeated interactions that patterns of relating are learned, reinforced, and perpetuated. A family can learn ways of communicating that transmit information but do not create understanding. A family can develop methods of decision making that minimize differences of opinion and emphasize the power of position with little concern about support and buy-in from those directly affected. A family can learn that conflict is bad, thus avoiding it at all costs through secretive silence, so that when differences do surface they quickly escalate them into knock-down, drag-out battles which reinforce the belief that conflict is always bad. Of course, good relationship skills are also learned over the years. Families learn how to handle crises by pooling resources and redistributing family responsiblities, or they encourage individual expression without undermining family cohesiveness.

Inside a family business the way interactions around the business itself turn out are also dependent upon Relationship Skill. When family and business are joined together, though, the outcome is not as optional as when family is separate from business. In other words, how issues are handled jeopardizes both financial and familly well-being. The impact of the level of Relationship Skill possessed by a family in business, derived from its shared history of learned ways of interacting, has an ongoing and direct impact on how the needs of the business get addressed. It can deprive the business of a unified sense of direction, clear roles and responsibilities, proper leadership, and responsible management. In other words, when it comes to how family history has set the level of Relationship Skill among family members, the stakes are higher, much higher, for a family business.

The lengthy relationship history has a similar direct bearing on the Relationship Paradigm that controls and directs the spirit, ethos, and culture of the family, and consequently their business. Relationship Paradigm is composed of expectations and prejudices that exist within the relationship. As we said in chapter 2, the particular Relationship Paradigm that a group functions with grows out of how it resolves three basic issues:

- Trust versus Mistrust—"How much can we rely on each other?"

- Optimism versus Pessimism—"What can we expect of each other?"

- Respect versus Disrespect—"How much do we value and regard each other?"

The first and most influential group with which we face these issues is our family. It is in the relationships between grandparents, parents, and siblings; aunts, uncles, and cousins that the family establishes its expectations and prejudices around these issues. We would expect the operative Relationship Paradigm to be a positive one in a family in which needs and problems are consistently attended to: expressions of caring and interest are freely and reciprocally expressed; and there is never a question about everyone's concern for others' welfare. On the other hand, for the family in which self-interest takes precedence over the needs of others, disappointment and hurt dominate interactions between people, and secrecy abounds. Here we would expect to encounter a negative Relationship Paradigm.

The important point is not that every family has an operative Relationship Paradigm that sets the context for the relationships between family members. This is obvious. The really important point is that this Relationship Paradigm, whether positive or negative, is brought directly into the business. Like leaven in a loaf of bread, it becomes a dominant source of the company's culture and spirit; the family is the architect of the culture of the business. Again, when a business is part of the family, the family's Relationship Paradigm doesn't just affect family celebrations and child rearing practices. It gets projected into the business, directly affecting basic business relationship needs related to trust, respect, confidence, teamwork, and responsibility. In some family businesses the motto of the employees is "We are great because we work for, and with, a great family." Unfortunately, for other family businesses the motto of the employees is "Family members are out to get each other so watch your backside and keep your mouth shut!" In both situations the Relationship Paradigm has deep roots in the family's history.

QFRs

- What has your relationship history taught your family about getting along in areas like handling differences, praising one another, surfacing problems, reaching out, resolving conflicts, achieving fairness, and maintaining equality?

- How do the teachings of your family's relationship history directly impact the connections betweeen family and business, both positively and negatively?

- For the benefit of your family business, what aspects of your family's history are worth preserving and which should be left behind?

UNDERSTANDING THE COMPLEXITY

THE THREE DOMAINS IN FAMILY BUSINESS

It's clear that Relationship Intelligence is essential to helping family businesses deal effectively and creatively with the lengthy and rich histories that characterize them, but another important relationship reality in family business also involves RQ. Everyone talks about the complexity of family business. This complexity is most often attributed to the fact that emotional issues contaminate business issues. Indeed, the emotional ties that bind in family businesses are important but by themselves don't fully explain the complexity. Even in family businesses where family members all have strong IQs and EQs significant relationship problems still derail everything from management meetings to succession planning. Behind "all the emotional stuff," family businesses are different because they are made up of three interlocking and intermingling domains: family, business, and ownership. Each of these domains has not only different, but inherently divergent needs, rules, and interests. The three-circle diagram originated by John Davis and Morris Tagiuri depicts how the three domains overlap.[1] It has become a popular symbol around the world for family business.

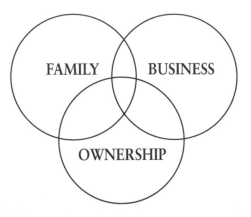

As you can readily tell, this diagram depicts multiple and overlapping relationships: the relationships within each of the three domains, among family members, among employees and managers, and among the owners of the company. In addition, multiple relationships develop among the domains themselves, as each one influences the other two, and vice versa. Each is interlocked with the other two in an intensely interdependent way. At the center of the family business all three domains are connected in a complex web of relationships. This situation only exists in the world of family business. Even in closely held businesses that espouse a "family-like atmosphere," it is not the same as a family business. Only in a family business is there an expectation about Thanksgiving dinner, Christmas gifts, or bar mitzvah celebrations. You can avoid it, but it's still there. Only in family business are people joined by irreversible family ties of birth, adoption, and marriage (marriage can be undone but not reversed, especially when there are children).

MANAGING THE DIFFERENCES

Separating the three domains and looking at each one separately makes the differences and tensions among them obvious. It's important to recognize and understand the differences because managing them well is essential to survival and success. While there is tremendous diversity in how familes and businesses function, some commonly accepted principles and assumptions undergird both.

Families exist to care for and nurture their members, and provide safety and refuge in an impersonal world. Family ties are natural, emotional, and especially in today's families, egalitarian. Individual needs are as important as, if not more than, those of the group. In a real sense membership is unconditional; you don't have to perform to become or remain a member of the family.

FAMILY
• harmony
• unity
• self esteem

Success in family is measured in terms of harmony, unity, and the development of happy individuals with solid and positive self-esteem. For example, loaning money to your brother or son interest-free is more an emotional than a rational business decision. You may do this because you care for him, not because he is a good credit risk. We know of an Italian family living in the United States that completely turned home and family life upside down for more than six months, in order to accommodate a relative from Italy who needed surgery that could only be performed in the United States. How many parents and families take a wayward son or daughter back into the fold when the person has failed at life and continues to sabotage all efforts at help? These are family decisions based on family rules and family measures of success.

BUSINESS
• production
• profit

Businesses, on the other hand, are economic entities where ultimate success is measured not in individual self esteem and interpersonal enjoyment, in spite of today's emphasis on employee empowerment and involvement, but in productivity. The needs of individuals are always subordinate to corporate goals and objectives. Continued inclusion in the business is conditional; it's based on performance, achievement, and contribution.

From the perspective of the business the value of an individual rests ultimately on that person's contribution to the company's strategies, competitive position, and profitability, the primary measure of success. For example, corporate downsizing and layoffs of individuals who have many years of dedicated service, for the purpose of improving productivity and profitability, is an accepted, if unpopular practice. Employees at every level, even in the most progressive companies that encourage intrapreneurial initiative, are expected to eschew personal agendas or priorities in favor of participation in, and support of, corporate strategies and goals.

The priorities of ownership are based on yet another set of rules: the rules of investing, not producing; on minimizing, not maximizing, risk. In the strict sense of the word, ownership means putting capital at risk for the purpose of realizing a desired enhancement of the investment. Success for owners is measured in terms of return on investment and the protection of ownership interests. It may also be measured in terms of owner values and philosophy of business; for example, how the company deals with issues of the environment, employee practices, and business ethics. Regardless, if owner priorities are not met, the expected result is a withdrawal of invested capital and reinvestment elsewhere.

In every family business these three domains are the ingredients that are mixed and blended. The final concoction of family business dynamics is measured by the degree and nature of the interdependence and overlap among them. Over time, the extent and effects of this overlapping fluctuates, but it never goes away. When people refer to "family business dynamics," the shifting and repositioning of the three domains is what they are describing. At any one time family needs may override business priorities or vice versa, or ownership concerns may take priority over business growth, and so on.

Portrayed in graphic form the comparisons among the three domains in family business look like this:

●●

FAMILY BUSINESS RELATIONSHIP RULES MATRIX

	Family	Business Management	Ownership
MEASURE OF SUCCESS	Harmony	Production	ROI and ROS (Responsibility of stewardship)
AUTHORITY	Equal	Not equal	Both equal and not equal
FINANCIAL REWARDS	Based on need	Based on productivity	Based either in what's taken or what's left over
LOCUS OF IMPORTANCE	Individual aspirations	Corporate goals	Profitability
RULES OF INCLUSION	Unconditional acceptance	Dependent on contribution	Either deserved or earned

●●

Even a cursory review of the Family Business Relationship Rules Matrix reveals the geometric complexity of relationship rules competing for attention in the family business. Not only are the assumptions and measures of success inherent in each domain different, in many ways they are in opposition. You could say that family business is designed not to work, yet it has worked for centuries and still works. A lot of things in this world seem as if they shouldn't work but do. For those of us who are not aeronautical engineers a 400 ton Boeing 747 should not be able to fly, but it does. For those of us who are not reptile specialists, a short-legged, slithering alligator should not be able to run 15 miles an hour, but it does. For those of us who are not cardiac surgeons, it should not be possible to take the heart from one person and transplant it into another, giving new life, but it is. Family businesses do work, and one of the greatest challenges of all is finding ways to manage their complexity so that they can.

COMPROMISE IS KEY TO SUCCESS

The truth is, and this is important, that the relationships among the domains inevitably require compromise. The needs of any one domain can never be fully satisfied as long as they are linked to the needs of the other two. We have often been asked, "How can you keep family and business separate in a family business?" Our response is always the same: "You can't, and still call it a family business!" Compromise, from our perspective, is not good or bad but an essential reality of family business. When compromise is managed well, there is a great payoff. Synergistic opportunity becomes the fruit of the compromise. When the family, business, and ownership each give something to the others, a greater, rather than lesser, result is achieved. For example, the family sets expectations of each other regarding performance that are very unfamily-like but needed by the business. The result is tremendous, and otherwise unattainable, opportunity for family members and extraordinary long-term loyalty by family employees to the business. Owners sacrifice some of their return on investment to provide key nonfamily managers with financial incentives that will keep them in the company since they will never achieve the top executive spots. The result is a marvelous combination of family and nonfamily leadership talent all pulling together rather than in opposite directions.

Within the family business an individual may participate in one, two, even all three, of the domains. Most CEOs, for example, are constituents in all three domains as head of the business, a member of the family, and a shareholder. Sometimes family members are shareholders but are not active in the business. In the majority of family businesses there is a family member working for the company who is not a shareholder.

Another of the many distinctive qualities of family businesses is that a family member who is neither a shareholder nor an employee can have a deep sense of "emotional ownership" of the business. This affection for and affiliation with the family's business keep even distant family members deeply interested and strangely attracted to what goes on within the walls of their family's company.

Several years ago we facilitated a family business retreat for a sizable plumbing company. Started by the father thirty years earlier, the company now employed the parents, a son, and a daughter. They also had four other children not active in the business. Also in the business was a man just two years older than their son who was "like a family member." Like their son he had been with the company for ten years. Their daughter had been in the business a year. The issue for the retreat was the parent's question as to whether it mattered to their children if the business stayed in the family. Five years earlier, the parents had established an interim plan to transfer ownership of the business equally to their son and the other young man. Dad believed at the time that it would take both of them to run the company should he die unexpectedly. Now with a daughter in the business and second thoughts about what he had done, the parents decided it was important to hear what all their children preferred. More or less expecting the consensus to be that it didn't matter to them, the parents were bowled over by the emotional way their children expressed their desire to see the business stay in the family. To their surprise, the parents heard that all their children kept up with how things were going in the company through their brother and sister. One daughter, an accountant living several hundred miles away, shared both her personal and professional opinions. No one knew they had such an interested and talented family member willing to help out. A son successfully employed in a Fortune 500 company suggested that they start a family newsletter for both family and business updates, and that he would take responsiblity for it. Not only the parents, but all twelve members of this family (including in-laws) were surprised and energized by the emotional ownership, the blood equity, that was expessed. The parents revised their estate plan to keep the business in the family while making appropriate long-term provisions for the man who was so vital to the company's operations. This one story is an example of a universal principle about the flexibility and compromise required to manage family, business, and ownership relationship systems. Relationship Intelligence is essential to flexibility and compromise. Remember that Relationship Paradigm controls the culture, atmosphere, and ethos of your family business. It is the filter through which experience and information are interpreted and understood. When a family business suffers from a negative Relationship Paradigm, flexibilty is interpreted as weakness and compromise as capitulation. Two very positive and necessary elements of healthy family business are translated into adversarial negatives. Failure to recognize how interdependent the three domains of family business are ignores one of the most important distinguishing characteristics of family enteprise. Failure to understand how essential Relationship Intelligence is to assuring that the domains relate in a harmonious way, ignores one of the most crucial steps to success in family enterprise.

QFRs

- How does the Relationship Paradigm in your family business interpret compromise and flexibility?
- What compromises have been made between family, business, and ownership in your family business to make it work?
- What compromises, from your point of view, have gone too far or cost too much?
- Would you describe your family business as more flexible or rigid, overall or in specific areas? Think of specific situations or events that illustrate your perspective.

NOTHING IS CONSTANT, EVERYTHING CHANGES

The relationships among the three domains are constantly changing and evolving. This occurs because of the inevitable cycles that famlies and businesses go through as they mature. Families move through multiple stages from young children, through launching young adults, to incorporating their spouses and families, into old age and the death of the parents. Businesses also have a natural cycle of evolution from start-up, through growth and diversification, into consolidation and professionalization, and ultimately into maturity, decline, or regeneration.

The changes that family and business cycles bring affect the relative magnitude of importance which one domain has at any given time in relation to the other two. Famles with children typically demand attention and resources that diminish for empty-nest families. Businesses that are growing rapidly are typically more demanding of energy and resources than those that are maturing, even though the latter can be very demanding in different ways.

In addition, the relative magnitude of importance placed on one domain over another also reflects the attitudes and perspectives of the current family ownership and management. In some family companies, everything revolves around the needs and activities of the business. The business domain dominates the other two. In other family businesses, the family is all-important and the business is valued largely as a resource and opportunity for family members now and in the future. As shareholders get older, the ownership domain often becomes more of a dominant force, overshadowing both the family and business domains, as the financial security needs of older owners draw capital away from the business. A common result of this change is controversy among family members as the desires of the younger generation conflict with the concerns of the older.

• •

One of the popular exercises in our Family Focus Meetings and Family Business Retreats is inviting family members to draw the three circles as they view them. In the first part of the exercise they draw the size of the circle representing the domain to indicate the magnitude of importance of that domain as they view it. The size of the circle represents the amount of energy and resource that goes into that domain. Also, the larger the circle the more importance they believe is placed on the rules of that domain as explained in the Family Relationship Rules Matrix. The degree of overlap that they draw between the three circles represents the extent to which each of the domains influences the other two. A large overlap between the family and business domains would indicate that each greatly influences the other. A very small overlap between the family and ownership domains would indicate that family matters and ownership issues are largely distinct, separate, and unconnected. Again, greater overlap would indicate that the roles, rules, and procedures in each of the two domains is greatly affected by those in the other. The result is greater confusion whereas less overlap represents less confusion.

Here are the drawings of five family members, all active in the business, as they completed this exercise.

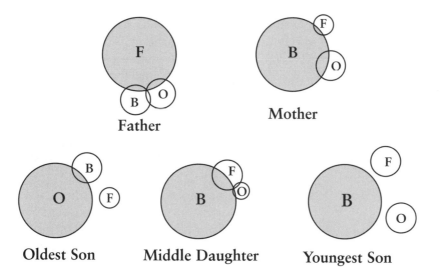

As family members share their drawings with each other, there often is, as you might expect, diversity as to how they view their situation. As they discuss the reasons and assumptions behind their drawings, important information is placed on the table about expectations and prejudices. In other words, the Relationship Paradigm that they share but never recognized before emerges from the individual drawings into the paradigm portrait for the family.

In the second part of the exercise they draw the circles as they would ideally like it to be in their family business. Once again they explain the reasons and aspirations behind their preferred drawing. As they discuss the differences between the first and second drawings, they begin to challenge the Relationship Paradigm they have been operating under. All of this is quite a revelation to the family!

● ●

ALIGNING RELATIONSHIPS

The three-circle diagram helps us see two additional dimensions of family business dynamics. The first is the relative magnitude of the three domains and the fact that they are ever-changing over the years. Magnitude is measured in terms of energy and resources consumed. The second is the degree to which each of the domains influences the others. This also changes and evolves over time. This influence is represented diagramatically as the amount of overlap among the circles. Greater influence is represented by greater overlap and vice versa. Influence is measured in terms of clarity versus confusion as to roles, rules, and procedures. Because of the inevitable overlapping and the constantly changing interactions among the three domains, the number one challenge is keeping the competition among the domains to an absolute miminum.

In some family businesses the influence of family rules over business is significant. This would be represented by a family domain drawn larger than, and largely overlapping, the business domain The best-known experience of this is the rule of primogeniture in which the oldest male family member is the heir apparent in the business, regardless of ability. A natural heirarchy in a family is superimposed on the business. But other forms are just as obvious: equal pay for family members regardless of position or responsibility in the company, use of company funds to help out a struggling family member, or a negative Relationship Paradigm in the family erupting into conflict among family managers about key business decisions.

This is just one possible combination. Every family business is different. For some the business domain is so dominant, and overlaps the family domain to such an extent, that family members relate to each other only through their business roles. In others, the ownership domain is so miniscule and overlaps the other two domains so little that family members never learn the responsibilities of ownership and company managers never understand the real desires and intentions of shareholders.

There is no ideal diagram, three equally sized circles with equal overlap is a fiction used only to illustrate the idea of the three domains and how they relate to one another. The true challenge for every family business is managing the ongoing process of trying to achieve the best balance or fit possible among the three domains. We use the word "alignment" to describe this balance and fit. To be aligned is to have the best and most beneficial relationship between two components that must work together. It is the mechanism by which the needs and interests, the rules and measures of success of each domain are synchronized with those of the others, and continue to be so over time.

QFRs

- Draw the three circles depicting the magnitude of each domain and the alignment between them as it exists today in your family business.

- Make a second drawing depicting the magnitude of each domain and the alignment between them as you would ideally like to see it in the future.

To illustrate alignment, think of the two front wheels on your car. These are the two major components of the car's front suspension, and they must work together to keep the car moving. The front wheels of a car must be aligned from time to time to make sure they are, together, pointing straight down the road. Alignment settings vary from car to car depending on how it is designed. Likewise, alignment between the moving parts of a machine tool is essential to avoid excessive maintenance and unnecessary downtime. As machine tools wear down over time, alignment settings have to be adapted to account for changes in the tools to make sure the parts are produced to desired specifications.

So it is with the relationships among the three domains in family business. Alignment in the relationships between and among the three domains is a never-ending and essential ingredient to success and survival. Lack of alignment is a sure predictor of trouble. Alignment problems often come to the surface in conjunction with major changes in the family business. Typical alignment-sensitive events in family business include the first time a next-generation family member comes to work for the company, ownership and management transfer planning, and formation of a sibling/cousin confederacy to run the business.

Here are a couple of real-life examples of alignment problems that surface around succession planning.

● ●

Case Example 1: "It Takes Two to Tango"

The founder and sole owner of a successful family business, in which his son and son-in-law were the top two executives, instructed his attorney to develop an ownership transfer plan for the company. When all was said and done, he had in fact paid for three different fully developed succession plans, each of which was collecting dust on the shelf. Neither his son nor son-in-law was willing to accept any of them. Although the owner was frustrated to the point of thinking about selling the business to a third party, the problem was that he had never consulted his family about the plans. He made decisions for them regarding how their future ownership would be structured and thus how they would relate together in the business. In one plan, the son-in-law would end up a minority owner, forever dependent on his brother-in-law for job and income: no good. In the second, the first problem was corrected, so the owner thought, by allocating equal ownership to the son and the son-in-law's wife, the owner's daughter, who was not active in the business. The rationale was equal ownership between the families, but the son-in-law's job and income were now dependent on his marital status: definitely no good. The third proposed the son's buying the business entirely from father, financed out of company profits on an installment basis. Some of the proceeds would go, through gifting, to the daughter and son-in-law to pursue their own business interests. The son insisted, however, that the business couldn't support the payments without affecting his income and besides, dad insisted on contingency clauses based on performance that kept him looking over son's shoulder: totally unacceptable. What would you do next?

● ●

Case Example 2: Doctor's Orders: "Get a Life"

Four siblings were assigned responsibility for running the company when dad, at age sixty-nine, suddenly decided to "turn over the reigns" after bypass surgery. He had been saying for as long as anyone could remember that he would probably never retire. "You know, die with my boots on as they say," he would comment with a chuckle. But reality sank in, as it has a strange way of doing when your best view is the ceiling tiles of a hospital room, and the picture of his ideal future changed. He convened a family meeting with his wife and two children in the business to tell them that his doctor ordered him to "get a life" outside the business. He was retiring from everything except Board duties. He and their mother would be going to their home in Florida for six months, and they planned to buy a smaller place up north for the summers. By the end of that month his office was cleared out and they were in Florida. Both of the successors naïvely believed they were ready to take over. As a family they all pulled together around the parents to deal with their crisis and to prolong their father's life. However, conflict quickly erupted between the brother and sister—it could have been predicted. They never had actually worked together as business partners, only as reactors to their father, who pulled the chains and levers. While both did a good job in the company, there had been no grooming of successor leadership and the exit of the charismatic founder left employees anxious and worried. Still firmly tied to him, they refused to follow the direction of the new president, appointed simply because he was the oldest son.

• •

In both situations, you can readily see the gigantic misalignment problems that created the failures. In the first example, the concerns and needs of family members were not in alignment with the needs and desires of the owner. In the second, the needs of the business for an orderly and orchestrated management transition plan were ignored by the needs and concerns of the owner and the family. While alignment solutions always involve compromise, as we discussed earlier, they will never be realized when the needs of one domain or another, are ignored.

REACHING OUT FOR RELATIONSHIP ISSUES

Alignment is achieving the best and most beneficial relationship between two components that must work together. Achieving this objective requires the ability that can only be provided by a sufficiently high level of Relationship Intelligence. In neither situation did the family business group (family members and nonfamily employees) possess the communication, problem-solving, decision-making, change management, and planning skills that they needed. In the first example, the Relationship Paradigm was essentially positive. The spirit and culture of the family/employee group contained high levels of respect, trust, and optimism. These could have been undermined over time by the lack of relationship skill, but fortunately they were not. Gaining new skills got them to their goal. Through outside help they learned how to create understanding and buy-in through good communication and how to negotiate rather than dictate.

The second situation, though, was different. The Relationship Paradigm was more negative. The son was viewed by employees as a "spoiled playboy" and the daughter as "nice but not very competent." Father was viewed as a benevolent dictator who expected unquestioned loyalty. This situation exhibited low levels of trust and respect, and there was a subtle but strong fear that the patriarch's departure would spell the end of the business. New Relationship Skills, though needed, would not solve the problem here. It actually required the father to get reinvolved for a while in the role of transition manager. With outside assistance he led the way in building bridges from the old Relationship Paradigm to a new one. He did this by helping establish optimism and confidence in the next generation and letting the company move forward with more professional methods of management and planning.

Without a shift to a more positive Relationship Paradigm new skills are often useless and can even be detrimental when used to manipulate the situation rather than to resolve it. Changing Relationship Paradigms takes an outside change agent with the knowledge and skill for managing relationships while not losing focus on the business. For any family business to succeed, it is essential that the needs and interests of family, business, and owners are in alignment with each other. This is an ongoing responsibility of family business leaders especially during times of change and turmoil. Relationship Intelligence is the essential ingredient in making this happen.

MAKING FAMILY BUSINESS WORK

The role of Relationship Intelligence in a family business is to provide the aptitude and attitude necessary for managing the multliple levels of relationship complexity and the decades of relationship history that are uniquely characteristic of family firms. This was certainly true for Jordan's Garden Centers, a fourth-generation chain of garden supply and gift stores. Started as a feed supply and small implement store, the business grew with each succeeding generation to an eight-store chain doing $18 million in sales. In each of the prior succession transitions, ownership was passed to the oldest male child of the next generation. This fact has not gone unnoticed by the other children but has never been discussed openly. In fact, the Jordan family has a very strong and rigid set of unwritten rules about family relationships. Everyone knows not to bring up emotionally charged issues. The few times it has happened the result has been a family feud that simmered and cut people off from each other for years. Also, everyone knows that this is a man's business. Even though modern machinery and facilities have eliminated much of the heavy labor, and the business draws about half its revenue from retail giftware sales, some in the family say, "Women are not suited to management or key ownership roles." This business-owning family prides itself for not displaying conflict and for keeping things "just the way grandpa Jordan would have liked."

The second succession transition from Robert to Robert Jr. in 1967 was more difficult than the first one when Robert took over the business from his father in 1935. Everyone expected Robert to become the owner and manager in 1935, after all, he was the oldest son, with a proven track record in the business. His younger brother Will also worked his whole life in the company, but his two sisters were never involved except as youngsters.

At age sixty-six, Robert sold the business to Robert Jr., the oldest of his three children. Robert Jr.'s two cousins, Will's children, have been employed for many years in responsible positions managing multiple store locations.

In 1996 Robert Jr. hit the wall as he began to lay plans for reducing his role in the company. His oldest son Frank, who is manager of garden equipment and supplies, is not his oldest child. His daughter Karen is Frank's senior by four years and has been giftware manager for ten years. Though Karen and Frank work together every day, they have never developed a sense of partnership; each separately goes to their father for direction and advice. Karen and Frank have each been rewarded for their efforts by being given ten percent ownership by their father. It has been assumed that Frank would eventually purchase the remaining eighty percent from his father. He, as oldest male successor, would become majority owner just as had been done in previous generations. Karen has never been asked what she wants and she knows the rule: Don't bring up emotionally loaded issues and don't question tradition.

Frank and Karen's two cousins successfully manage two stores in different adjoining communities. Having far less allegiance to family tradition and grandfather Jordan's legacy, they are now demanding an ownership stake in Jordan's. It is clear that without ownership, they will take their experience, ability, and customer relationships and open competing stores.

What's the problem here? Why are problems arising at the point that the business is doing so well and provides record-setting opportunity to support the Jordan families? Robert Jr. looks at his children Karen and Frank and his nephews and says, "I think it all boils down to greed; they've got so much and now they want more!" What the Jordan family doesn't have are the fundamental tools of Relationship Skill and the requisite positive Relationship Paradigm needed to manage the succession transition. They are bright and capable people, each in their own right able to manage significant aspects of the company. But when it comes to dealing with their relationships they become almost paralyzed confronting thorny problems, handling uncharted dynamics of changing family relationships, and confronting one another in both a confident and caring way. It is likely that the Jordan family has a Relationship Intelligence somewhere between Level 1 and Level 2. The first challenge in getting beyond their stalemate will be for them to make some improvement in their Relationship Skill by learning how to create better understanding through communication, dealing with their individual differences, and developing a cohesive plan for the future. This will lay the groundwork for them to experience increased optimism, trust, and respect in their relationships as they learn tools that build their Relationship Skill. In turn, the increase in Relationship Skill will build the foundation for taking a new look at how they define their relationship and beginning the process of establishing a more positive Relationship Paradigm than they have ever had.

The good news, once again, is that Relationship Intelligence can develop throughout life, even into advanced adulthood. The skills and abilities, the expectations and prejudices that make up Relationship Intelligence can be developed through learning and practicing new ideas and new ways of doing things that are guaranteed to strengthen Relationship Intelligence. It requires having access to the necessary skills and tools and, most importantly, having the willingness to adapt expectations and prejudices. You simply cannot manage the complexity of your family and business relationships, nor avoid being held hostage by your family history, with a low level of Relationship Intelligence.

Note
1. John Davis and Morris Taguiri. "Bivalent Attributes of the Family Firm." *Family Business Review* (reprinted) vol. ix, no. 2 (summer 1996).

4 Improving Relationship Intelligence
Tools and Methods

When we formed our family business consulting practice in the late 1980s very little information existed about the special needs of family businesses. In the succeeding years of consulting with family businesses, we have developed and adapted a number of tools that have proven to be very effective. Our desire to provide resources that were responsive to both sensitive family issues and the realities of running a business required new approaches. We turned to the fields of business management, organization development, psychology, sociology, and family therapy for approaches that would be beneficial to family businesses. In addition, we forged new tools out of our work in helping clients find solutions to problems that went beyond traditional approaches.

The aim of our work has always been not merely to find a solution to a particular relationship problem, but to teach our clients how to manage their relationships. As our particular style of consulting to family companies came together, we noted that the real benefit did not come from the resolution of their present problem, or help for individual family members, as beneficial as these things were. The real benefit was in their becoming better problem solvers as a group and more able to understand and benefit from the principles and practices of Relationship Intelligence. It was very much like watching the growth in intelligence that teachers observe as their students absorb new learning. We were helping develop a unique kind of intelligence that increased their ability to create effective family and business relationships.

After understanding what Relationship Intelligence is and how it develops, the most important question to ask is how to improve it. We will be discussing ways of doing just that in the following chapters. Remember, as we said in chapter 1, it is the relationship-first family business that has the best chance of success and survival long term. Without desire and motivation to invest in improving family relationships, it is more or less a matter of time before the family's joint business interests will come to an end. It is best to get help far enough ahead of time to avoid significant damage to the business, as well as the family. Everyone loses when deteriorating relationships are allowed to linger and infect others.

There are four principles that govern the process of improving Relationship Intelligence in a family business. We will outline them here and go into more detail about them in later chapters.

- **Relationship Intelligence—Principle I:** The skills that comprise Relationship Skill can be learned by anyone. Learning new skills causes changes in behavior that are beneficial to the relationship. For example, learning communication skills improves the quality of interactions; learning decision-making skills improves how the group reaches an agreement on complex issues.
- **Relationship Intelligence—Principle II:** The expectations and prejudices that comprise a Relationship Paradigm change slowly and then only when those in the relationship commit to new ways of behaving with each other consistently over time. For example, agreement to talk directly rather than behind each other's backs builds new trust; listening for the purpose of understanding rather than to debate creates new openness.
- **Relationship Intelligence—Principle III:** Neither learning skills nor correcting expectations and prejudices is sufficient alone to improve relationships; it takes work on both areas. Relationship Skill and Relationship Paradigm are interdependent in that Relationship Skill provides the tools needed to conduct the business of relationships, and Relationship Paradigm provides the drive, motivation, and attitude that fuels the desire and willingness to use the tools.
- **Relationship Intelligence—Principle IV:** There is a sequence by which improvement in Relationship Intelligence occurs. Improvement in RQ always takes place sequentially from one level to the next; for example from Level 2 to Level 3, never from Level 2 to Level 4. Getting from Level 1 to Level 2 or from Level 3 to Level 4 (horizontal growth) requires focus first on the Relationship Skill dimension, with the learning of new skills in the areas described above. This then is followed by work on changing expectations and prejudices in the paradigm dimension. Going from Level 2 to Level 3 (vertical growth) requires focus first on the renegotiation of expectations and the rehabilitation of prejudices in the paradigm

dimension. This is followed by the learning of the new skills required to support the increased expectations that accompany improvements in Relationship Paradigm.

Interest and motivation for improving Relationship Intelligence is generally not evenly shared by every member of the family business group. Everyone may be aware of the need to improve relationships within the family business group. Yet, in spite of a high level of unhappiness, not everyone will jump on the band-wagon to start a program of improvement. In fact, there are times when those who stand to gain the most from improved RQ are the most resistant to helping make it happen.

MOTIVATING PEOPLE TO CHANGE

Recently, a family business owner called complaining about his son, who he said "is running his division of the company into the ground, but he thinks he knows everything and won't listen." He called to find out how we would handle a situation like his. He was obviously very disturbed. Evidently the company was suffering, but he rejected as useless, irrelevant, or unworkable, every question or suggestion that focused on the breakdown in the relationship between him and his son. It became clear that he had decided his son, not their relationship, was the problem and was soliciting support for his position. Most likely his son was, at the same time, trying to convince someone on his end that his father, not their relationship, was the problem.

What is the source of this apparent lack of desire to improve relationships, especially when it's clear that doing so would dramat-ically improve the situation? Is it because some people simply prefer misery over happiness? Perhaps misery does offer some payoff at times as a way to justify keeping the battle going. However, to change how we do things, even to stop being miserable, requires energy. There has to be sufficient motivation to overcome the iner-tia and move forward. Most of the time the resistance to improving the quality of relationships, does not relate to love of misery or even fear of change. It relates to one of the most fundamental aspects of human behavior: motivation.

Understanding what motivation is and how it can be strengthened is therefore an important element of any program designed to improve Relationship Intelligence. In fact, there is a for-mula for motivation, and it goes like this:

$$Vp \times ESp = M,$$

where **Vp** is perceived value; **ESp** is perceived expectancy of success; and **M** is motivation. Value is the extent to which something is perceived as desirable and important to us. Expectancy of success is the extent to which those involved have confidence that they can successfully achieve that which is valuable. Motivation will be high if the end to be achieved is perceived as both desired and important as well as possible to achieve. On the other hand, if the end to be achieved has little desirability or importance, even if the likelihood of achieving it is high; or, if the end has high desirability and importance, but there is little confidence that it can be achieved, there will be very little motivation to proceed.

Let us illustrate. Suppose you are offered ten dollars to deliver a package to a destination a hundred miles away within the next day or so. Most likely you would turn the offer down, not because of your lack of perceived expectancy of success (to get the package there on time), but because of the lack of value. Most likely you would conclude that it would cost more than that much in gasoline and that wasting half a day is not worth ten dollars. You would have no motivation. If, on the other hand, the offer were sweetened to one thousand dollars for the same job, your level of motivation would rise dramatically; not only because you could do it but also there's value in doing it. Change the deal again slightly. What happens if the offer is still a thousand dollars, but now you must deliver the package to its destination a hundred miles away within the next hour or you are paid nothing? Once again, your motivation drops to zero unless you can fly an airplane or helicopter, because you know you can't possibly drive that hundred miles in one hour.

When it comes to improving Relationship Intelligence, the willingness to do so depends upon the motivation level of those involved. If either the perceived value or the perceived expectancy of success on the part of the group is minimal, expect to encounter resistance. A group of family shareholders may see little perceived value in developing a good buy-sell agreement because everyone plans to will their stock to their children when they die and pay the taxes with insurance. In their minds a buy-sell agreement would not only be unnecessary but it might interfere with what they've already decided to do. A group of siblings or cousins may not be motivated to grab the reins of leadership of the family business together because they have little perceived expectancy of success since their values and personal aspirations are very different and frequently the source of disagreement.

To fully understand how to improve RQ, it is also important to understand the process of change that is involved. Motivation is a key ingredient in the first of three stages of change originally spelled out by sociologist Kurt Lewin. Lewin said that change always involves three stages: (1) unfreezing, (2) transition, and (3) refreezing. The change itself occurs in stage two, the transition, but it will never happen if those affected by the change aren't willing to embrace it. Stage one, unfreezing, creates the openness and readiness of those involved to accept and support the change. Lewin says further that once the change has been made, it is essential to bring the change process to a close in stage three. The changed condition is the way things will be for a while; people can count on a period of stability. Without refreezing, change becomes ongoing and leads to turmoil and chaos.

When a change effort fails, it is because the change process was initiated without sufficient unfreezing, without people being open and receptive to new ideas or practices. Yet, it is common practice to initiate change efforts at stage two, completely bypassing the essential unfreezing process. A few people get together and begin talking about how something could be done differently and become convinced of the benefits. Because they have the power to do so, they inform the others that this change will be made, naïvely expecting that everyone else is at the same point of readiness to move ahead, that everyone else has bought into the benefits which change will bring for them. When the change effort fails, either because of active resistance or stonewalling, everyone scratches their head, wondering why. A common example is when many companies began using computers. Management made the decision behind closed doors. One day the van backed up to the company and one hundred computers were unloaded and set up. Training classes began the next day; however, three months later most computers had not been turned on. Why? Stage one, unfreezing, which creates readiness for change, was skipped over. There should have been numerous information meetings and question-and-answer sessions with employees before the computers arrived. The age-old question, "What's in it for me?" needed to be answered by everyone and it was not.

Unfreezing depends on motivation, and motivation requires a sufficiently good mix of perceived value and perceived expectancy of success. As you consider improving Relationship Intelligence in your family business, think about these basics of motivation and change. Have efforts in the past to make things better failed because everyone was not on the same page; they were not motivated, ready to move forward? How have past failures at change affected those who tried to make it happen? Is lack of motivation to improve

Relationship Intelligence in your family business, coming from a Relationship Paradigm that perpetuates mistrust, disrespect, pessimism, fear, suspicion, helplessness, and self-interest? Or is the lack of motivation based on inadequate Relationship Skill, a lack of relationship building tools, that results in repeated frustration to move ahead in spite of everyone's desire to do so?

Everyone thinks they understand relationships. Perhaps it is because relationships are such a common part of everyday life. We are so accustomed to the relationship dimension of life that we take it for granted. Like the old adage that a fish doesn't know that it's swimming in water, we don't stop to realize that we live each day in our own sea of relationships. It's a bit like a traveler in an unfamiliar place without a map saying, "How hard can this be? I know how to drive a car and read road signs, and besides I know that where I'm going is north of here!"

LSi's RELATIONSHIP ROADMAP

Renegotiating relationships within a family business does not just happen because people know how to talk to each other. It requires a roadmap and perhaps an experienced guide to assure that you don't short circuit the process of reaching agreement. Such a roadmap is at the heart of our work with family businesses in helping them build their Relationship Intelligence. We call it LSi's Relationship Roadmap. It describes how effective relationships form and how they deteriorate, if not attended to. While LSi's Relationship Roadmap can be applied to any and all kinds of relationships, it is especially useful for business-owning families who must deal with complex roles and a lifelong shared history. LSi's Relationship Roadmap provides an integrated and action-oriented way to understand such common family business issues as: managing change, dealing with conflict, and clarifying agreement expectations as family members, business partners, and co-owners. It also focuses on learning specific aspects of Relationship Skill, such as communication, issue management, renegotiation, and maintaining flexibility and accountability. LSi's Relationship Roadmap is a guide, sorting out the prejudices and beliefs of our Relationship Paradigm as well.

Perhaps the Roadmap sounds a bit complicated; however, the following diagram will help you see the whole relationship-building process. We will break it apart to describe how the individual segments of the process work.

LSI's RELATIONSHIP ROADMAP

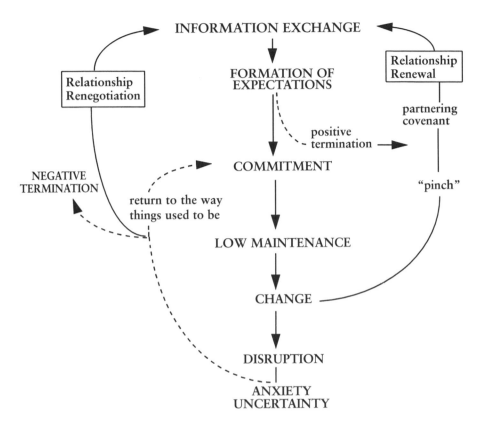

THE PLACE WHERE EVERY RELATIONSHIP BEGINS

Study the Roadmap for just a minute. Relationships form over time by a process that begins at the top of the diagram, proceeds to the bottom and back to the top again. As we said above, LSi's Relationship Roadmap depicts how relationships develop, change over time, and possibly break down. As we explain how the Roadmap works, it will be helpful if you can be thinking about an important relationship in your life today. Doing so will help you put real-life meaning into the diagram.

Sherwood and Glidewell (1972) originally conceived of this as depicting a process of organizational change that helps organization development consultants understand the work they do. We then began adapting their insights into our work with family businesses. The communication specialists of Interpersonal Communications,

Littleton, Colorado, have also done a nice job of applying Sherwood and Glidewell's idea specifically to communication. Over the past ten years, we have integrated their original work with many of our own ideas and now use the Roadmap as a centerpiece of our consulting and seminar work.

STEP ONE: EXCHANGING INFORMATION

All relationships begin at the same place, with "information exchange." The more important a relationship is, the more time we invest in the exchange and sharing of information. When I park my car I spend very little time exchanging information, except to find out the cost and make sure my car will be there when I return. On the other hand, if I am hiring an employee, considering a business partnership, or contemplating marriage, the amount of information that is exchanged becomes considerable. If you are married, think back to your courting days. Many couples can remember how they spent hour upon hour talking, sharing, and discussing. They will say, "It was like we had known each other forever; we were so comfortable with each other and had so much to talk about." Then, as the story goes, you get married and the talking stops!

Interviewing an applicant for a position in your company is a daunting responsibility. We will use this situation to exemplify how the Roadmap works. The exchanging of information when interviewing a prospective employee is an important and often arduous job. The first pieces of information exchanged are typically a job ad and a resume. This is followed by a series of interviews along with reference checks and perhaps even ability and drug testing. Many hours are spent in this initial stage of information exchange; the more important the job to the company, the more time is typically invested on all sides.

STEP TWO: FORMING EXPECTATIONS

As information is exchanged something very interesting begins to happen at a subtle level; expectations begin to form as to what this relationship will be like. At the outset of the initial job interview, expectations in the relationship are based on minimal written information, a resume and perhaps a brochure about the company. Quickly though, expectations begin to solidify based on additional information provided: how people are dressed, their manner of speaking, and how they conduct themselves. As expectations get clarified, the relationship begins to take on a particular shape and style, which is either positive enough to move to the next phase or not. The shape and style of the relationship depends on how the three basic relationship dilemmas are dealt with: trust versus mistrust; optimism versus pessimism; and respect versus disrespect.

STEP THREE: MAKING A COMMITMENT

At some point, expectations are formed and negotiated to the extent that the participants in the relationship arrive at a commitment. If it is an employee interview, we decide to continue our relationship into employment or go our separate ways. The commitment we reach grows out of our process of negotiating and clarifying expectations. This commitment represents the Relationship Paradigm that we have just established together, the beliefs and biases we have created together about our relationship. This sets the context of our relationship as we move forward with it. We have decided, for example, that we can rely on our relationship, we believe we can meet each other's expectations, and are confident that we can trust what will happen between us. This is what happens when expectations are fully clarified and a relationship forms well. When it doesn't, because the stage of information exchange and clear expectations is short circuited, we don't know what to expect. If that happens, we are building a relationship not on solid ground, but on sand.

STEP FOUR: ENTERING INTO LOW MAINTENANCE

Assuming that all has gone well, our relationship moves into its most wonderful period of all. It is the kind of relationship we all yearn for. A relationship characterized by stability, productivity, and *low maintenance*. In marriage it is known as the "honeymoon"; a descriptive notion that has been used as a metaphor for this wonderful period in many other types of relationships. We can all recall the first time we have a run-in with a new employee and another manager says to us, "Sounds like the honeymoon is over!" During the low-maintenance period, no one in the relationship is investing energy looking over her shoulder, concerned as to whether expectations are being met and commitments carried out. As the employee, I know what my job is; as the employer, I trust it will be done.

STEP FIVE: MEETING UNEXPECTED CHANGE

The one inevitable characteristic of this period of low maintenance is that, as you have guessed, it will come to an end. It will be interrupted because of another inevitable fact of life: *change.*

The reason change has such a profound impact on relationships is that it disrupts our shared expectations. Some changes come from outside, from the environment. Other changes come from inside the relationship, from changes brought on by previously undisclosed or new information from individuals involved. Let's return to our illustration of the newly hired employee to see how change from the inside or outside disrupts expectations. Let's say this employee was hired as the director of marketing and sales. One day the boss calls in the marketing and sales, and operations directors. Ms. Boss says, "Our sales have been fifty percent less than expected this quarter. I'm working with the research director to try to understand what's happening. I don't think we'll have to lay people off as yet, so please don't get overly concerned. I just wanted both of you to know we are studying the situation. I will have another meeting next week at which I'd like each of you to present your ideas about what's gone wrong and what we need to do about it. Please keep this information to yourselves for now and don't worry." Mr. Marketing walks out of the meeting. Do you think he forgets it? If you said, "no" you are beginning to understand how change from the environment—from outside either person in the relationship—causes a disruption to the relationship. Mr. Marketing is saying to himself, "Boy, I better polish my resume . . . she says 'don't worry,' but she looked right at me when she said 'sales were down,'" and so on and so forth. The newly hired employee does not know if he can trust the original commitment he made to the job and the employer made to him, as being an integral part of their management team. This is change that comes from the outside because of a change in the marketplace.

Now let's look at change from the inside. Our new employee reads about an eighteen-week weekend master's program in marketing and sales. One of his personal, long-range goals is to get his master's. So, he approaches his boss to ask if he could have every other Friday off for eighteen weeks to get his degree. He says, "I think this would open up new doors and opportunities that had been closed to me before." Ms. Boss notices how excited her marketing person is about attending this program, but is taken aback by the "sudden" change in expectations. The boss denies the employee's request saying it's impossible now, what with the employee already needing to put in fifty to sixty hours a week to manage the company's rapid growth. Mr. Marketing not only hears his boss's words, but sees the look of dismay on her face. So, he quickly says, "I understand, forget I brought it up, and leaves the boss's office. But neither of them really forgets the impact of this interaction. Inside, Ms. Boss is questioning the employee's long-term commitment, and the employee is disappointed because he sees the master's program as his ticket to being able to build a marketing and sales department to handle the company's growth.

STEP SIX: ANXIETY LEADS TO FALSE AGREEMENT

Whether from the inside or outside, change will disrupt expectations and *create a period of anxiety and uncertainty in the relationship.* The opposite of the "honeymoon period," this period in the relationship is marked by high, and increasing, relationship maintenance costs. People are confused and wary because they no longer know what they can expect from one another. The answers to the three relationship dilemmas are no longer valid so mistrust grows, pessimism escalates, and respect deteriorates.

This is an awful period in any relationship. When change is not managed well, this anxiety leads to what we call *false agreement.* Let us explain false agreement.

The period of anxiety and uncertainty is so difficult and painful that people typically attempt to push through it by simply reinstating the previously workable commitment. The group reminds itself of the original commitments and expectations: "Let's get back to the way things were or are supposed to be." You will hear angry or pleading statements that begin with "But you agreed to . . . ," "You promised me that . . . ," "I don't know what happened but we have got to get back to the way it's always been." As people capitulate to the pressure and pleading, they make peace by picking up the shell of the old commitment but it is now devoid of the energy and integrity it originally had. Their lukewarm and cautious "yes" is really just a "maybe" at best and more likely an "if I have to I will" response. The path of false agreement is found on the left side of LSi's Relationship Roadmap.

This approach works in the short term. A new period of low maintenance and stability ensues, but is not as stable or as enduring as the original period was. This is because this renewal of commitment is built to a large degree on false agreement.

PATH OF FALSE AGREEMENT

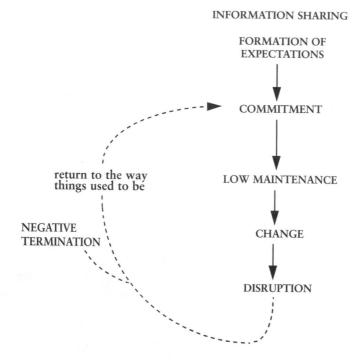

INFORMATION SHARING

FORMATION OF
EXPECTATIONS

COMMITMENT

LOW MAINTENANCE

return to the way
things used to be

NEGATIVE
TERMINATION

CHANGE

DISRUPTION

In our example, the employer and employee agree to return to the way things were and to pretend that the expectation altering issue of a master's program was never mentioned.

Remember our old friend change? The reality of disruptions in expectations because of change is not a one-time event; it is a recurring part of the life of every relationship. When the rush to get beyond the anxiety and confusion of disrupted expectations causes a reinstituting of the previous commitment, the next disruption when it occurs will be greater than the last one. A cycle develops in which the periods of low maintenance become shorter and less stable, and the disruptions become greater and greater until the relationship breaks down completely. As the positives of the relationship give way to negatives in the relationship it comes to an end as the participants opt out. Either they opt out psychologically or literally end their contact with one another. In marriage these are called either apathy or divorce, while in business they're called work slow down, quitting, or being terminated. These possibilities are noted on the left side of LSi's Relationship Roadmap.

When a relationship ends because of a cycle of deteriorating disruptions, false agreement, change, and further disruptions, open interpersonal wounds are left that will take years to heal. Stories about how awful it was will take on a life of their own and circulate in the family and business for years, becoming a negative part of the legacy. The end result is inevitable and always destructive: there is always a negative termination of the relationship.

STEP SEVEN: RELATIONSHIP RENEGOTIATION

Fortunately, there is a way to reestablish clear expectations and restore commitment through the process of relationship renegotiation in which the now obsolete expectations are revisited and revised by the group. The path of relationship renegotiation is found on the far left side of LSi's Relationship Roadmap.

Unlike the natural inclination to return to the old commitment, relationship renegotiation takes everyone back to the stage of Information Exchange. In much the same way as occurred when the

PATH OF RELATIONSHIP RENEGOTIATION

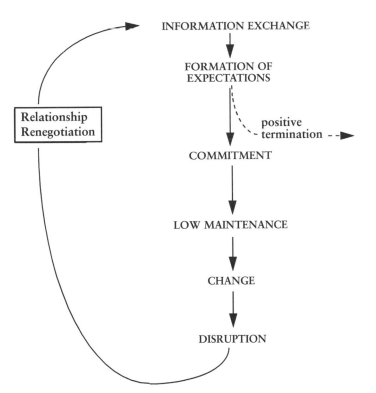

relationship was formed initially, there is a frank and open discussion about expectations. Practically speaking, any person in the relationship who is being affected by the mounting cycle of increasingly painful disruptions brings the group back to Information Exchange and renegotiation of expectations.

The three relationship dilemmas connected to trust, optimism, and respect come back onto the table as the group members air their differences, express their feelings, and state their positions. It is truly a process of renegotiation that relies on Relationship Skill for successful results. Relationship Intelligence is the essential ingredient required for this process of relationship renegotiation to succeed. Both dimensions of Relationship Intelligence, Relationship Skill and Relationship Paradigm, must receive attention by the group as it moves to redefine itself.

Returning to our employer-employee example, Ms. Boss calls her employee to her office a few days later, having observed the tension between them and her employee's lack of original enthusiasm. Getting right to the point, Ms. Boss asks, "How do you see the master's program assisting you here in your job responsibilities?" Mr. Marketing responds, "The company is growing rapidly, our approaches to marketing need to be more sophisticated. I'd like to expand my knowledge and skills in this area, which will give our marketing efforts greater focus." Ms. Boss is greatly relieved. She had begun to form a negative paradigm about the new employee, thinking maybe he just wanted the company to pay for his education so he could move on to greater things. But after a heart-to-heart talk, sharing expectations two ways, and listening to each other, she was able to trust even more deeply in his sincerity and commitment. It was agreed that he would put off the program for a year and continue organizing the marketing department. He would hire an assistant within the next six months; and after a year, he could pursue the master's program. The company would also offer 75 percent tuition reimbursement. And Mr. Marketing was delighted at the new expectations and commitment they arrived at together.

There are two potential outcomes of the successful renegotiation of expectations. One of these, as we have indicated, is a renewed commitment, that leads to a new period of low maintenance that is just as enduring as the first period was. The inevitable next disruption resulting from change will not be any greater than the first was. The cycle of deteriorating disruption and false agreement has been replaced by a roadmap to renegotiation. It is also possible that the relationship may still come to an end. Renegotiation of expectations may result in the group deciding that it is in the best interest of all concerned to part ways, whether it's a group of two or twenty. There is, however, a world of difference when a relationship ends not because of an endless cycle of disruption and breakdown, but as the result of renegotiation of expectations. The former is always a negative termination whereas the latter, even though difficult and uncomfortable, is always a positive termination. In our case example, Mr. Marketing could have decided not to wait a year and could have voluntarily left the company. But in this case renegotiation led to a renegotiated set of expectations and a strong commitment to undergird the relationship.

STEP EIGHT: RELATIONSHIP RENEWAL OPTION

There is yet a third, and even better option than Relationship Renegotiation, the pathway on the left side of LSi's Relationship Roadmap. The best alternative of all is called Relationship Renewal. It is preventive, rather than restorative, in focus and sets the stage for avoiding much of the difficult disruptive fallout that comes from change. Relationship Renewal is shown on the right side of LSi's Relationship Roadmap.

Relationship Renewal is initiated when the expectations or commitments within the relationship are negatively impacted by a change that takes place. It can be as minor as an unexpected change in

PATH OF RELATIONSHIP RENEWAL

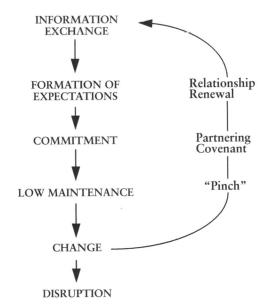

an appointment or as major as a failure to follow through on an important assignment. Glidewell and Sherwood refer to this as a "pinch."[2] While a "pinch" is the same thing as we refer to as an "issue," we like the word "pinch" because it dissipates much of the defensiveness and reactivity that typically arises when a negative issue is brought up. Another helpful way to think of a "pinch" is that it is any experience of a loss of personal freedom in the relationship. Whenever you have the experience that limitations are placed on you, or that you have been given unwanted constraints, you have experienced a "pinch." Furthermore, what is a pinch for one person may not be experienced as such by another. The cardinal rule of "pinching" is that if it's a pinch for the person experiencing it, then it's a pinch and needs to be dealt with as such.

The secret to successful Relationship Renewal is the agreement that any member of the group experiencing a "pinch" not only has the right, but the obligation, to bring the issue to the table for discussion. It is the responsibility of the person who experiences the "pinch" to bring it up, as soon as possible, with the person(s) who are involved. It is an obligation based on caring about the relationship. There is an agreement that unresolved "pinches" are destructive to relationships. During a family business retreat many years ago a family member said, as we were explaining relationship renewal, "Oh, I get it, if you don't deal with the pinches, they pile up and become an ouch!"

Let's go back to our first story about Mr. Marketing and Ms. Boss talking about sales and profits being down. He really senses that the boss is not happy with his performance, but that she hasn't said anything directly. He's felt this for the last month and now he really feels "pinched" by not being included in the "research" about what the problem is. He has a choice to ignore it, in which case mistrust and uncertainty can cause an even more serious disruption. Or he can go to the boss and ask for some performance feedback. He decides to do just that. They have a good conversation and Ms. Boss acknowledges that she has been going behind his back, picking up pieces of uncompleted projects. They make a "Partnering Covenant" to meet weekly to evaluate sales performance and to identify problems and solutions together. But, what are Partnering Covenants?

STEP NINE: ESTABLISHING PARTNERING COVENANTS

As you can see from LSi's Relationship Roadmap, Partnering Covenants are a very important aspect of Relationship Renewal. Partnering Covenants are nonlegal yet binding agreements among the members of a group as to how they will manage their relationships. Partnering Covenants typically cover recurring issues that are actual or potential sources of significant conflict or difficulty. We recommend that you develop the fewest number of Partnering Covenants needed, not more than three or four. The reason for this is that everyone needs to be able to remember all of them, and they should only be developed to deal with especially problematic relationship situations. We almost inevitably suggest that family business clients establish a Partnering Covenant establishing their obligation to return to information exchange whenever someone experiences a pinch. It is usually worded something like this:

> Because we care about our relationship and want to do everything we can to make it a good one, we believe that it is our obligation, not just our right, to bring up any and all pinches that affect us. Therefore, we agree to bring up pinches immediately, or as soon as possible after we experience them, with those involved in order to make sure that we keep our expectations clear and our commitments current. We also agree to bring in an outside resource whenever any one of us feels we cannot resolve the pinch ourselves.

Partnering Covenants work well in situations where there is sufficient good will and commitment to make sure they are kept. A central element of every Partnering Covenant is that it is binding upon those who agree to it, and family members are expected to maintain accountability for keeping it. We have found that spouses of family members in the business are frequently willing and able to provide support and accountability for keeping Partnering Covenants. For example, we once worked with a family business that involved a father and two sons. For several years there had been fairly severe conflict among the three of them that included arguments and disparaging and downright demeaning remarks made in front of employees. This was carried home to their spouses, who often had to suffer through lengthy tirades by one about the others. The father would complain to his wife about what good-for-nothings her sons were, and the sons complained to their wives about their unreasonable father-in-law and about betrayals at the hands of their brother-in-law. The mother and two daughters-in-law had always enjoyed good relationships until this started. The heavy input of disparaging comments from their husbands was driving them apart. They couldn't help being affected by the constant demeaning language. They didn't know what to do, feeling stuck between loyalty to their husbands and their love for each other. The men were also becoming aware that their behavior was destructive and not appropriate, but they didn't know what to do either. We developed a Partnering Covenant among all six of them that stopped the viscious cycle. Essentially, their Partnering Covenant went like this:

> We agree from now on, that while it is O.K. for us (John, Jack, and Rod) to talk to our wives about a bad day at work and even from time to time discuss how difficult our relationships are with each other, we will not do so in a way that is demeaning or disparaging of one another. Such talk drives a wedge between everyone that is unnecessary and is particularly distasteful to our wives. Therefore, we agree that we will not use language that disparages or demeans one another. If we do, we ask our wives to remind us that they do not want to hear it, such a reminder being accepted by us willingly and with appreciation.

Just as in Relationship Renegotiation, Relationship Renewal relies for its success on Relationship Intelligence. The Relationship Skill tools of active listening, esteem enhancement, Partnering Covenants, and issue management are all crucial to Relationship Renewal. This offers a great opportunity to redefine a Relationship Paradigm through the use of LSi's Paradigm Kaleidoscope, which we will also discuss in this chapter. Through Relationship Renewal the group, through its Partnering Covenant, returns to exchanging information to fully understand what happened, why it happened, and what can be done about it. When this occurs on a regular basis, the discussion may take only a few minutes, or it may require several meetings if the situation is more serious.

GUIDELINES FOR DEVELOPING A PARTNERING COVENANT

- Focus on those areas where you consistently run into significant problems in your relationship; remember to have no more than three or four Partnering Covenants at one time.
- Write down in one or two sentences what the problem is within your relationship that you want to address and agree on it. Don't move on until this is done.
- Discuss what you believe can be done to minimize or eliminate the problem and agree on that.
- Put your agreement into writing, describing the new or changed behaviors that you will put into practice.

- Add a final clause that describes what you will do to remain accountable to your agreement (e.g., solicit other family members to monitor your behavior, bring in a coach, etc.).
- Review your Partnering Covenants on a regular basis, but at least once a year, and revise as necessary. Eliminate those that have become unnecessary, decide if any new ones are needed, and reaffirm your commitment to them.

Let's turn next to the tools of Relationship Skill required for developing Relationship Intelligence.

BASIC TOOLS OF RELATIONSHIP SKILL

COMMUNICATION

Relationships *are* the language of family business, and good communication is foundation of that language. Everyone agrees that communication difficulties are the biggest problem in family business, even in those that are working well. In the early 1980s the need to improve the quality of products and services among U.S. companies generated a rush of attention from academics, consultants, and business executives who produced a library of books, tapes, and articles, along with seminars and training classes, promoting quality. The result of this effort has been questioned by many who contend that with all the effort, overall quality is no better today than it was back then.

Similarly, countless books, seminars, tapes, articles, and workshops have been produced to teach families in business how to communicate. Yet ineffective communication still dominates the field of contenders for enemies of successful family enterprise. Why is this so? We believe that part of the reason lies in the fact that while the techniques of communication can be studied from books, tapes, and seminars, the practice of good communication can only be learned from hands-on experience. Because bad communication practices are so ingrained, learning new communication tools usually requires some experienced coaching from someone who can keep the group focused and motivated. Otherwise, it is like learning the craft of cabinet making by reading a book without an apprenticeship. Somehow, reading about complex mitered joints and cutting them perfectly are two different things. Similarly improving communication skills usually requires an apprenticeship. In addition, interpersonal communication has been taught and promoted as techniques that emphasize "how" to communicate, but miss the point as to "why." Without the reason, the method is empty.

We became interested in this strange phenomenon as we heard families in business talk very intelligently about all the communication techniques they had learned, yet also admit that they continued to communicate poorly. We started asking families who attended our seminars and workshops "What is the purpose of good communication?" The responses would always be the ones you'd expect: to exchange important information, make good decisions, keep everyone informed, avoid confusion, etc. But the major purpose of communication, at least from our perspective, was almost always left out, that is, to create understanding. Remember that the three levels of intellect, from lowest to highest, are knowledge, understanding, and wisdom. The same can be said of Relationship Intelligence. In our relationships the production of information creates knowledge. The use of that information to effectively manage a relationship creates understanding, and the synergistic process of the group, which takes it far beyond the individuals involved, creates wisdom. Communication in family businesses all too frequently stops at the lowest level, the level of producing information. However, it is the satisfaction and reward of jointly produced understanding that reinforces our use of communication techniques, that keeps us interested and motivated. *Unless communication results in understanding, families in business become disillusioned and frustrated with techniques which then fall into disuse.*

This is what we think is behind the unfortunate phenomenon of learning communication techniques, trying them out, and then discarding them. Relationship Intelligence requires understanding, and the development of Relationship Intelligence demands constant effort at creating deeper understanding. In light of this, we teach two tools of good communication and emphasize that they are to be used not to produce information, but to build understanding between people. Those tools are: the process of active listening, and understanding how communication affects *self-esteem*.[3]

ACTIVE LISTENING

Active listening is a communication tool that goes back to the earliest days of relationship enhancement and therapy programs. It emphasizes the notion that listening is not a passive process, sitting patiently as you take in what the other person is saying. It also emphasizes that Relationship Intelligence requires the tool of knowing how to listen, not just how to express ideas and feelings. These may seem like self-evident and simplistic ideas, but if lack of communication is the biggest problem in family business, the absence of proper and effective listening is, without question, the biggest problem in communication.

Bernard Guerney in his book *Relationship Enhancement,* which we cited in chapter 1, distinguishes between "two modes of communication" this way:

> One set of behavioral skills is called the *expressive mode.* This mode of communication is designed to enable the individual to express . . . emotions, thoughts, and desires clearly and honestly without generating unnecessary hostility and defensiveness. The second basic set of skills is called the *empathic mode.* This mode of communicating is designed to convey acceptance of another's communication and the ability to identify with another's perceptions, thoughts, and feelings. It is not essentially different from what is sometimes called *reflective listening.* In our view, however, the term *empathic responding* connotes the depth, the intensity, and the giving, illuminating, enhancing qualities . . . better than the phrase *reflective listening.*[4]

Our preference is to use the term *active listening* instead of "reflective listening" because it emphasizes that a good listener has real work to do, because good listening is an active process.

Think for a minute about what is going on inside you when you are listening to other people talk; your mind is anything but inactive. You are trying to figure out their motive, you are taking in and processing their nonverbal gestures and facial expressions, you are remembering previous conversations about the same topic, and you are preparing your response. Yes, you are very active, but most of the activity is not directed to understanding; it is focused on interpreting and preparing your response. Stephen Covey's "Habit 5" in *The 7 Habits of Highly Effective People* says simply and eloquently "If I were to summarize in one sentence the single most important principle I have learned in the field of interpersonal relations, it would be this: *Seek first to understand, then to be understood.* This principle is the key to effective interpersonal communication"(p. 237). Usually in listening we are not working to create understanding, we are working to create a response. As we do so we are only listening half-heartedly, with one ear so to speak, because the brain cannot take in information in an unbiased manner and prepare to respond to it at the same time. The response that we give, therefore, is based on partial, biased, and faulty information. Words are filtered through the Relationship Paradigm and we fully believe we know from the beginning how this exchange is going to turn out. When this form of listening predominates in family business relationships, conflict can escalate in seconds, as all those involved push to be understood. There is a lot of talking and much information gets produced, but it does not lead to understanding. What a difference it makes when everyone is pulling toward shared understanding!

You may think this sounds simple. We challenge you to try it. It is even more difficult to create enough emotional and psychological space actually to experience the feelings, aspirations, fears, and concerns that other people are expressing along with their words. This is indeed a very high level of Relationship Skill when the undisclosed truth is, as we often tell clients, *"It's like you know each other so well, you can't hear what each other is saying."*

The following dialogue between two brothers, Bernie and Ron, in a family business illustrates how active listening works.

Bernie: We've been over this a hundred times, Ron. You are simply creating too much disruption in the sales department. I've really had it this time. We are going to lose our V.P. of sales because you keep going around her and giving orders directly to the reps that are directly contradictory to hers!

Ron: She's a troublemaker! She doesn't like me, never has since you hired her. Look, Bernie, it's either her or me. I can't stand by and watch her screw up major accounts because she's intimidated by some of the reps. But what really bugs me is that you listen to her, as if it's gospel and then question everything I say. I'm you're brother for God's sake!

Bernie: Look, this is going to get us nowhere. I thought we could discuss this calmly but my blood pressure is going up and yours is, too. You're right, you are my brother, and I am yours. I hate this battle that's going on between us. Grandpa and Dad would be so disappointed in us.

Ron: (after what seemed like a five-minute silence) You're right Bernie, I know you're right. What's the real problem between you and me?

Bernie: Well, Ron, I think you're really concerned about how the V.P. of sales is handling Frankfort Industries and Milltown Products, and you're worried she's going to lose our biggest customers. That's why you go around her and you don't think I'm taking the situation seriously enough, right?

Ron: Yeah, that's part of it. I just don't think the reps respect her either. She has never spent any time with them, making customer visits like you and I used to do. The reps complain to me and what am I supposed to say?

Bernie: So, you're also feeling caught in the middle. But, what's this thing about her not liking you and being a troublemaker?

Ron: Well, it's just some of the things I hear from other people and I resent that she talks to me like I should stay completely out of her area, she knows it all.

Bernie: So it's comments from other people and her hostile attitude, is that it?

Ron: I guess. She's not really hostile, just pushy. But where are you on this Bernie, I feel like you're focused on me as the problem.

Bernie: That's a fair question, and no I don't think you're the only problem. I don't think I did a very good job integrating her into the company or coordinating her joining us with you. I can see that now. I think she has one picture of things and you have another; and probably I and the sales reps have two others. I think she has some excellent skills, part of which is her assertiveness which we need, but we're going to have an explosion on our hands if we keep going on this way. Does that answer your question, or better, what do you hear me saying?

Ron: I don't think I see it that way . . .

Bernie: Wait, wait. What did you hear me say, you asked me how I see the situation, right?

Ron: Right! Well you think she has excellent skills and we need her style of assertiveness and that we're going to have a blow up if something doesn't change. And, you said we all have different expectations about her role and authority.

Bernie: I also said, I feel I haven't done my job integrating her into the company. I take responsibility for that and I need to correct it. Did you hear that too?

Ron: Yes, I did. I'm sorry I missed that. Do you think we're on the same page about this situation or not, Bernie? If we're not then . . .

Bernie: *I'm not sure Ron, but I think I understand better why you're so frustrated and I hope you understand I am not out to get you.*

Ron: *No, Bernie, I hear you say that you could have done some things better in bringing her on board and you're going to correct that. I really don't think you're out to get me, but we've got to do something . . . and I think you understand that now.*

Bernie: I've been waiting for things to improve, to give her some time to settle in. I've probably waited too long. I'd like to think about what to do next and talk with you about it on Thursday, will that work for you?
Ron: See you Thursday, thanks!

The tool of active listening is learned by discipline and practice. It is not difficult to master but it does require conscious and intentional effort to achieve understanding. Bernie, without making a big deal out of it, simply redirected the conversation with Ron that was quickly escalating. No, it wasn't easy, especially with the head of steam the two of them were building up, but it worked to avoid an explosion. Next time they meet, we would encourage Bernie and Ron to agree at the beginning of the meeting to use the rules of active listening throughout their meeting. They are, remember, that the listener must repeat, in their own words, what the speaker said, to the speaker's satisfaction before the listener can respond. The responder then receives the same active listening treatment as was just given.

Getting in shape physically is not difficult for most people, but it does require disciplined and intentional effort. The greatest enemy of good listening, just as it is of good physical condition, is the lack of will and motivation. There is no greater joy, nor security and satisfaction, than when you have listened to someone with whom you are in conflict or disagreement and created genuine understanding. LSi's Relationship Roadmap gives you direction as to when this communication tool is most essential; when you are working on renegotiating or renewing expectations and commitment. You can get by with casual listening elsewhere, but not when mutual understanding is crucial to your creating effective relationships.

COMMUNICATION AND SELF-ESTEEM

Self-esteem is a relationship phenomenon. Not only do we form our baseline of self-esteem in relationships with parents and other significant people in our lives but, as adults, our self-esteem fluctuates based on how our relationships are going. We have all experienced how we have great self-esteem in one group where we are confident, strong, and positive, yet in another our self-esteem is lousy. One of the groups where many people experience low self-esteem, unfortunately, is in their families. In esteem-diminishing families, relationships foster self-doubt, lack of confidence, and negative self-image. It's no wonder family members quickly disengage and attach to esteem-enhancing groups where they can experience a relationship that promotes the opposite.

One of the cardinal rules of self-esteem is that we will migrate toward those relationships that are esteem enhancing and away from those that are esteem diminishing. We believe that it is inherent for human beings to strive for positive self-esteem. All people want to feel good about themselves, to enjoy and celebrate their core of goodness. Sometimes this need has been so frustrated that people will do bizarre things to get recognition and elevate themselves even in homicidal and self-destructive ways. The case of the Unibomber, Theodore Kaczynski, is a tragic example. In his personal journal in which he chronicled his attacks on innocent people, he wrote, "I have not the least feeling of guilt about this—on the contrary, I am proud of what I did."[5] His mental illness and isolated childhood left him desperate for a way to enjoy and celebrate the feeling of pride in himself. Fortunately, such tragedies are the exception, but a frustrated drive to feel good about, and value, ourselves is why families fall apart, marriages end in divorce, and good employees leave well-paying jobs.

In family businesses the situation is, as you might expect by now, more complicated. Because of the economic interdependence, the tie that binds family members together, it is often not possible simply to make a clean break from an esteem-diminishing relationship to one that is esteem enhancing. The pressure-cooker environment that develops can be overwhelming as relationships become convoluted, conflicted, and empty when they are empty of esteem-enhancing energy. Thus, it is not uncommon to find family businesses in which people carry out responsibilities in perfunctory ways, collect their checks, and find any excuse possible not to spend time together. (Recall if you will, the left side of LSi's Relationship Roadmap where a person terminates the relationship "psychologically.") At times, the need for an esteem-enhancing relationship even drives family members into disgruntled nonfamily employee groups, where they become victims of employee efforts to divide and conquer the family ownership and management. Yes, self-esteem is a relationship phenomenon and it is essential to understand it in family business.

THE SELF-ESTEEM CYCLE

As we said, the need to feel good about ourselves and to value who we are is innate to human beings. Achieving this requires that our encounters with others result in our having a feeling of success and of being understood and appreciated. These two dimensions of esteem enhancement must occur on a consistent basis and they are, in fact, mutually reinforcing. In other words, the experience of being listened to, understood, and appreciated feeds a good feeling of success in the encounter. My feeling of success encourages me toward trust, optimism, and respect in the relationship. As we know from our previous discussion of the building blocks of relationships, these three dimensions, in turn, promote further relationship success. Since the need to feel good about ourselves, to value and appreciate ourselves, is universal, our esteem cycle is interdependently woven into the cycles of others. Our experience of success leads us not only to be open to being listened to by others but also it fuels our desire to listen openly and trustingly to them as well. As we do so, their experience of success, like ours, is strengthened, creating greater openness, trust, and desire to achieve understanding. It is a circular process that is virtually perpetual and self-reinforcing. We depict this as follows:

ESTEEM-ENHANCING RELATIONSHIP CYCLE

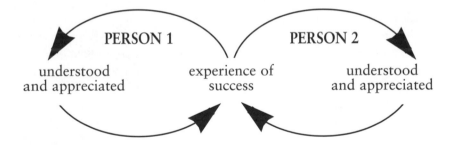

PERSON 1   PERSON 2

understood and appreciated   experience of success   understood and appreciated

In this simplified diagram each person in a two-person relationship is represented by one of the two circles. They are linked together by their common need for esteem enhancement. The cycle functions in such as way as to create the visual sign of infinity symbolizing that the cycle of esteem enhancement can go on forever.

Unfortunately, the experience of troubled families in business is the opposite. Day in and day out, they participate in a perpetual and self-reinforcing esteem-diminishing relationship cycle. It is just the opposite of the above: experiences of being ignored and depreciated fuel a deep feeling of failure in the relationship. The feeling of failure, in turn, causes mistrust, pessimism, and disrespect that easily drain away any interest in being open, understanding, and appreciative. In fact, in this eye-for-an-eye relationship, the experience of failure promotes ignoring, depreciating, and defensive behaviors that further contribute to the failure. This painful but common cycle is depicted as follows.

ESTEEM-DIMINISHING RELATIONSHIP CYCLE

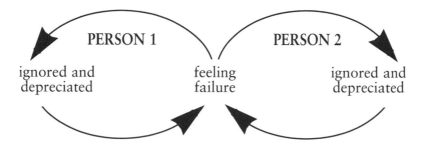

You will know which kind of cycle predominantly operates within your family business. Recognizing what you are doing to each other that results in everyone feeling bad about themselves and avoiding each other is the first step toward changing things. As long as the esteem-diminishing relationship cycle is in operation, it will be impossible to implement LSi's Relationship Roadmap. Perpetuating mistrust and bad will undermines even the best efforts. Converting the esteem-diminishing relationship cycle to an esteem-enhancing relationship cycle takes time, but it can be done. It takes time because the experience of being put down or ignored fuels a negative Relationship Paradigm, a deeply imbedded belief that either you or we are hopeless.

As with the learning of new communication tools, reversing the esteem cycle in your family business requires discipline and intentional effort. As you attempt to reverse the cycle, you will experience the pull of the old esteem-diminishing patterns like the undertow of a powerful river pulling you down as you swim frantically toward safety. Progress occurs in small things, small changes and improvements. It may simply be the decision by the group to recognize one positive virtue of each person each day, or practicing effective active listening with each other. In many ways, doing the things that cause others to experience understanding and appreciation is merely common sense. Remember the Golden Rule: "Do unto others as you would want them to do unto you." When the esteem-diminishing relationship cycle is deeply ingrained within the relationship paradigm, you will need help turning it around. Someone with a boat is essential to keep you from being pulled right back into the negative and powerful undertow. When you know you want out but you just can't break the cycle yourselves, reach out for help. Don't wait too long, though; otherwise you will be like the frog who became accustomed to the pot of simmering then boiling water. The negativity will destroy your own esteem and that of other family members so much that you will all think it's an impossible situation.

ISSUE MANAGEMENT

Issue management stands alongside Partnering Covenants and effective communication as the third key tool in relationship renewal. An issue is a problem waiting to happen. Put another way, when issues go unresolved, they compound into problems. An issue is anything about which a decision needs to be made. In this sense, an issue can be anything from whether to eat in or go out to dinner, to internationalizing a company. When issues go unresolved, when no decision is made, they become encrusted with emotional residue; this is when they become problems. This is why issues are much easier to resolve than problems. In family businesses a very common place in which issues escalate into problems is in the area of accountability. We can recall a family business run by three brothers. Two of the brothers had been with the company for over ten years when their younger sibling Dan joined the business. Dan replaced the retiring purchasing manager. At first all three were excited to be working together, but an issue soon emerged. The performance and productivity of the purchasing department began to decline almost from the beginning. When his two older brothers talked to Dan about their concerns, his response was always the same. The problems he was having came from too much demand on the department, too few staff, and problems left over from his predecessor, who had been with the company for twenty-five years. Suggestions for improving the situation were always rejected by Dan, who said he had to do it his way. After a year and a half, the situation was so bad that Dan's brothers reassigned him to manage the maintenance department, which was a new position in the company. They never resolved the issue of Dan's lack of ability to lead the purchasing department because talking about it always led to an argument. After three months of managing the maintenance department, the same problems developed. Again,

Dan blamed the problems on lack of staff, bad equipment, and unreasonable demands of production. By now, the *issue* of Dan's lack of competence in management had become the *problem* of Dan's incompetence. As always happens, there were several layers of emotion that made it impossible for the three brothers to discuss the problem and know what to do about it. Now it would be much more difficult, costly, and time consuming to resolve, than if they had dealt with it only a few months earlier.

The majority of problems faced between family members in family businesses exist because an issue was ignored or neglected at an earlier time. Identifying and managing issues before they become problems is a central tool in the Relationship Skill toolbox.

This is not to say that a method or system for resolving problems is unimportant; there will always be problems. In writing about the promotion of healthy family relationships, the well-known family therapist and researcher Dr. Froma Walsh says:

> Problem solving is a crucial process in families. Well-functioning families are characterized not by the absence of problems but by effective problem-solving ability and conflict management, requiring open disagreement with good communication skills for resolution. Epstein and his colleagues . . . identify sequential steps in the problem-solving process. Negotiation and compromise are important, and can be hindered by competition and struggles over power and control. Mutual accommodation and reciprocity over time are crucial for long-term relationship balance. Families need to develop effective strategies to resolve normal problems in daily living as well as crises that may arise. How well the family, as a functional unit, masters these adaptational challenges will reverberate throughout the system, impacting the well-being of all members. (190)[6]

Yes, having a method for problem solving is essential to success and survival in family business. However, it does nothing to create a system whereby future problems can be minimized or avoided. It's a bit like bailing water on the Titanic after it's hit the iceberg. It's better to avoid the iceberg in the first place. This is what issue management is all about and why it is so essential to any business-owning family wanting to improve their level of Relationship Intelligence. While the issue management process can be utilized at any level in the company, it is especially helpful for family executives and owners. It is even helpful in resolving issues with and among family members not actively involved in management or ownership of the business.

Implementing issue management involves three things: (1) establishing a Partnering Covenant to support it, (2) developing the protocols for implementing it, and (3) holding one another accountable for sticking to it. One of the reasons issues grow into problems in family businesses is that people, in a meeting or a hallway conversation, will say something like, "We really have to do something about . . ." or "We are going to have big trouble if we keep . . ." There are a thousand variations but the end result is always the same: someone dumps an important issue on the group, it is acknowledged by the others, yet everyone walks away forgetting about it until the next time it's mentioned.

Issue management therefore begins with the creation of a Partnering Covenant that establishes the group's desire and commitment to this new way of working together. Every family business will have their own wording and style regarding Partnering Covenants, but one of our clients established the following:

> Knowing how much problems cost us as a company and that the toll on family relationships has been great in the past, we agree to establish and follow protocols necessary for identifying and managing issues to avoid having them turn into problems. We further agree that this is a major duty and responsibility we have to one another; and will support each other in following the protocols and willingly accept, as individuals, the accountability of the group when we do not.

The issue management protocol, supported by the Partnering Covenant, provides the guidelines for implementing the process. The following can serve as a helpful guide.

ISSUE MANAGEMENT PROTOCOL

ISSUE OWNERSHIP

Whoever identifies an issue verbally or in writing, owns the issue and is responsible for the successful completion of the issue management process regarding that issue. It is not this person's responsibility to single-handedly resolve the issue. The person who owns the issue is the facilitator of the issue-management process for that issue. Resolution of the issue, per the Partnering Covenant, is the group's responsibility. In some cases, a person other than the one who brought the issue to the table is best suited, and willing, to take ownership of the issue. This is perfectly O.K., as long as everyone in the group supports the transfer of ownership.

ISSUE MANAGEMENT PROCESS

The issue management process involves the following steps. The owner of the issue will use an Issue Management Worksheet (see page 92) for communication with all involved and to track the implementation of the process. If this is an emergency situation, as defined by the group, the following process is still very helpful. But needless to say, the time frame must be condensed to perhaps hours rather than days. Particularly in emergency situations, it is easy to mismanage an issue, to overlook an important aspect of the situation and create a solution that winds up causing more issues than it resolves. This process helps avoid this common mistake.

Step 1: Ownership of the issue is determined.

Step 2: The owner of the issue completes the Issue Management Worksheet (see below) so that it can be distributed and the next meeting scheduled as soon as possible.

Step 3: A preliminary list of people involved is developed by the owner of the issue; these people receive the completed worksheet. Each person is asked to provide his or her written comments about all the items on the worksheet to the owner of the issue, prior to the meeting. In some cases the owner of the issue may be the only one involved but members of the group should still receive and comment on the Issue Management Worksheet. When several people are identified, some may be involved in only certain aspects of the process.

Step 4: The meeting of the group to discuss the Issue Management Worksheet should be scheduled as soon as possible following identification of the issue. For particularly sensitive or critical issues this should happen within seventy-two hours.

Step 5: By the end of this meeting, or within a couple of days, a detailed task plan is completed by the owner of the issue spelling out the chronological steps in the resolution process. Each step includes a description of the task to be completed, the persons involved, identification of any resources needed, and projected completion date.

Step 6: In the case of more complex issues, regular reviews of progress are done in group meetings. Focus should be on getting to resolution as quickly as possible without jeopardizing the quality of the outcome.

ISSUE MANAGEMENT WORKSHEET

Issue owner _____

- Write a clear definition of the issue (what's going on that needs to be changed?)

- Relevant background (how the issue developed, what has been done in the past to resolve it, who is involved)

- Impact of issue on business process (finances, operations, family relationships, employees, sales, etc.)

- Resolution options (identify at least two)

- Pros and cons of each option listed

- Additional information needed to resolve the issue

- People who need to be involved in the discussion and resolution of this issue

- Proposed resolution date _____

- Proposed date of meeting to discuss _____

DOCUMENTATION OF ISSUE RESOLUTION

When resolution is reached it is documented in some form such as a memorandum of understanding, a policy or procedure, a revision of the corporate bylaws or shareholders agreement, or entry in board minutes.

SHIFTING YOUR RELATIONSHIP PARADIGM

The Relationship Intelligence model says that skills alone are not enough to successfully manage a relationship long term. Of equal importance are the spirit and ethos, the culture of the group—in short, its Relationship Paradigm. The Relationship Paradigm controls the exchange of information and emotions in a relationship like the customs booth controls the exchange of visitors and citizens at the airline or ship terminal. It can create huge bottlenecks and interpersonal snarls, yet without it there would be chaos. To carry our analogy one step further, dishonest customs agents prey on innocent people just as a negative Relationship Paradigm destroys all the potential in a relationship. Along with building Relationship Skill, Relationship Intelligence requires the creation of a positive Relationship Paradigm. Altering a Relationship Paradigm is always more difficult than learning relationship skills.

Every Relationship Paradigm has a history. Some are longer than others. We all have lifelong Relationship Paradigm histories with our families. Each of us also has been involved with a group that developed its particular style of prejudices and expectations within a few months or even weeks. The basis of a Relationship Paradigm can be found in such shared history, and it grows out of the experiences the group has, the meaning they attach to those experiences, and how the group is affected emotionally as a result. Experience, meaning, and emotional impact have great bearing on how the three relationship dilemmas discussed in chapter 2 are resolved. The group will either develop trust, optimism, and respect, or mistrust, pessimism, and disrespect. Its actions and commitments will reflect its paradigm.

Since a group's Relationship Paradigm develops through experience, it makes sense that it can likewise be changed through experience. We call these *corrective paradigm experiences*, and they happen either by planning or serendipity. Serendipitous positive Relationship Paradigm changes are somewhat rare and risky because they are left to chance. It seems that they can turn out negative just as easily as positive. Many years ago we met two brothers who had been through such an unplanned, serendipitous, positive Relationship Paradigm change. As the third-generation owners of a $35 million distribution company, they had "decided" years before that one of them was the optimist and the other the pessimist in their relationship. They would say of their relationship, "Jack is always seeing the light at the end of the tunnel and Rich is always blowing it out!" For years, their relationship revolved around this central tenet of their Relationship Paradigm. They became known, not only in the company, but in the industry as "the flip brothers" because they always took opposite sides of the coin. As is predictable in relationships such as theirs, Jack and Rich became polarized and petrified into their respective positions. The company organized around them, and the unwritten rule among employees was if you wanted a "yes" answer you went to Jack, knowing Rich would likely say "no." Neither Rich nor Jack liked the stereotype but that's how a Relationship Paradigm works.

Their Relationship Paradigm changed because of a major crisis. The same day that they received word that their largest customer had changed vendors, their building burned and they lost 80 percent of their inventory, computers, and equipment. Jack was devastated, this was an account he had brought into the company and always said was untouchable. Being six years older than Rich, Jack was ready to throw in the towel. It would be mind boggling to start all over again. But Rich, being more pragmatic and detail oriented, provided the spark that ignited the rebuilding of the company. Within three days, working day and night, he had created a program to rebuild the company and make it even more efficient than before. Everyone was amazed that what was always seen as a battle over optimism versus pessimism was in reality a potentially creative difference. Rich always looked for details and was cautious until he found them, while Jack was energized by the dream of a new and better tomorrow and couldn't get there fast enough. The crisis created an openness, not just between Jack and Rich, but on the part of the entire company, to a new set of expectations and prejudices about their relationship.

LSi's PARADIGM KALEIDOSCOPE

The path of Relationship Renewal must pass through revision or reaffirmation of the Relationship Paradigm. Typically, when expectations become altered due to change (cf. LSi's Relationship Roadmap), and a "pinch" ensues, some alteration of the Relationship Paradigm is in order. This is a planned approach to changing Relationship Paradigms by opening the paradigm up and making its basis explicit. LSi's Paradigm Kaleidoscope is a structured process that is used in Relationship Renewal in combination with the tool of active listening discussed above.

We chose the name "Paradigm Kaleidoscope" to describe this aspect of Relationship Renewal because it reminds us of how the turning of a kaleidoscope changes the perspective of the viewer or of what is being viewed. Even though what we see is really only a rearrangement of colors or a different refraction of an image through the lens, each view appears as new. Several people observing the same event will have their own version about it like looking at it through their kaleidoscopes. It is also possible to alter our own perspectives on the same event by changing how we view it. Viewing a person who is verbally attacking us as doing so because he is vicious and intentionally mean is very different than viewing the same person as emotionally troubled and unstable. Being offered a new way to look at things is like turning our own kaleidoscope and bringing a different view into focus. LSi's Paradigm Kaleidoscope provides the mechanism to get the perspective and clarity we must have to continue the journey of relationship renewal.

There are five facets of LSi's Paradigm Kaleidoscope, like the five facets of a lens in a kaleidoscope. Depending upon which facet we look through, we see a different component of our Relationship Paradigm.

LSi's PARADIGM KALEIDOSCOPE

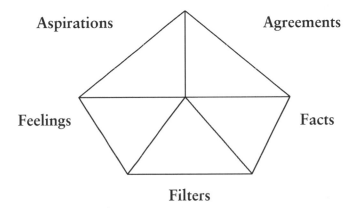

Facts, filters, and feelings are the three facets of the Paradigm Kaleidoscope that define the operative Relationship Paradigm. They form the foundation of the Relationship Paradigm. Facts are the observable events and occurrences upon which we base our perspectives. They are the raw data from which we later draw inferences and make assumptions. This is easier to describe than to experience, since most of us are oblivious to the facts of a situation. We often use the analogy of two people seeing an automobile accident take place. They heard the screech of tires and the metal-crumpling sound of the impact. As they look out their window a young man jumps out of one car. He looks twenty, long unkempt hair, rings on his hands and in his nose, and loud music is blaring from his radio. An elderly man slowly and carefully emerges from the other car. He has thick glasses and walks with a cane. There are noticeable dents already in his car and a little dog is jumping back and forth between the seats barking wildly. Those are the facts, observed by hearing and sight, no judgment about them, like a movie camera recording the event.

We don't stay long with the facts, though. Within an instant the facts are making their way through our filters of expectations, prejudices, beliefs, and interpretations. We apply meaning to the facts, and the meaning is based on the filters we have. One of us says, "Look at that, I bet that kid's on drugs . . . they ought to lock him up for a long time!" The other of us says, "I don't know why they let people drive when they're too old to see and their reflexes too slow to react . . . they should take his license away from him!" Same facts, different meanings given once we filter them. It happens routinely and automatically, until we know enough to stop and scrutinize our filters.

Facts filtered through expectations, prejudices, and beliefs have an emotional impact on us. One of us observing the accident will feel enraged at the young man, sorry and worried for the elderly man. The other of us will feel disdain and frustration with the elderly man, sympathy for the younger man. The emotional impact of our prejudices and beliefs, powers and reinforces our Relationship Paradigms. If a Relationship Paradigm revolves around mistrust, pessimism, and disrespect, each time an event takes place and makes its way through the filters of that paradigm, the emotional impact of divisiveness, anger, and hopelessness feeds the paradigm.

The aspirations (what we hope for) and agreements (what we are willing to commit to) that operate within our relationship are formed and shaped by this foundation of facts, filters, and feelings. Like the tip of an iceberg, what we experience most commonly in negative Relationship Paradigm situations is the fragmentation of aspirations and the breakdown of commitments. But, below the surface is the observing, filtering, and feeling process that supports everything else.

Understanding LSi's Paradigm Kaleidoscope puts you in the position to make important changes in your Relationship Paradigm, both below and above the surface. Each facet of the Paradigm Kaleidoscope offers a different perspective on things. Some people typically lead with their expectations or beliefs when describing a relationship. They will say, "Nobody trusts anybody else," or "This is such a great place to work because of the team spirit," or "We simply cannot work together as a family." The pronouncements are made as gospel fact, when in truth they are really expectations and prejudices. Our experience is that two-thirds of us, when describing a situation, typically lead with telling about our filters, not with facts or feelings. The second most frequently expressed perspective flows out of feelings, the emotional impact the situation has. When describing a situation from this perspective people will say, "It's very frustrating," or "This family is so hurtful I feel embarrassed around employees," or "It's such a joy seeing all of my kids working together." The majority of us find it very difficult to start right out presenting the facts, the raw data, upon which we are basing our conclusions. For example, I will most likely tell you I think you're disappointed in me, not that I just saw you grimace or heard you tell someone you'd rather be working on the project with them.

There is no better method for identifying, discussing, and revising a Relationship Paradigm than LSi's Paradigm Kaleidoscope. In using this method any group of people, especially family members, can objectively and progressively lay the groundwork for Relationship Renewal, clarifying of expectations, and arriving at a new commitment. It is a vital element in successfully returning to the information exchange stage of LSi's Relationship Roadmap and the promotion of an ongoing pattern of preventive maintenance for relationships.

Through the process of clarifying the facts, filters, and feelings of the group, a new and more positive level of understanding is developed. In addition, the process promotes trust, builds empathy, fosters respect, and restores optimism. All of this happens because the paradigm information that is so critical to everyone, yet is usually kept under the surface, is brought out into the open and explored. You can imagine how refreshing this is for people used to arguing over "pinches," now able to join together in productive and successful dialogue about them. *This is why the practice of genuine active listening is so vital to the use of the Paradigm Kaleidoscope.* As everyone in the group contributes to the collection of facts, filters, and feelings, the group begins to understand itself in a new way. Expectations and prejudices that caused the pinch are placed on the table, not for the purpose of argument, but for understanding. Our experience in using this method with family businesses struggling with years of pinches is that the divisiveness and polarities begin to evaporate as everyone comes to understand the facts, as perceived by others, the beliefs through which those facts were filtered, and the emotional impact all of this has had on the group. Any pinch or issue, can be unpacked and understood using LSi's Paradigm Kaleidoscope method.

USING LSi's PARADIGM KALEIDOSCOPE

The first step is to describe the pinch. For example, "I thought we were all going to be involved in making the decision, not just the two of you"; or "It was a real pinch for me when you jumped right over my idea, and went on to discuss Fred's!" We usually suggest that the person who experiences the pinch, take time to identify the facts as she or he observed them, along with the meaning given to the facts (their filters) and the emotional impact that resulted. For example:

> I thought we were all going to be involved in making the decision, not just the two of you (pinch). You never discussed your ideas with us and now we hear that you two met a week ago to come up with a plan that you are proposing we adopt today (facts). It looks to me like you could care less about our input and that your only intention is to railroad us into your own position (filters). Frankly, that really disappoints and irritates me about both of you (feelings).

Everyone in the group, whether two people or twelve, should do the same. It must be understood and agreed that everyone's facts are, for them, true and that their filters and feelings are to be accepted, not debated. Understanding grows through this recognition and it is destroyed through inappropriate judgment. A worksheet like this one can be used by everyone to help in recording.

LSi's PARADIGM KALEIDOSCOPE WORKSHEET I

1. FACTS: what behaviors, actions, or words
   you observed in conjunction with the pinch

2. FILTERS: the meaning you place on the facts, your
   beliefs and interpretations of them

3. FEELINGS: how the facts and filters affect you
   emotionally

As we said earlier in this chapter, the purpose of communication is to create understanding and promote low-maintenance relationships. Supported by the communication tool of active listening, LSi's Paradigm Kaleidoscope is a communication-oriented method that helps to permanently redefine relationships.

By working through the facts, filters, and feelings, a group is then prepared to state their aspirations and agreements. Aspirations are statements of desire and hope based on real understanding. Agreements convert aspirations into commitments . . . the goal of Relationship Renewal. Along with the Paradigm Kaleidoscope Worksheet I, the following can be incorporated on the back of the same sheet.

LSi's PARADIGM KALEIDOSCOPE WORKSHEET II

4. ASPIRATIONS: how I hope we can resolve this pinch. . . for myself and for our group

5. AGREEMENTS: the commitment(s) I am willing to make to help achieve my aspirations

---

As everyone presents and discusses their aspirations and agreements, it is important to combine them into a consolidated statement of aspirations and agreements for the group as a whole. Some individuals may have their own specific agreement to carry out but it must be coordinated with, and approved by, the group. We must make it very clear, once again, that the process of Relationship Renewal is never completed. It is an ongoing process that is necessary for maintaining successful relationships. It is central to creating the next level of Relationship Intelligence.

Notes
1. Kurt Lewin. "Quasi-stationary Social Equilibria and the Problem of Permanent Change. In *The Planning of Change*, ed. W. G. Bennis, K.D. Benne, and R. Chin. New York: Holt, Rinehard, Winston, 1969.
2. John Sherwood, and John Glidewell. "Planned Renegotiation: A Norm Setting OD Intervention." In *Contemporary Organization Development: Approaches and Interventions,* Warner Burke, ed. Washington D.C.: NTL Learning Resources Corporation, 1972.
3. Interpersonal Communications Programs, Inc. 7201 South Broadway, Littleton Col. 80122
4. Bernard Jr., Guerney. *Relationship Enhancement*. San Francisco: Jossey-Bass Publishers, 1977, p. 26.
5. "Sentence Closes Door on Unibomber Saga," *Chicago Tribune,* May 4, 1998, p. 12.
6. Froma Walsh. "Healthy Family Functioning: Conceptual and Research Developments," Family Business Review, VII, no. 2 (Summer 1994): 190.

5 Assessing Your RQ

Assessing RQ is what this chapter is all about. There are two methods for assessing RQ. The first is the inquiry-based evaluation method and the second uses the RQ Questionnaire, which we have developed to provide you with a more definitive assessment of the level of RQ in your family business. The two methods go hand in hand, and though they can be used separately, together they provide a much more reliable assessment. Advisors/consultants working with family businesses may find in the inquiry-based evaluation a method for assessing the RQ status of a family business client when the RQ Questionnaire cannot be used. For families in business the inquiry-based evaluation provides a way of exploring and discussing aspects of their relationship that are problematic and for which they have been unable to get more than a vague handle on. Being able to understand the reasons for both problems and successes is key to preventing the former and capitalizing on the latter. The inquiry-based evaluation focuses attention on the reasons, thanks to the understanding gained through RQ.

The RQ Questionnaire is a simple but very effective tool to be used by a family business in confirming the observations made from the inquiry-based evaluation, or by itself to arrive at a good estimate of the level of RQ in the group. We will also discuss what to do once the level of RQ has been identified for your family business.

USING INQUIRY-BASED EVALUATION OF RQ

A good inquiry-based evaluation of RQ in your family business focuses on the two dimensions of RQ, Relationship Paradigm and Relationship Skill. We should reiterate a very important point that we made in chapter 2 where we described the RQ in a group as like a collage of individual perspectives. Obviously, a group has no eyes or ears except for those of the members, and members will vary to one degree or another in their evaluation of the group. Everything

101

we say about inquiry-based evaluation applies to the combined views of all the members of the group together. In other words the inquiry-based evaluation will require discussion and at least basic agreement about the elements of Relationship Paradigm and Relationship Skill that exist. This is probably not all that difficult since you only have to agree as to whether your Relationship Paradigm is essentially negative or positive and your Relationship Skill is high or low. If you simply cannot agree or even come together to discuss the questions, it's a pretty good indication that you are struggling with a Level 1 RQ that is destroying the motivation even to try. Advisors/consultants using the inquiry-based evaluation need to remember the importance of the combined perspectives as well. Many times you can talk to several family members and be convinced that they are neither in the same family or business together given the disparity of their perspectives. To get the full picture of RQ the advisor/consultant must ask the questions and make the observations of all those in the group either individually, or preferably together. Each perspective is like the individual colors on the artist's palette and only when blended together do they paint the portrait of the family.

What needs to be asked and observed to evaluate the RQ within your family business? Let's first look at the Relationship Paradigm dimension. You will need to evaluate how your family has resolved the three relationship dilemmas described in chapter 2.

- Trust versus mistrust
- Optimism versus pessimism
- Respect versus disrespect

Trust in a relationship is built by an enduring spirit of openness, sincerity, predictability, and reliability. Mistrust is built by secretiveness, duplicity, deceitfulness, and disappointment.

Optimism in a relationship is built by an enduring attitude of appreciation, positive anticipation, and confidence. Pessimism is built by depreciation, hopelessness, and fear.

Respect in a relationship is built by an enduring perspective of high regard, positive recognition, and gracious conduct toward one another. Disrespect is built by ingenuousness, derisiveness, and self-centeredness.

These are the qualities and characteristics that will let you know whether your family business operates with a more negative or more positive Relationship Paradigm. Here are the specific areas you will want to have in mind as you evaluate your group's Relationship Intelligence. First we will look at questions related to assessing Relationship Paradigm. Ask yourself, "To what degree do our relationships reflect these characteristics? In which areas do we have problems or get stuck?"

- Is there open and honest sharing and exchanging of information within your group, or is there secretiveness and intentional screening of what people say to each other?
- Do members of your family business group follow through on what they agree to do, or is there convenient forgetting about commitments made to each other?
- Is information shared in a consistent manner, or are there efforts to create different perceptions or understandings depending on whose agenda is being served?
- Is there willingness and desire to support, encourage, and appreciate each other's talents, or do people use every excuse to criticize and demean one another?
- As a group are you positive, hopeful, and eager about your future together or are you discouraged, unempowered, and dreading it?
- Is praise and recognition expressed willingly and freely among the members of your family business group, both to each other and to those outside the group, or is there back-biting, finger-pointing, and undercutting?
- Do you, as a group, sincerely express interest and compassion for each other, or does everyone complain about too much being expected of them by others?

A major part of your inquiry-based evaluation related to your Relationship Paradigm will come from observing how all of you together conduct yourselves around the issues identified above. It's important that you read between the lines and listen with a third ear as you observe and listen to one another. Advisors/consultants also need to listen with a third ear as the members of the family business describe their situation and problems. For example, secretiveness can be seen as timidity or inability to answer questions. The tone and atmosphere of the meeting will convey optimism or pessimism. Lack of eye contact, strained and hostile remarks, and requests of the advisor/consultant, to take sides are indicators of mistrust and fear.

QFRs

- Based on your observations about your family business relationship, do you think that your level of Relationship Paradigm is more positive or more negative?
- Do you think others in your family business would agree with your

evaluation? Why or why not?

• Have each person in your family business individually write out his or her answers to the Relationship Paradigm questions. Make sure all answers are supported by at least one specific example that illustrates it. Then meet as a group to share what you each have written and arrive at an estimate of your level of Relationship Paradigm.

Now, let's take a look at the Relationship Skill dimension. You will need to evaluate the ability within your family business group to:

• establish understanding through good communication;

• develop and carry out plans;

• keep differences between people and interpersonal conflict from negatively affecting family and business relationships;

• keep changes in the family, business, and ownership from destroying family harmony and eroding company performance; and

• effectively manage the routine as well as unusual problems with which they must deal.

Relationship Skill is more easily evaluated than Relationship Paradigm, by directly asking some objective questions. In other words, it is less necessary to read between the lines when it comes to Relationship Skill.

• Does everyone have a clear and consistent understanding about where the business is going?

• Do you have written guidelines for making decisions about the conditions under which a family member can come to work for the company?

• Does your company have a long-range planning process that contains specific implementation plans with assigned responsibility for getting them done?

• Do you have methods for resolving conflicts or do the same conflicts keep resurfacing?

• When problems arise, how do you resolve them? Is it effective, or do the same problems keep coming up over and over again?

• Do you work well together as a team; are you able to collaborate, compromise, and keep a unified focus on your tasks?

QFRs

• After you have answered the questions rank them, based on your answers, from 1 to 6, with 1 being the most important area where your family business needs to develop Relationship Skill and 6 being least important.

• Meet as a group to discuss everyone's responses to the questions and their ranking of importance.

Based on the answers to these questions and your observations related to Relationship Paradigm, you will be able to identify the issues related to RQ within your family business client. Again, this is not a precise measurement as to the specific location of your family business within one of the four quadrants. Nevertheless, knowing what issues related to RQ you are operating with will help greatly in knowing what areas you most need to work on, where you will have the greatest difficulty, and what's possible or what's not.

THE RQ QUESTIONNAIRE

Another method for assessing Relationship Intelligence is through the use of the RQ Questionnaire. The RQ Questionnaire was developed to assess the level of Relationship Intelligence among family members working together in the business. It provides a way to identify which of the four quadrants family business relationships fall into. Using the questionnaire results in comparison to your inquiry-based evaluation of RQ and in relation to the case examples will give you a comprehensive assessment of RQ. It has thirty-five items, which can be grouped into three categories: Relationship Paradigm, Relationship Skill, and Motivation.

Relationship Paradigm items deal with the spirit, morale, and culture of the family working in the business. This determines such important factors as the level of trust, hope, respect, confidence, and openness within the family business as a group. Relationship Paradigms cause us to experience our interactions with others as succeeding or failing, as positive or negative fulfilling, or as fulfilling or frustrating.

Relationship Skill items deal with the working family's collective ability to maximize their joint capability in dealing with problems and opportunities: Relationship Skill is the ability we have to create and sustain particular relationships in a satisfying and successful manner.

Specific relationship skills include managing differences, resolving conflicts, creating intimacy, having fun, solving problems, adapting to change, carrying out joint tasks, and experiencing a sense of mutual understanding.

The degree of Relationship Skill plus Relationship Paradigm expressed and experienced is the measure of a group's Relationship Intelligence.

Motivation items deal with perceived value and expectancy of success that a group shares. Motivation provides the emotional energy for a group to work at improving RQ. If either the perceived value or expectancy of success about and with relationships of a group are low, you can expect to encounter resistance for working together to make things better.

Unlike IQ, an individual's intellectual intelligence, RQ is a *shared ability*—it resides within the interactions you have with people in a particular group. Experience shows that there is something intangible, yet very real within our relationships that causes some to succeed better than others. High RQ makes it possible to create and sustain satisfying and productive relationships within a particular group.

HOW TO ADMINISTER THE RQ QUESTIONNAIRE

The RQ Questionnaire is administered by having all family members working in the business, and/or those who actively participate as owners, complete the thirty-five-item questionnaire. It may be best to keep individual family member responses anonymous unless using a family business consultant or facilitator to help interpret and discuss results.

RQ QUESTIONNAIRE

1. No effort is made to solicit and understand family members' ideas regarding the business.

a. Always ○   b. Frequently ○   c. Sometimes ○   d. Seldom ○   e. Never ○

2. It is easier for us to avoid conflict than to risk a breakdown in family relationships.

a. Always ○   b. Frequently ○   c. Sometimes ○   d. Seldom ○   e. Never ○

3. Family members have a shared and inspiring vision for the future of the business.

a. Always ○   b. Frequently ○   c. Sometimes ○   d. Seldom ○   e. Never ○

4. In our family, expressing personal opinions and ideas is considered disruptive or is discouraged.

a. Always ○   b. Frequently ○   c. Sometimes ○   d. Seldom ○   e. Never ○

5. Upon entering the business, family members clearly know the kind of behavior that is expected of them and what they must do to get ahead.

a. Always ○   b. Frequently ○   c. Sometimes ○   d. Seldom ○   e. Never ○

6. Family members feel safe enough with each other to acknowledge mistakes and to ask for forgiveness.

a. Always ○   b. Frequently ○   c. Sometimes ○   d. Seldom ○   e. Never ○

7. We meet regularly to review long-range goals and implementation plans.

a. Always ○   b. Frequently ○   c. Sometimes ○   d. Seldom ○   e. Never ○

8. We can count on each other to follow through on commitments.

a. Always ○   b. Frequently ○   c. Sometimes ○   d. Seldom ○   e. Never ○

9. There are definite topics family members avoid discussing.

a. Always ○   b. Frequently ○   c. Sometimes ○   d. Seldom ○   e. Never ○

10. We avoid being together as a family outside of the business whenever possible.

a. Always ○   b. Frequently ○   c. Sometimes ○   d. Seldom ○   e. Never ○

11. Family employees receive regular objective performance appraisals based on specific feedback of both individual contributions and areas for improvement.

a. Always ○   b. Frequently ○   c. Sometimes ○   d. Seldom ○   e. Never ○

12. Family members show support, encouragement, and appreciation for each other's efforts and talents.

a. Always ○   b. Frequently ○   c. Sometimes ○   d. Seldom ○   e. Never ○

13. We can easily discuss problems and arrive at mutually acceptable solutions.

a. Always ○   b. Frequently ○   c. Sometimes ○   d. Seldom ○   e. Never ○

14. Our actions reflect the unwritten family rule of "Think it, but don't speak it."

a. Always ○   b. Frequently ○   c. Sometimes ○   d. Seldom ○   e. Never ○

15. Speaking out will usually get you in trouble in our family.
a. Always ○   b. Frequently ○   c. Sometimes ○   d. Seldom ○   e. Never ○

16. Employees recognize that family members work together mainly for the good of the business rather than individual or family gain.
a. Always ○   b. Frequently ○   c. Sometimes ○   d. Seldom ○   e. Never ○

17. Family members can freely express their feelings, values, and beliefs.
a. Always ○   b. Frequently ○   c. Sometimes ○   d. Seldom ○   e. Never ○

18. Family members have to deal with unclear expectations, roles, and responsibilities.
a. Always ○   b. Frequently ○   c. Sometimes ○   d. Seldom ○   e. Never ○

19. We set aside time to plan together and to create specific strategies for growing and managing the business.
a. Always ○   b. Frequently ○   c. Sometimes ○   d. Seldom ○   e. Never ○

20. We experience the present and anticipate the future with a shared sense of hope and optimism.
a. Always ○   b. Frequently ○   c. Sometimes ○   d. Seldom ○   e. Never ○

21. Family members do not fully understand what is expected of them.
a. Always ○   b. Frequently ○   c. Sometimes ○   d. Seldom ○   e. Never ○

22. We relate in an open and honest way about family and business issues.
a. Always ○   b. Frequently ○   c. Sometimes ○   d. Seldom ○   e. Never ○

23. We do not resolve issues fully and similar conflicts keep recurring.
a. Always ○   b. Frequently ○   c. Sometimes ○   d. Seldom ○   e. Never ○

24. Family members undermine or criticize one another either directly or indirectly.
a. Always ○   b. Frequently ○   c. Sometimes ○   d. Seldom ○   e. Never ○

25. Family members really understand each other's point of view.
a. Always ○   b. Frequently ○   c. Sometimes ○   d. Seldom ○   e. Never ○

26. Working together in the business is a real benefit both for the family and the business.
a. Always ○   b. Frequently ○   c. Sometimes ○   d. Seldom ○   e. Never ○

27. Family members find it easy to collaborate, compromise, and reach consensus.
a. Always ○   b. Frequently ○   c. Sometimes ○   d. Seldom ○   e. Never ○

28. Information is shared with all family members in a consistent manner.
a. Always ○   b. Frequently ○   c. Sometimes ○   d. Seldom ○   e. Never ○

29. We have created separate structures and procedures for addressing family, management, and ownership issues.

a. Always ○   b. Frequently ○   c. Sometimes ○   d. Seldom ○   e. Never ○

30. We avoid discussing controversial issues.

a. Always ○   b. Frequently ○   c. Sometimes ○   d. Seldom ○   e. Never ○

31. We have a clear and comprehensive understanding of where the business is going.

a. Always ○   b. Frequently ○   c. Sometimes ○   d. Seldom ○   e. Never ○

32. Family members' input is actively sought in regard to all major family business decisions.

a. Always ○   b. Frequently ○   c. Sometimes ○   d. Seldom ○   e. Never ○

33. I believe there is no greater work or career opportunity for me than working with the family business.

a. Always ○   b. Frequently ○   c. Sometimes ○   d. Seldom ○   e. Never ○

34. Family members feel very confident of their combined abilities for managing the business together.

a. Always ○   b. Frequently ○   c. Sometimes ○   d. Seldom ○   e. Never ○

35. I believe that we, as a business-owning family, have the kind of supportive and trusting relationship to face whatever difficulties that come our way.

a. Always ○   b. Frequently ○   c. Sometimes ○   d. Seldom ○   e. Never ○

SCORING THE RQ QUESTIONNAIRE

First have individuals score their own questionnaire.

Step One:

1. Twelve item numbers are boxed in: 1, 2, 4, 9, 10, 14, 15, 18, 21, 23, 24, 30 (e.g., 1. , 2. , etc.)

2. Put a 1 (one) next to each of the twelve boxed items for which you answered (D–Seldom) or (E–Never).

Step Two:

1. Place a 1 (one) next to each of the 23 other items, which *are not boxed in*, for which you answered (A–Always) or (B–Frequently).

Step Three:

1. Circle the 1's (ones) you have entered in front of all the *even* numbered items 1 thru 32 *only*. (*Do not* count questions numbered 33, 34, or 35 as yet.)

2. Count the circled even numbered 1's. This is your Relationship Paradigm Score.

3. Count the remaining 1's (ones) in front of the *odd* numbered items 1 thru 32 *only*. (*Do not* count questions numbered 33, 34, or 35 as yet.) This is your Relationship Skill Score.

Step Four:

1. Return to items numbered 33, 34, and 35. Place a 1 (one) next to each of these three items for which you answered (A–Always) or (B–Frequently).

2. Count the 1's (ones) in front of items numbered 20, 26, 33, 34, 35. This is your Motivation Score.

3. Record your individual scores below.

> Relationship Paradigm_____
> Relationship Skill   _____
> Motivation   _____

Category	Relationship Paradigm	Relationship Skill	Motivation
Respondents 1			
2			
3			
4			
5			
etc.			
Total			
Average			

(Average = Total ÷ by number of respondents)

Step Five:

1. Appoint someone to record and add all of the individual Relationship Paradigm, Relationship Skill, and Motivation scores in each of the three columns: Divide the sum of each by the number of family member respondents. The average becomes the score for this particular group.

2. Record your family's average score for:

> Relationship Paradigm _____
> Relationship Skill   _____
> Motivation   _____

INTERPRETATION

An average score of 8 or less equals *low Relationship Paradigm or Relationship Skill*. The midrange score for Motivation is 3 on a scale of 1 to 5. Motivation helps to qualify how optimistic or pessimistic family members are about successfully being able to work together toward common goals while working through differences or conflicts. The higher the level of motivation a family has that falls within Level 1, 2, or 3, the greater the possibility for working together to improve Relationship Paradigm or Relationship Skill. For example, if a family's RQ falls within Level 1 or 2, but they have a Motivation score of 4 or 5, this indicates that it is well worth the effort to work at improving Relationship Skill or Relationship Paradigm, as indicated. However, if a family's RQ is at Level 1 or 2 and Motivation is a 1 or 2, it will be much more difficult to get the family to work at improving Relation ship Skill or Relationship Paradigm. In such a situation, they should seriously address the question: "Should we continue to be in business together?"

An average score between 9 and 16 equals *high Relationship Paradigm or Relationship Skill.* Your family's Relationship Paradigm and Relationship Skill average will help you identify which of the four quadrants of Relationship Intelligence at which your family is operating. See the Relationship Skill Matrix below:

RELATIONSHIP INTELLIGENCE MATRIX

POSITIVE

	LEVEL 3 Positive Relationship Paradigm Low Relationship Skill	LEVEL 4 Positive Relationship Paradigm High Relationship Skill
RELATIONSHIP PARADIGM LOW		HIGH
	LEVEL 1 Negative Relationship Paradigm Low Relationship Skill	LEVEL 2 Negative Relationship Paradigm High Relationship Skill

NEGATIVE

RELATIONSHIP SKILLS

In general, the higher the level of RQ and Motivation together, the better prospects there are for family members being successful in business together.

Knowing which level of RQ a family is confronting is extremely valuable in making decisions about a family's readiness and ability to im prove their Relationship Intelligence. The following four hypothetical family business scenarios, one for each of the four quadrants, can be used to compare the results of your inquiry-based or RQ Questionnaire assessment. Think of them as descriptive templates against which to check your observations or the average scores obtained on the questionnaire.

CASE EXAMPLE—LEVEL 1 RQ
Situation:

Two sons, a daughter, and their father are equal owners of the $27 million distribution business started by the father. Father, now in his seventies, is no longer active in the business, but he and his wife are very dependent on it for a six-figure annual income. Father has always been rigid and dictatorial with both employees and his children. Mother, also in her seventies, has always been a very anxious and dependent woman. She focuses her anxiety about security on her husband's lack of financial planning and their dependency on their children for financial security. The three children were told by their parents that if they did not enter the business they would have no part in the parents' estate. The apparent reason for the mandate was the parents' belief that the business would serve as the glue to keep their loosely connected family together. After ten to fifteen years in the business, two of the children have become aware of how much they resent being in the business, but feel trapped. The family members are economically dependent on the business. They cannot afford to sell the business because its sales have declined and thus the value eroded due to the family conflict. The children have persistent emotional struggles individually and among them over, on the one hand, their family feelings of loyalty and deference to their parents and, on the other hand, feelings of indentured servitude as executives in the business. Relationships between the sibling families are nonexistent. Relationships between the grandparents and grandchildren are distant and strained at least partly because of the negative comments the grandchildren hear from their parents about their grandparents. The children have all grown up in the business with no formal business education, so the company has no planning processes and very weak management structures. The revenue of the company is dependent on strong product lines and several excellent sales reps who virtually call the shots, do their own thing, and pull down huge commission incomes.

Evaluation:

On the outside this looks like a successful distribution company with solid, though flat, sales. However, the situation is chaotic and fragile on the inside. The Relationship Paradigm of the group is obviously very negative. Mistrust is rampant and causes parents, children, and siblings to be defensive and skeptical about one another's intentions. The parents believe that at least two of the children could care less about the parents' financial security, siblings are looking out for themselves, and employees are building silos in the company in which to hide and push their own agendas.

The Relationship Skill of the group is likewise very low. There are many words, but little understanding; conflict explodes and goes underground only to explode again in a destructive cycle; there is no formal planning either by the business, ownership, or family. This leaves all three groups highly vulnerable, and decisions essential to the well-being of the business are never made, so the same issues and problems keep coming up over and over again.

CASE EXAMPLE—LEVEL 2 RQ
Situation:

A third-generation agribusiness, involving several related types of agricultural operations, is in the hands of five third-generation family members. They each have varying percentages of ownership in the various entities, given to them by their grandparents and parents. Only two of the five are actively involved in management of the group of businesses. Nevertheless, all depend upon the profits of the operations, to one degree or another, for their family incomes. All of the third generation are well educated. One is a CPA with a small public accounting firm, another is an attorney specializing in tax and estate law with a small law firm, another is a clinical social worker in private practice, and the other two are married to business managers, each a mother of small children and very active in community organizations.

The major concern of the third generation is what they should do with the family business in the future. The agricultural industry is very different than it was when their grandfather and father were in it. Today, foreign agricultural producers, consolidation within the industry, and lower profit margins without government subsidies, make it a very demanding business. Only the two third-generation family members active in the business actually have the interest and skill to manage it. However, there is a significant amount of land involved which has no tax basis, having been passed down three generations; selling it would trigger huge capital gains taxes. Both the family CPA and attorney are vehemently opposed to having this happen and are constantly scheming between themselves about how to avoid taxes.

In terms of family relationships, there is a strong unspoken commitment to avoiding conflict and not making waves. Even the mildest questioning of the two family members managing the business is viewed as an indication of mistrust, disloyalty, and lack of appreciation. Several in-laws have had major blow-ups with other family members, even during their one and only family meeting five years earlier, because they asked the wrong questions or pushed for too much information. Those not in the business have no information about how the two family managers are compensated nor how "loans" to family members from the business are dealt with. There is a precarious but precise dance between siblings active in the business and those who are not. The latter are, on the one hand, grateful for the income they get but, on the other hand, they constantly wonder and talk behind the scenes about why there is a lack of information, apparent secrecy, and vagueness regarding the operations of the company. Concern is growing that should something happen to the two active managers, no one else in this generation could take their places and no one in the fourth generation is either ready or interested in getting involved in the family business.

Evaluation:

This is the kind of family business that finds it very difficult to recognize their need for help or to ask for outside advice and consultation. In part, this is because as a group they have a better than average level of Relationship Skill. They plan and implement successful family gatherings and vacations. Issues and problems are solved for the most part by deferring to the designated problem solvers, meaning the two family executives who each have well-defined areas of responsibility. They have executed a Shareholder's Agreement that provides for all of the standard contingencies except there is no liquidity for owners during their lifetimes. The companies are all profitable and apparently well run by managers chosen by the two family executives. The one glaring deficiency in their Relationship Skill is communication. There is an unacceptably high degree of false agreement among family members because of the prohibitions on voicing personal expectations that are taken negatively. Communication therefore serves not to create understanding but to preserve tranquility and pass limited information about sensitive business topics.

Relationship Paradigm, which is essentially negative for this family in business, is the real problem area here even though it might not appear as such at first glance. A higher level of Relationship Skill can mask a negative Relationship Paradigm with artful application of Relationship Skill tools. Nevertheless, it's apparent that mistrust is very much present although veiled, there is thinly covered pessimism about their ability to improve their communication and about the future of the business, and the deference that has previously been viewed as respect is weakening. Interestingly enough, their attempts to resolve the long-term issues have all focused on becoming more skilled, not on improving their Relationship Paradigm. They attend seminars on communication and planning and use their advisors to educate them. They choose this approach because they are already better than average in Relationship Skill, and this is the less risky avenue to follow in terms of getting into interpersonal issues. However, for reasons we will discuss below, their long-term situation will improve only by redefining their Relationship Paradigm and making it more positive, a more threatening and intimidating path for this very educated group.

CASE EXAMPLE—LEVEL 3 RQ
Situation:

Father, stepmother, two sons, and one of the son's wives are actively involved in the $10 million manufacturing company that dad and a former partner purchased fifteen years earlier. Dad and his partner bought the business, at the time a very small operation, when it was a division being sold off by its parent company. The business grew modestly and the partner wanted to retire, so dad bought him out. Since then the company has quadrupled in size and his second wife is in charge of all office and administrative functions. Dad never envisioned his company becoming a family business even though his family meant everything to him. He had supported his two sons in their educations and beginning careers: one in mechanical engineering and the other in working for a government agency. The family has always been very close and the children weathered their parents' divorce very well. The children have good relationships with both their mother and father, and have established a comfortable and warm relationship with their stepmother.

Five years ago, dad started reading about family businesses and, having a successful growing business, became increasingly excited about the idea of his sons working with him in the company. He began to imagine how they would complement each other in abilities, remembering how well they got along growing up, and still do today. While his intention all along was to sell the business to a couple of key employees or to a third party, he began to think about his two sons someday owning the business he had built. After some discussion his oldest son, the engineer, and his son's wife decided to relocate and join the business with the intention of eventual owner-ship. Two years later the younger son approached his father with the notion of leaving his somewhat unsatisfying government job and joining the business to eventually own it with his brother. Dad and younger son discussed the possibility and dad, happy to have both sons working with him, announced without discussion with his older son, that his younger son would be coming into the business as well. Six months later both sons were actively involved in the company, each managing one of the two locations. Over the next two years dad and both sons came to respect each other's abilities and contributions. When the younger brother's location began to struggle financially, in spite of the fact that his older brother's loca-tion was doing very well, family members came together around concern and support, not blame and criticism. The younger brother solved the problem, which helped deepen the respect and confidence that he had gained with his father and brother.

Problems arose as dad began to take a less active role in the company, putting the decision making and planning on his sons' shoul-ders. Friction developed in what had been a great relationship between them and they began to avoid each other. Both felt bad about what was happening and it was beginning to affect life in their larger family. Dad's attempts to mediate the friction usually ended up with him mak-ing the decisions he wanted his sons to make. The two brothers began to think that a business partnership between them wasn't a good idea and might, in fact, destroy the good relationship they had always had as a family. Managers and employees who had a great respect and admiration for the family members also became increasingly concerned about their futures. They could not understand the friction developing between the sons and wondered if dad's stepping out had unleashed some deep-seated sibling rivalry that would destroy the company.

Evaluation:

Obviously the triggering factor here is dad's taking a less active role in the business and handing over more of the responsibility and author-ity to his sons. As the entrepreneur-founder of the business he had been the one pulling the chains and levers, a reality with which his sons and other employees were comfortable and confident. The Relationship Paradigm in this family business is very positive. Both in the family, and now in the business, there is significant trust built on the reliability, openness, and sincerity that characterize relationships. Optimism has never been at a higher level (although it has declined a bit due to the friction) because the future is bright and family members and employees alike are confident that these two brothers have the right stuff to continue growing the company. Respect, which has always been present in the family, is now deepened and extended into the business. Dad's overt appreciation for employees over the years is echoed by his sons, and their proving themselves in their respective locations impresses even seasoned managers.

The problem here is with the other dimension of RQ, Relationship Skill, which in this family business is at the low level. While everyone has always gotten along well as family, the sons and father have never taken the time to redefine and structure their relationship as business partners. Rules and skills that build success in families are, as we discussed in chapter 3, not the same as those for business. As father steps out of the role he has solely occupied in decision making, problem solving, planning, and managing change, neither he nor his sons realize that they do not have the tools needed to fulfill these functions. Neither of the sons has been trained in management or had the opportunity to be mentored and supervised in skills essential to a business partnership. Each individual is bright, a good problem solver, and technically skilled, but they do not know how to manage issues together, plan together for the entire company, clarify and integrate their roles and responsibilities, confront and negotiate their different styles, ideas, and conflicts, or establish true understanding through being attentive listeners.

Building on their positive Relationship Paradigm, the two brothers, their father, and stepmother can develop their Relationship Skill by:
- learning how to become better listeners;
- implementing the system for issue management described in chapter 6;
- instituting a family business strategic planning process that begins by making sure everyone is on the same page and ends with clearly defined responsibilities and accountability;
- the two brothers completing a career assessment program, which will help them define their executive roles and responsibilities as business partners; and
- each of them joining a CEO education and support group to learn from other CEOs and presidents about what it means to own and manage a business.

Family businesses at Level 3 are often eager for professional assistance because their lack of Relationship Skill threatens the high regard, appreciation, and enjoyment they have in their relationships.

These are the families that say, without hesitation, "If the business is going to destroy our family, we'll get out of the business." It isn't the business but the lack of skill that is destructive, and their desire to keep both family and business together, as a relationship-first family business, is a great catalyst for change.

CASE EXAMPLE—LEVEL 4 RQ
Situation:

A large third- and fourth-generation electrical engineering and contracting company has three third-generation owners who, along with two outside directors, comprise the Board of Directors of the company. The only third-generation family member active in the company is the oldest, age sixty-four, who is the president and CEO. While the company represents a sizable portion of the estate of each of the third generation, none are financially dependent upon their one-third ownership. Over the years the company has provided tremendous opportunity for all family members to launch businesses and careers of their own. The two third-generation owners not active in the company each own successful retail businesses. The fourth generation has likewise been blessed with talented individuals who have been well educated and are now executives in Fortune 500 companies, physicians, and business owners. Only two of the fifteen fourth-generation family members work in the family business. They are young and have lower-level positions, but are doing well and progressing. Each of the three third-generation families and the seven fourth-generation families among the married cousins have close family relationships. The families gather twice a year, in the summer and during the holidays. Inevitably, some can't make one of the annual gatherings, but will almost always be at the next one.

Estate planning has been completed by all of the third-generation families and several of the fourth. As for the stock in the business, the arrangement as of today allows each owner either to transfer it to their children or have the company purchase it from them or their estate. The Board of Directors has a succession plan that specifies one fourth generation family member from each "branch" of the family who would, in the event of his parent's death, replace the parent on the board.

The question before the current owners is whether they should aim toward transferring ownership to their children, as is currently the plan, or sell the business. The current president and CEO wishes to step down in two or three years and neither of his siblings, who are, respectively, two and four years younger, is interested in taking his role. If some of the fourth-generation family members want to own and manage the company, or even a part of it, the current owners will not sell it. The problem is that the family has never gotten together to discuss this issue, and thus the current owners are in the dark as to the level of interest, or even awareness of what opportunity exists, on the part of their children. If younger fourth-generation family members are interested, the current president and CEO has already identified a fifty-five-year-old executive in the company who would serve as mentor and bridge manager until the family member is ready to take over. In three years he would become chairman and CEO, making the mentor president of the company. However, the third generation have decided that if no fourth-generation family members want to manage the company, it will be sold.

A family meeting involving all the third- and fourth-generation family members and spouses was convened by the board. Twenty-two people attended. The facilitator of the meeting used premeeting questionnaires and small groups to get dialogue going about the intentions and concerns of each generation. The president and CEO made an in-depth presentation to the fourth generation about the company, the opportunities that exist for the future and, on behalf of the third generation, summarized their own plans. The two generations then met as groups in separate rooms to formulate questions for the other. The third generation worked on elaborating the conditions under which they would pass ownership and management to their children, and the fourth generation developed their response to the question about whether or not they were interested in ownership and management of the business. The whole group reconvened and each generational group made a presentation to the other about their respective meetings. The outcome was great clarification of expectations on both sides and the formation of a fourth-generation task force consisting of four people interested in the future ownership and management of the business, as well as the president and CEO. The task force was to take the reports from the two generational meetings and develop a possible succession plan to be presented to this same group in nine months.

Evaluation:

Here is a family business that is clearly at Level 4. Their Relationship Paradigm is very positive and their Relationship Skill is high. While they could have conducted the family meeting without professional facilitation, the president and CEO wanted to participate fully and knowing that he would be asked to run the meeting, was concerned that because of his position some younger family members might not speak up as freely. In addition, the facilitators, while making sure no one dominated the dialogue, were able to affirm the family's strengths and abilities from an outside authoritative position. In addition to the task force the group also decided to initiate a family newsletter, which several family members willingly agreed to start.

USING YOUR EVALUATION TO SET YOUR RQ DIRECTION

Now that you have identified the family's level of RQ, you can evaluate what must happen next. In many situations, the best alternative for severe Level 1 family businesses is for the family simply to get out of being in business together. When a very negative and entrenched Relationship Paradigm along with extremely poor Relationship Skill is carved out of decades of repeated disasters and pain in the family and business, motivation to restore relationships is likely to be nonexistent. Of course, there is motivation to stop the destructive negative cycle but not to restore the relationship. On the other hand, being at Level 1 does not mean all hope of relationship restoration should be abandoned. If the members of the family business would like to restore the family and business relationship, it is worth working to build a higher level of Relationship Skill. You need to be aware, however, of the strong current you are swimming against. The litmus test of ability to rebuild your family business relationship is in the extent to which you are able, without considerable support from the outside, to maintain the improvements in Relationship Skill. When a family in business continually slips back into old destructive patterns of communication, bad problem solving, and poor management of change, even with intensive focus on skill development, it is likely an indication that you should go your separate ways.

A great many family businesses can be placed either at Level 2 or Level 3 of RQ. If you are at Level 2, as can be seen in the scenarios described above, you are ready for and need to progress in Relationship Paradigm. You are among those bright and capable families in business with successful companies who just can't seem to get beyond relationship bottlenecks and hindrances that keep them from even greater success. A skilled process-oriented consultant can help you redefine and restructure your relationships, thus creating a new level of Relationship Paradigm that unleashes the potential of your business and opens new avenues to enjoying yourselves as a family. At Level 2 your family business does not need, nor will it benefit from, additional development of Relationship Skill until your Relationship Paradigm improves. Many Level 2 family businesses, motivated by new hope and possibility, seek out seminars, classes, and other educational experiences to add to their toolbox of Relationship Skill, only to find that their relationship is not progressing. This is because skill development is not what they need. What you need is a redefinition of Relationship Paradigm, and that cannot be achieved in seminars and classes.

If you are at Level 3 you are ready to build on your growing positive Relationship Paradigm and the basic set of Relationship Skill tools you have worked so hard to develop. You are among those families in business that need opportunities to build high-level Relationship Skill tools and structures. Individualized seminars and workshops that build on what your particular family business needs to, and can do are very effective. It is at this level that the development and implementation of the structures described in chapter 6 are essential and very rewarding. It is often through these structures that you are challenged to achieve new heights of Relationship Skill within the family, the business, and ownership groups. Implied here also is the fact that even a Level 4 family business must invest resources in their relationships. The good news is that many do make this investment because they've worked too long and hard to get where they are to take the important relationships for granted.

QFRs

- Based on the existing level of RQ in your family business, what can you do that will help the most in advancing it? Are there some hard and uncomfortable realities and decisions that you must face about your level of RQ and the implications for your future together as a family business? Are you a Level 2 RQ family business that is finding it difficult to recognize your need for help?

- To what extent are you putting development efforts in the wrong places, e.g., working on Relationship Skill too long or trying to improve your Relationship Paradigm before you have the tools to do so?

As you can tell by now, RQ provides a comprehensive way of understanding and improving relationships in your family business. As we have said, RQ integrates important perspectives and insights from the psychology of families, individual development and groups, organizational development, business management, mediation, change management, and human motivation. We have found that the complexity of family business relationships necessitates such an integrative approach in truly understanding and improving both Relationship Paradigm and Relationship Skill.

The four-quadrant RQ Matrix is reminiscent of a four-paned window. We like to think of it as the window that gives you a great view of the relationship landscape in your family business. In the past the view has been much more limited because the window was only one of the perspectives that have been incorporated in the RQ model. Looking through the RQ window requires that we provide you with a way of assessing the RQ in your family business. The two methods of assessment, along with the case examples provided in this chapter, should put you well on your way to understanding your family's level of Relationship Skill, Relationship Paradigm, and Motivation. Combining all three provides an assessment of the family's level of Relationship Intelligence.

6 The Architecture of Family Business

Most family businesses, even very large ones, operate with an unstructured and informal organizational style that is not in keeping with the magnitude of their situation. Some of these companies, and the families that own and lead them, fear becoming bureaucratic and losing their spontaneity and freedom. Most others have just never gotten around to thinking about how the business should be structured and organized. Even third- and fourth-generation family businesses often perpetuate a seat of the pants kind of organization of the company that was set in place by the founder and reinforced by the second generation. It's as if the business has the body of an adult but the skeleton of a child, or no skeleton at all, leaving it unable to bear the weight of its many essential tasks and functions.

When family businesses do establish more formalized structures of management and organization, they often emulate styles that are written about in textbooks and used to exemplify great organizations, most of which are nonfamily publicly held companies. While these may be excellent models to provoke thoughtfulness about getting organized, they do not fully take into account the unique complexities of family businesses that we have been describing and discussing. In other words, the great examples of organizational structure that capture the attention of Wall Street and the interest of management gurus don't fit when it comes to family business. This chapter provides some practical ideas and suggestions about creating the organizational structures needed to support established multigenerational family businesses. We have described RQ as the technology of relationship management in family business. Now we are adding to that technology what we call the architecture of family business. The structures we are presenting in this chapter provide the blueprint for the internal organizational and management systems that are needed to support a family business with multiple generations and multiple owners. This is an important point because like most everything else we have discussed, the necessity for structure becomes more and more paramount as the business moves into and beyond the second generation.

WHY STRUCTURE?

Most successful family businesses are run by entrepreneurs, sales-oriented people, or technicians, none of whom have much use for structure and organization. Entrepreneurs fear structure will fence them in and douse the fire of that entrepreneurial drive. Sales types are just opposed to the meetings, rigid expectations, and paper work they associate with structure and organization. They get charged by roping in the prospect and making the sale, not following protocol. Technicians' eyes glaze over at the thought of structure and organization because they love to do what they do, they're great at it, and for them managing an organization is a mind-numbing distraction. But running a business is a lot like having a child; the process of making the baby is wonderful, the anticipation of this blessed new life is exciting, and the early years are a constantly thrilling evolution of parenting skills. But the baby will grow into adulthood whether we like it or not. From adolescence through all the stages of adulthood, whether curfews for teenagers, house rules for the young adult, or balancing holiday traditions with in-laws, the family must develop new structures or you will face turmoil. Like it or not, the joy of success in family business will ultimately require the creation of appropriate organizational structures or face problems in all three domains of family, business, and ownership.

On more occasions than we can count, we have had families in business tell us that they have had a family meeting several years earlier. Gripes were aired, people got issues on the table, discussed them, and left the meeting all smiles, feeling they had refreshed their relationships with one another. But it didn't last. Within anywhere from a few weeks to a few months things were back to the way they'd always been, as the afterglow of the meeting faded away. We have heard similar stories about family meetings that were professionally facilitated by a consultant or advisor which resulted in a great feeling of relief and apparent progress. This lasted for a while but that also faded along with the memory of the event.

Why do such things happen? The answer to this takes us back to something we briefly addressed in chapter 4 about the process of change. You will recall that we discussed the three stages of change, identified by sociologist Kurt Lewin, unfreezing-transition-refreezing. The importance of the third stage, refreezing, is that once a planned change has successfully occurred, it is essential to make the change permanent by bringing the change process to a close and locking in the desired new conditions. The new state of affairs that has been established is the way things will be for a while, and people can count on a period of stability and knowing what to expect. Without refreezing, the change dissipates either because things go back to the way they used to be or changes continue to occur unchecked leading to turmoil and chaos.

Establishing and revising a structure and organization that reflect the changed conditions is a very important way to accomplish the refreezing stage of the change process. If there is no structure to support and sustain the changes that have taken place one must be established. For example, if it is agreed that family employees will henceforth be compensated and held accountable for their performance just like any employee, but there is no structure for setting compensation or doing performance reviews, the new expectation, or agreement, will never be fulfilled and the "old way" will creep back in and continue. Or, if it is agreed that owners should begin to specify their expectations regarding their return on investment, based on business conditions and owner needs, but there is no structure as to how and when this will be discussed, decided, and communicated to management, the change invites chaos. The directive from each quarterly board meeting is different than the last as owners individually lobby the board. In other words, nothing gets nailed down, changes are made repeatedly, and there are no firm ground rules to count on.

If, on the other hand, a structure does already exist, new conditions may necessitate only a revision rather than the creation of something new. For example, suppose family members have met regularly to discuss both business and ownership concerns, and they agree that combining them is confusing and that the issues need to be discussed separately. The meeting format is revised to incorporate two separate meetings, one for business issues and the other for ownership issues, each with a specific agenda that focuses exclusively on the issues appropriate to that meeting. However, to agree that there is great confusion in meetings when ownership and business issues are comingled and then decide that this will no longer be done, but fail to revise the structure to reflect new expectations, guarantees that business and ownership issues will continue to be brought up in inappropriate places.

Along with the importance that structure and organization have in maintaining desired new conditions or expectations, there is another place where they are especially relevant to family business. The dynamics of family business, you will recall, consist of the compromises that must be made among the measures of success that characterize each of the three domains of family, business, and ownership as they interface and adapt to changing conditions over time. You will also recall that it is the optimal alignment among the three domains that serves as the benchmark of a healthy functioning family business. Compromise is an essential ingredient to this alignment.

For compromise and alignment to occur the needs, interests, concerns, measures of success, and priorities of each domain must have a way to be expressed and taken into consideration. As with any compromise involving people and relationships, if you don't know and understand what each side needs and wants, you cannot achieve an agreeable compromise. Further, in family businesses in which those needs and wants have no way to be represented, they don't just evaporate, they find another outlet. You can compare this to what happens when one person is really angry but doesn't express it for fear of the other person's retaliation. The anger will come out in another place and be inappropriately directed at a totally innocent third party. Psychologists call this "displacement," meaning that the emotion is displaced or redirected toward someone who is safer or more available. It's the source of the old story about the woman who is angry at her boss, comes home and yells at her husband who yells at the kids who kick the dog that bites the cat. Unexpressed need or emotion will always find an outlet, and if the appropriate one is unavailable, an inappropriate one will do. An employee who feels underpaid and wants more money will, in lieu of any other way to resolve the problem, finds back door ways to express himself by becoming less productive, stealing from the company, or sabotaging important projects.

The principle of displacement also holds true when it comes to the relationships among the three domains of family business. A common problem in family business is that issues related to one domain seep into, infect, and demand attention in another. The constituents in each of the three domains need a voice through which to express themselves. This voice is provided through the structure specifically established to address the needs and concerns of that domain and represent it in interactions with the other two. When, for example, there is no structure to provide for discussion and resolution of issues within the family domain, those issues will come up and be discussed in one of the other domains: in a management meeting, a board meeting, a strategic-planning session, or a shareholders' meeting. The family issue will not go away and it will find a way to get expressed through one of the other domains that give it a structure and a voice. The same holds true of issues appropriate to business or ownership that have no way to be expressed, addressed, and resolved. Perhaps the most notable examples are ownership issues that find a voice through board meetings, because there's nowhere else to talk about them. Board meetings turn into shareholder meetings, which usually means that neither board issues nor shareholder issues get adequate attention.

The importance of structures for each of the domains is especially relevant for those family businesses intending to be relationship-first family businesses. Relationships depend for their long-term health and vitality upon achieving the highest level of the two dimensions . . . of Relationship Intelligence, the beliefs of a positive Relationship Paradigm and the tools of good Relationship Skill. Along with this, relationships only thrive in an environment in which there are clear and consistent boundaries that tell people where they and others belong and provide the rules and guidelines for their interactions. The structures we are discussing in this chapter provide these boundaries and guidelines.

THE ARCHITECTURE OF FAMILY BUSINESS

The architecture of the family business consists of the structures and organization needed to provide voices for each of the domains. This architecture is important both to the management of change and to the alignment of the measures of success between the family, business, and ownership domains. For the family the primary structure and organization is the **Family Forum** along with the planning it does and functions it carries out. For the business the primary structure and organization is the **Board of Directors,** supported at the operational level by the leadership structure and the management team. For ownership the primary structure and organization is the **Shareholders' Council** along with the functions it carries out. Expanding the three-circle diagram to include the structure and organization, it looks like the diagram on the following page.

In the rest of this chapter we will be presenting specific ideas and suggestions about the kinds of structure and organization that create the architecture of the family business.

ARCHITECTURE OF THE FAMILY BUSINESS

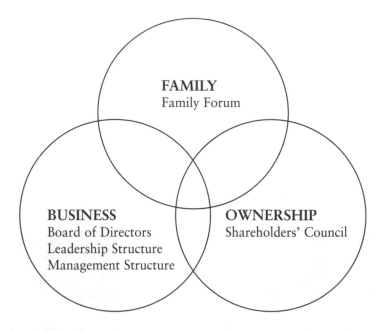

ARCHITECTURE FOR THE FAMILY

One of the greatest blessings and curses for a family in business is the requirement that it have more structure and organization than other families. It's a curse because of the time and effort required to create and maintain it. Family meetings and retreats, family newsletters and written charters, skill development and introspection about the family Relationship Paradigm take time, money, and a significant emotional investment. To a business-owning family it can sometimes seem that other families can go bumping and meandering along without these demands and really have it easy. While that may seem true, it is also true that being a business-owning family provides tremendous opportunities to deepen and solidify family relationships because of what they must face and deal with together.

The common business interest and the interdependency it creates is truly a tie that binds in two ways. It is a force that creates both restrictions and unity. For virtually all of our clients convening together and learning how to work together, to deal with the snags and potholes of making business, family, and ownership function more harmoniously together has created the opportunity for strengthening the emotional and historic ties they share. They learn to enjoy, not regret, the old adage that you can choose your friends but not your family. If it weren't for the business, they would never have gotten to know each other as intimately or learned to appreciate each other as fully.

Let's review briefly the measures of success within the family domain. You recall that families exist to care for and nurture their members, provide safety and refuge in an impersonal world. Family ties are natural, emotional, and especially in today's world, egalitarian. The norm is that individual needs are as important, if not more than, those of the group. In a real sense membership is unconditional, you don't have to perform to become or remain a member of the family. Success in family is measured in terms of harmony, unity, and the development of happy individuals with solid and positive self-esteem.

For families in business these needs, priorities, expectations, and measures of success related to family matters all exist in relation to those within the business and ownership domains. We have identified a number of related interface issues that must be addressed on behalf of the family.

- Expectations of family members about participation in the business.
- Education of family members about the business and about the meaning and value of business ownership.
- Balancing business needs and family expectations.
- Incorporating family values into business strategies and goals.
- Coordinating extended family estate planning to avoid problems with future ownership.
- Deciding about options related to keeping, or not keeping, the business in the family.
- Exploring how being a business-owning family can be a source of opportunity other than employment for family members.
- Linking ownership, family, and business through a family foundation and other philanthropic activities.

These are the areas for which the family domain needs a voice, a structure and organization through which they can be expressed, discussed, and resolved. The Family Forum is the framework that helps make it happen.

THE FAMILY FORUM

The Family Forum provides the structure, place, and time in which to deal with the interface issues between family and business, and between family and ownership. The Family Forum typically meets once a year, and meetings focus primarily on information, education, and relationship building.

IDEAL Industries, a large international manufacturer of equipment for electrical contractors, has an annual family meeting serving these three purposes. President and Chairman David Juday describes how as many as thirty-five family members ranging in age from thirteen to eighty gather each year at the company headquarters in Sycamore, Illinois, for a family business gathering. The meeting includes a family softball game and barbecue, meetings with company executives to discuss new products and other developments, meetings that include company advisors to discuss financial information and other technical matters, and an information-oriented discussion led by the president and chairman about company and ownership philosophy, values, and direction. During one such meeting the president and chairman sailed, Frisbee-style, a leather coaster made at one of the company's plants in Canada and imprinted with the company logo, to each family member who asked a question at the annual meeting. As he said, "Little things like that add fun to our meetings and help reinforce that its purpose is to inform and educate family members."

The role of the Family Forum will vary depending on the complexity and magnitude of the interface issues. A first-generation family business with parents and children actively working in the company and ten or fifteen years away from transferring ownership and management may see little need for a Family Forum structure. The interface issues that come up are dealt with on an informal basis over lunch or a Saturday morning discussion when everyone is in the office. However, as in-laws come into the picture, even if they don't work in the company, and when multiple siblings and cousins are involved, the necessity of the Family Forum structure becomes a high priority. At this level of complexity the problem-solving and developmental functions of the Family Forum become virtually indispensable. As a problem-solving structure, the Family Forum can keep misinformation, gaps in understanding, confusion about people and priorities, and festering relationship problems from blossoming into full-blown disruptions. The Family Forum also provides an excellent setting through which senior family members can help recall and record the legacy they have built in the family business.

For one family business we know, it was within the Family Forum that a project for writing the founder's memoirs was conceived and completed.

Here is an actual annotated agenda from one of the meetings of the IDEAL Industries Family Forum.[1] We think it is an excellent example of just how enriching and productive family meetings can be.

●●

THURSDAY

1:00–4:30

Welcome, NLJ (5 min)

Special Feature. CLL (25 min for the baby pool) (Note: One of the family members, Erica, was expecting. The pool was that each attendee picked a date, time, weight, and sex of the baby, and whoever was closest got to name the child. Erica wasn't informed in advance of the prize for winning the pool. She didn't think that was a very good idea, but we really laughed at the process.)

IDEAL Operations Update. DWJ (1.5 hr) (Note: This is a financial performance report as well as strategy updates, including new products, market changes, etc.)

Break. (15 min)

Tour of Sycamore Plant. DWJ (1 hr plus 15 min to walk over)

FRIDAY

8:30–12:00

Congratulations to and Updates from Matt and Dan. (15 min) (Note: Recent college and h.s. grads.)

Executive Council Report. SJG (30 min)

Internship Policy. NLJ (15 min) (Note: Policy covering family members working here during college summers.)

Family Getaway. PAJ, SJG (15 min)

Family Project. SLJ, SRG (30 min) (Note: A part of our "mission" is to take on a charity project. It has included creating an endowment for the local library, new doors for the local sheltered workshop, etc.)

Break. (15 min)

Meet Bob Lane. DWJ (1.5 hr) (Note: Bob is the new presdent.)

Lunch with Bob in the atrium.

1:00–4:30

Report from Margaret on her trip to China. (15 min)

IDEAL Strategic Planning Update. DWJ (1 hr)

Break. (15 min)

Electronic Commerce Update. CLL (30 min) (Note: Chris is the fourth–generation family member who works in that area for us.)

Datacom Product Demonstration. DWJ (1 hr)

(We have a half hour to catch up or can break early to help set up at Chris and Cory's)

SATURDAY

8:30–12:00

Report from Patty and Frank on their new house. (15 min)

EC Report re. LFBI Seminar. DWJ, SLJ, BDJ (30 min)

IDEAL Foundation. MAB (15 min)

IDEAL Share Transfer Restriction Agreement. NLJ (45 min) (Note: This is our buy/sell agreement.)

Farm Report. LWB (15 min) (NOTE: The family owns a farm locally.)

Break. (15 min)

Split Session. (1 hr)

Fourth generation to discuss topics and recommendations for next meeting. Old folks to discuss IDEAL capital structure. (Note: This was the beginning of the S Corp discussion that culminated in this year's activities.) (Author's note: This will be discussed in the section on shareholders' agreements later in this chapter.)

●●●

What should be noted in the agenda is the masterful way family, business, and ownership issues are woven together in informational, fun, and relationship-enhancing ways. Every family business will have its own style and format for Family Forum agendas.

The Family Forum, as you can easily see from the agenda of

an IDEAL Industries meeting, also provides the place, time, and structure to inform and educate family members about a host of important matters such as:

- how family businesses work;
- what the business does and how it operates;
- opportunities and expectations for family involvement;
- relationship skill development for family members;
- understanding and preserving family and business legacy; and
- principles and philosophy of business ownership.

Woven throughout all of this is the added benefit of strengthening family bonds in a very profound way. Family Forum meetings are a combination of family reunion and business meeting that provide the opportunity for family members to relate at multiple meaningful levels. One comment we often hear from family members at the initial formation meeting of a Family Forum is, "This is the first time as parents and children, brothers and sisters, nieces and nephews we have met together as adults to discuss the business and have enjoyed each other as family at the same time." What they mean by this is that they have discovered a way to meet as a business-owning family, wearing family, business, and ownership hats, and have gotten to know each other in ways other families will never be able to experience.

The specific purpose, structure, and organization of your Family Forum will depend on your needs and situation. With the understanding provided above as to what a Family Forum is and does, the first step in establishing a Family Forum, is to ask the question, "If we were to establish a Family Forum what benefits would it bring to us as a family in business and would it be worth the effort?"

This question should be posed to all family members who in some way are affected by the interface issues between family and business and between family and ownership. This would include family members active in the business and their spouses, all owners and spouses, and family members above the age of fifteen with possible future interest in employment or ownership. Usually, this initial step is spearheaded by a senior family member who is willing to take on the task. Each person asked to respond is provided a summary of what a Family Forum is and does. They are asked to answer the above question anonymously. You can, of course, have a small group of interested family members simply convene a meeting for the purpose of establishing a Family Forum and see who shows up. The principles and practices of Relationship Intelligence, however, would urge getting all interested people involved from the earliest point of consideration in order to encourage their buy-in and participation down the line. You don't need a majority of support to move forward, but knowing that a core group representing a cross section of the types mentioned above provides reinforcement to put the effort into it.

The first meeting of your Family Forum is the formation meeting. At this meeting you will need to establish the basic purpose, structure, and organization of your Family Forum. You may already be having regular family meetings of some kind, but if you haven't done the formation work we recommend below, we suggest you take a step back and do it now. Specifically, you will need to decide about the following items:

- A Statement of Purpose—which describes in a few paragraphs what your Family Forum does and why this is important.

- Structure of meetings—how will the format and agendas for meetings be developed and what should be included on a regular basis?

- How often will you meet, where, and for how long? As we said above, most Family Forums meet annually but can be convened more frequently if desired or necessary. Some families in business will decide during the first year to meet twice, or even quarterly in order to get organized.

- Organization—who will fill the necessary roles to organize your Family Forum? These include convener, record keeper, leaders of projects, communications coordinator, meeting planner(s), etc. How will people in the leadership roles coordinate their work? In some cases the convener coordinates it all, while in others the leaders form a planning council that meets once or twice to plan the Family Forum meeting.

Here is a hypothetical example, actually a composite from several family businesses, that illustrates how a family in business might document the formation of a Family Forum.

STATEMENT OF PURPOSE
BOWLES FAMILY FORUM

The purpose of the Bowles Family Forum is to provide the mechanism by which we can honor our past, celebrate our present, and anticipate our future as a business-owning family. We recognize the great responsibility and opportunity that has been passed down for three generations from John and Mildred Bowles, who started our family and our business. It is our desire and intention to strengthen family ties and support a great business by being as informed, educated, and unified as we can.

We recognize that those who participate in the Bowles Family Forum will have diverse levels of interest in future involvement in the business. Being involved in the business is not expected of, nor encouraged upon, those who participate in the Family Forum. Our Family Forum is for any family member interested or curious about the business as a source of information, understanding, and learning about our family, our business, and what they mean to each other.

We recognize that being a business-owning family places us in a special category of obligation and opportunity. We are responsible for assisting the success of both a family and a business. We will do this by stating in writing what it means to us to be a business-owning family, writing down our desires, hopes, and dreams for the future (Family Charter) and, in cooperation with company owners and leaders, establishing participation guidelines for family members who have interest in employment by the business (Family Participation Plan).

Structure:

The Bowles Family Forum will meet annually on the third weekend in June at the company's headquarters. During this first year, two task forces will be established and given the responsibility to gather ideas and input and draft a Family Charter and Family Participation Plan to present at our next annual meeting for discussion.

We intend to keep our Family Forum gatherings informal and enjoyable. Each meeting will provide opportunity to have fun together and leave with a better understanding of ourselves as a family, of the business and how to make the relationship between, the two work as smoothly as possible. How this happens is up to the people who do the planning.

Organization:

Every three years we will select from among family members someone to be the Family Forum Convener. The job of the Convener is to oversee the planning and conducting of each year's meeting and to make sure that whatever task forces or project groups are established get their jobs done and coordinate with each other as necessary. Also, every three years we will select a Family Forum Recorder who will write up and distribute to all participants a brief but complete summary of our annual meetings, especially any documents we prepare or agreements we make. The Convener and Recorder will each recommend two people to replace them, and anyone may volunteer. Selection will be done by written ballot.

From time to time, special projects or tasks will need a champion to lead them. We will ask for volunteers to help with these as they come up.

The company will pay all expenses associated with the annual Family Forum meeting except for travel.

• •

We are frequently asked who should be included in the Family Forum. In good consultant style we answer, "It depends." Every family in business is different so the makeup of Family Forums varies. However, we offer some guidelines that may be helpful. Remember, this is not a meeting for ownership issues nor matters that need to be handled by the company's Board of Directors. Family Forum members are usually family members above the age of fifteen who have an interest in the business and how it affects the family. Obviously, this includes:

- family members who have ownership or employment in the business;
- spouses of these people;
- family members who have a definite interest in future employment or ownership; and
- younger family members who will benefit from learning about the opportunities and responsibilities of employment and ownership.

Our bias, given the purpose and functions of the Family Forum, is to invite rather than to exclude a family member who does not neatly fit into one of the above categories. Typically you will find that those who have little interest will self-select out of membership in the Family Forum.

FAMILY FORUM PLANNING AREAS

The two planning areas that are often addressed by the Family Forum are the:

- Family Charter, and
- Family Participation Plan

The **Family Charter** is also referred to as the family mission statement or the family creed. It is a written statement about the guiding philosophy and values of the family, its priorities, principles, and aspirations. The writing of the Family Charter is best done by first developing a questionnaire that is distributed to Family Forum members. The questionnaire will ask the following kinds of questions:

- What values and principles do you believe should guide our family business now and in the future?
- What aspects of the history of our family business are important to preserve and transmit to future generations?
- What commitments and contributions should our family business make to society, the communities we are in, employees, and customers now and in the future?
- What kinds of opportunities should our family business provide to family members, and what responsibilities and obligations should accompany the opportunities?
- Why is it important to you that we continue as a family business?
- What philanthropic or charitable activities should we be involved in and what would be the best way for us to do this?

Using information from the completed questionnaires, a small group writes an initial draft that is presented at a Family Forum meeting for discussion, changes, and acceptance.

The second planning area developed by the Family Forum is the **Family Participation Plan** (FPP). The FPP is a written statement that establishes the guidelines for present and future family involvement in the business. While the Family Forum accepts responsibility for developing the FPP, it is done with the input and approval of the Board of Directors and owners of the company. It is important that the Family Forum take responsibility for this important planning work because the plan specifically affects family members and sets the standards by which the family, as a talent pool for the business, will hold itself accountable. Most FPPs cover at least these four key areas of family involvement in the company:

- Roles and responsibilities
- Personal behavior
- Experience
- Compensation and benefits

We will now discuss some of the issues that need to be resolved in each of these four areas.

WHAT FAMILY MEMBERS ARE SUPPOSED TO DO

Family businesses have different philosophies about providing employment for family members. For some there is always a job for a family member. For others, there must be an available position to move a family member into. In any case, specific job responsibilities, performance expectations along with a method of review, and a level of authority may never really be clarified.

The family business employer assumes that family members will, out of loyalty and family obligation, do a good job. For the family member employee, the lack of clear expectations and guidelines, while at first interpreted as trust and opportunity, can lead to confusion, a lackadaisical attitude, or even the building of the family member's own fiefdom with its own rules. Without clearly defined responsibilities, there is no objective way to measure performance, and it all degenerates into purely subjective perceptions and emotional reactions. Precisely because of the intermingling of family and business, family employees are best served when duties, responsibilities, and expectations are clear and understood by all.

HOW FAMILY MEMBERS BEHAVE

Closely related to role and responsibilities are problems associated with the personal behaviors of family member employees. A feeling of entitlement or lack of sensitivity can result in behaviors that are disruptive and would not be allowed with nonfamily employees. Without clear guidelines there can be abuse of paid time off, lack of adherence to company work hours, inappropriate language or behavior with other employees, unacceptable personal dress and appearance, gossiping with employees about personal family issues, and harmful representation of the company in the community. Family CEOs often complain that in situations in which they would fire other employees, they feel stuck in dealing with family employees who ignore repeated warnings.

This can be especially painful when the personal behavior problems result from addiction to drugs, alcohol, gambling, or from mental illness. One reason for this particular difficulty is that the family itself is often in denial about the problem or is protective of the family member suffering from the addiction or mental illness. The family mandate to preserve and protect its image and its members makes it very difficult, especially for the CEO, to objectively handle a work-related behavior problem with an affected family member.

GO ELSEWHERE FIRST

Successful outside work experience prior to joining the family firm is generally seen as a desirable, if not essential, component in family entry into the business. This is because it eliminates nagging second thoughts by the family member, and others, over whether the person could really cut it elsewhere. It also brings new business and management ideas to the family business, which can become very ingrown. One of the greatest benefits is the experience of being supervised and held accountable by a nonfamily employer according to customary business standards. This can help avoid the scenario in which a family employee complains of unfair treatment when expectations are actually no greater than they would be in any business situation.

Often, though, the benefits of prior outside work experience are more of a concept than reality. There are many reasons for this. Everyone may be excited about the new college graduate joining the family business. The need for outside experience is rationalized away. The business may have a current need for exactly the skills and training possessed by the inexperienced family member. Going to work in the family business seems like a perfect fit. It allows the business to avoid hiring a stranger, and the family member avoids the arduous task of job interviewing.

In the worst case, the family member has been unable to find and/or hold gainful employment elsewhere. There is absolutely nothing to support the idea that such a person will, in fact, become successful simply by going to work in the family business unless the underlying reasons for their failures elsewhere are determined and corrected. Even then, *successful* outside experience has still not been achieved.

HOW FAMILY MEMBERS GET PAID

Along with attitudes and practices related to hiring family members in the first place, families in business have varying philosophies about how the company should support the lifestyles of family members in the business. Some will say that the business should provide all family members, active or not, with a "good and comfortable" lifestyle. This financial expectation is unrelated to the performance of duties that benefit the business. In second and third generations, this can become a huge problem as siblings bring their children into the business with expectations for their children's compensation based on the family's historical, and highly inflated, entitlements.

In other situations, it is believed by parents who don't want to show favoritism that all family members in the business regardless of the scope of their responsibilities or position, should be paid the same. Others view ownership, or even the appearance of ownership via the right surname, as carte blanche access to perks, even ones not given to other employees. This can include things like cars, trips, club memberships, company credit cards, taking of company merchandise, commandeering of an employee's time for personal projects, just to mention a few. As decades go by, the company becomes larger and more complex, second- or third-generation family is running things, nonfamily managers are a vital force in the company, and growth is stretching capital resources. This is when it can all come to a head, and after all those years it is neither pleasant nor simple to resolve. Major fallout on both the business and family often occurs as nonfamily managers demand that the reins of family perks be pulled in and family conflict erupts over inequities in how members are treated.

The old adage "An ounce of prevention is worth a pound of cure" is nowhere more true than with family participation in the business. Most of the pitfalls can be avoided when families in business establish their own FPP up front, writing out and agreeing to the guidelines that direct how family members will enter the business and what happens once they're in it.

It begins with a statement about the family's intentions in providing ownership and employment opportunities for family members. (What follows illustrates how an FPP would actually be written, though it is not a plan from an actual company.)

●●●

THE SMITH FAMILY BUSINESS PARTICIPATION PLAN

Based on the Family Charter established by our family, the following guidelines for family involvement in our business are established to assist current and future family member employees, managers, and executives of the company.

Our intent and commitment is to keep the ownership of Smith Enterprises solely within the bloodline of our grandmother and grandfather. Family members are encouraged to consider making Smith Enterprises a place to invest their talents and express their career aspirations, but only when it is a great fit for both them and the company. Under no circumstances is there an obligation on either side to the other. Smith Enterprises will always have the very best professional management available, whether family or nonfamily, will adhere to common business practices of planning at every level, and will review the performance of family member employees against those plans.

Family members are expected to have the education, training, and skills needed to fulfill the job requirements of any position for which they apply or in which they are employed. Family members will not be hired by Smith Enterprises without three to five years of successful previous employment, achievement of a least one level of promotion in their previous employment, and an overall above-average performance evaluation. Every family member will be subject to the same hiring procedures (including preemployment testing and screening, interviewing, and application procedures) as any other applicant for the position.

Family members will not be hired into a position without an approved job description, will be paid at market rate for their position, and will receive approved company benefits appropriate to their position. Income from ownership to family members active in the business is considered completely separate from the compensation they receive for employment. Every family employee will, for at least the first five years of employment, be supervised by a nonfamily manager subject to the same hiring, performance, and termination rules that apply to other employees.

Family member employees are expected to adhere to a higher standard of conduct and contribution to the business in complying with company policies regarding dress code, use of company time, and equipment and behavior. In addition, family member employees are expected to exemplify a positive, courteous, and professional standard of personal conduct in all their interactions with other employees, customers, and vendors. While this may not be considered fair or just, we believe this is an appropriate and necessary level of responsibility and obligation in light of the great opportunities the company provides to family members.

This Family Participation Plan was developed by the Smith Family Forum on October 23, 1993, and was approved by unanimous consent. Signatures of all those participating appear on the other side to attest their agreement and support.

The relationship technology required to make your Family Forum successful is found in RQ. The Family Forum provides the family-oriented structure through which Relationship Skill can be taught, developed, and nurtured. Family Forum meetings should always have at least one component dedicated to educating and reinforcing the tools of effective communication, problem solving, conflict resolution, change management, issue management, and good planning. The Family Forum also provides the opportunity to explore, understand, and improve the Relationship Paradigm of the family. Through use of the exercises like the ones in chapter 4, and skilled facilitation of these components of Family Forum meetings, the Relationship Paradigm of the family, and thus of the business, will cause old patterns to be broken and replaced by new ones. As Relationship Skill improves and a more positive Relationship Paradigm evolves, the RQ of the family grows. In this way the Family Forum plays a major role in improving RQ throughout the family business.

ARCHITECTURE FOR THE BUSINESS

The business needs a voice, too. While it may seem that of the three domains of family, business, and ownership, the business gets the lion's share of the attention, the fact is that this very often is not the case. What sounds like the voice of the business may actually be the voices of special interest groups or the day-to-day clatter and clamor of a challenging and complex enterprise. Most executives, managers, and employees of family businesses regularly complain that they go from crisis to crisis putting out fires. The true voice of the business gets drowned out by the noise. The company has no compelling long-term vision because everyone is so focused on today. The core competence upon which the business was built gets ignored, underutilized, and lost in a revolving door of programs and projects aimed at the noble causes of fending off competition and improving profitability. The well-being of employees and effective coordination of the management and operation systems fall prey to special interests and neglect.

If yours is an established multigenerational business an active and effective Board of Directors, a strong leadership structure, and an established, well-functioning management team are essential in assuring that your business has the voice it needs. These are the structures that express the needs, interests, and concerns of the company in relation to the family and ownership domains. Recall the measures of success that define the business domain. The business is an economic entity for which ultimate success is measured in productivity and profitability. This requires a high degree of focus on the right priorities, determination of the most effective strategies, precise allocation of human and capital resources, and responsive flexibility to adjust to a constantly changing environment. These are the places where the business must have a way to stand up for itself and make itself heard above the competing internal voices of family and ownership, and the incessant external noise of the marketplace.

Typical interface issues between the business and the other two domains include the following:

- supervision and accountability of family employees;
- setting of compensation and benefits for family employees;
- managing financial practices and performance;
- balancing business needs and family expectations;
- long-range planning that reflects family owner values with business strategies and goals;
- integration of owner expectations regarding ROI with company performance;
- deciding about use of profits, for example, as distributions versus acquisition versus capital expenditures; and
- making sure that nonfamily managers are not driven away by family and ownership problems and are offered opportunities for satisfying, long-term careers.

A powerful family (and what business-owning family isn't powerful?) can pressure and coerce the business in ways it shouldn't go. Senior-generation owners, with their expectations and needs for financial security, can drain the company of financial resources needed to capitalize renewal and growth. Remember that the measures of success in family and ownership compete with those of the business. Without a voice, the business is overexposed and underprotected from the pressures of family matters and ownership demands.

THE BOARD OF DIRECTORS

The Board of Directors provides the primary architecture of the business domain: a place and structure to address the long-term, big-picture needs of the company. The work and challenges facing the board of a family business are unique because of the complexity of the family business. The Board of Directors is confronted with the interfacing issues brought by the dynamics of the family, whose members are also the owners of the business. Family business boards typically handle such issues as:

- setting of company policies;
- compensation and benefits of officers;
- evaluating company financial practices and performance;
- establishing and monitoring long-range planning that balances family owner values with business strategies and goals;
- integrating owner expectations regarding ROI with company performance and capital needs; and
- reviewing senior-management performance and management succession planning.

Several excellent books have been written about the Boards of Directors in family businesses.[2] Establishing and maintaining an effective working Board of Directors is a major commitment, but it is well worth the effort. As with the Family Forum structure, the exact size, composition, and organization of family business Boards of Directors vary widely. Part of this depends on whether the owning and managing family members are willing to include outside directors on the board. The majority of family business boards that have both inside (family) and outside directors maintain a majority of inside (family) directors. Some family business boards consist only of owners. One danger here is that board meetings can easily become shareholder meetings. The other danger is related to the fact that a Board of Directors provides a link and buffer between the interests of the owners and the needs of the business. This function can be jeopardized when the board is comprised only of owners. Other family businesses have board members that are company managers or are the professional advisors and consultants to the company. The rationale is that this makes needed areas of expertise available to the board. For several reasons we strongly recommend against this practice, with the exception that the company CEO is a member of the board. In the first place, the board should be reviewing and scrutinizing the company's advisors and consultants. It represents a conflict of interest when the advisor or consultant is a member of the very same company board that should be reviewing and critiquing the professional's work for the company. In addition, the company is already paying for and should be receiving the full benefit of the manager's, advisor's, or consultant's input, so there is no added benefit to their being a director of the company. Any input that is needed from these individuals can be provided just as effectively through reports or presentations to the Board. A good Board of Directors brings an outside perspective that is challenging, objective, and informed.

One family business board structure that can work well consists of five members: three inside directors and two outside directors. The inside directors consist of the CEO, who is typically a family member, a director elected by the Family Forum, and another director elected by the Shareholders' Council (discussed below). The two outside directors are business executives in companies that are currently of the size and organization that your family business desires to be in the future. They also are selected because needs for outside perspective in specific areas, such as finance, sales, operations, or human resources. In many instances, these outside directors are not the CEOs of other companies but are at the second or even third tier of management. Such individuals are often extremely capable, knowledgeable, and very excited by the honor and opportunity to serve on the board of another company.

Board meetings of established multigenerational family businesses are best held quarterly even though it appears that more than 50 percent of all family business boards meet only once or twice a year. Typically, board meetings are a half-day to a whole-day long. It's a good idea to make one of the quarterly meetings an annual planning retreat of a couple days in length. At this planning meeting the board reviews management's accomplishments for the past year, discusses the current strengths and weaknesses of the company along with the threats and opportunities in the environment, and approves plans for the coming year. It is often asked how much directors should be paid. Surveys indicate that two-thirds of family businesses pay no director's fee or stipend. For those family businesses that do pay a stipend, it is generally less than $1,000 annually per director. We believe it is best if the directors of established multigenerational family businesses, both inside and outside, are paid a director's fee not just because of the time it takes, but because it communicates the reality that this is a job requiring commitment and expertise. The amount varies depending on the size of the business, the length of the meetings, and the amount of work, such as committee assignments outside of regular board meetings. Whatever the amount, it should be sufficient to reflect the commitment of the owners and the business to take the work of the Board and the Directors seriously.

Along with the Board of Directors the architecture of the business has two additional structures. They are, in a sense, substructures of the board, but each has its own focus and responsibilities to carry out. The first of these is the leadership structure; the second is the management structure. In every business, and family businesses are no exception, the focus of leadership is managing change while the focus of management is managing complexity. This is well illustrated in a metaphor: workers are the people chopping their way through the jungle with machetes, managers are the people sharpening the machetes and calling out words of encouragement to keep moving forward, and leaders are the ones climbing up into the tallest palm trees, yelling, "We're in the WRONG jungle!" The Board of Directors, leadership, and management together form the complete structural triangle of the architecture of the business.

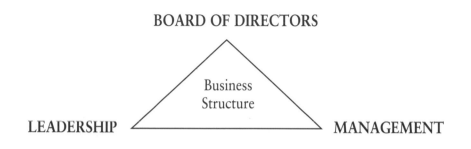

THE LEADERSHIP STRUCTURE

Providing for the leadership of the company is one of the primary responsibilities of the Board of Directors. By assuring consistency and quality of leadership the board makes sure that the many internal and external changes to which the company must adjust are well managed. While some family business boards get involved in operational matters, this is not the role of the board. Responsibility for the day-to-day operation of the company is delegated by the board to the CEO and other company executives. It is therefore essential that the board, especially for a family business in which the CEO is a family member, structure leadership well. It is true that every employee, every manager, and every team in the business, no matter what level, is called on to provide leadership in some way. However, in this discussion of structures we will focus only on the senior executive leadership of the company.

In owner-managed, entrepreneurial, first-generation family businesses the CEO, or president, of the company is usually both the sole owner and a senior family member. There is no Board of Directors and little need for one. The founder CEO is not only making sure the company is in the right jungle, but chopping the brush and sharpening the machetes all at the same time. There are instances when a family business goes from first to second generation and remains an owner-managed company. This happens when only one of the current generation's offspring continues to own and manage the company. Here, the leadership situation remains clear and relatively uncomplicated even though it is a second-generation family business.

However, for the family business that is established with a second tier of executive management and is multigenerational in terms of family ownership and involvement, the leadership situation gets more difficult. Now multiple family members and owners must either select one of themselves or someone else as the CEO. They must also figure out how to organize into a cohesive leadership structure. If the available talent from this generation makes it obvious to everyone that one person is clearly the most qualified to be CEO, and the others are happy to take supporting roles, a leadership structure can be established fairly easily. On the other hand, as is very often the case, if there are multiple qualified candidates, the potential for a leadership struggle is very strong. In chapter 9 we specifically address the special challenges of leadership in the family business and successor development planning. Here we want to discuss leadership structure by itself.

The purpose of the family business leadership structure is to accomplish the following objectives:

- Make sure that the company develops and successfully implements a long-range plan through which it anticipates and creates the future. You must not assume that the future is no more than an extension of it. Simply extrapolating from successes in the past is no guarantee of continued success in the future.
- Assure that all of the functional areas are operating effectively and in coordination with each other.
- Maintain significant external relationships with the industry, customers, suppliers, and the community.
- Engender positive and productive employee morale throughout the company.
- Be a guardian of the company's financial and human resources, protecting and allocating them.

In carrying out these objectives the traditional hierarchical leadership structure continues to dominate in family business. The reason for this is that most of the time it works. Typically this type of leadership structure incorporates a CEO or president and, reporting to the CEO/president, one or more vice presidents and perhaps an executive vice president, or chief operating officer. By definition leadership means that there is a leader, someone in the top of the palm tree. The responsibility of the leader (the CEO/president in this structure) is to make sure that the objectives identified above are fulfilled both directly and through supervision of the other executives who make up the leadership team. A simple leadership structure looks like this:

TYPICAL TRADITIONAL HIERARCHICAL LEADERSHIP STRUCTURE

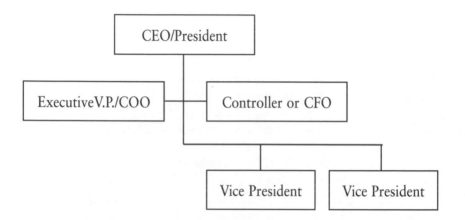

Clearly, there are many versions of this structure with additional second- and third-tier positions. However, this is a typical version of the traditional hierarchical leadership structure to which company managers who directly supervise other employees report.

As we have said, implementing this leadership structure has been, and continues to be, a major dilemma in those family businesses with multiple successors who are both qualified for and desiring to lead the company. Parents, and other current generation owners, frequently feel torn about having to decide among children, grandchildren, nieces, and nephews who are competing for the position of CEO of the company. A recent survey conducted by Mass Mutual and Arthur Andersen indicates that the problem will become even more pronounced as four out of ten family businesses surveyed say they will have more than one family member serving as co-CEOs in future generations.[3] Currently, about one in ten of family businesses have more than one CEO.

The potential emotional and organizational turmoil of choosing the future leadership for the company should not be underestimated. Nevertheless, the decision to choose a co-CEO leadership structure can prove disastrous. In far too many situations such a leadership structure is selected as a way to avoid having to grant the mantle of leadership to one person among a field of qualified family candidates. An even worse situation has been created by family businesses that opt for a rotating presidency model in which different family members, usually siblings or cousins, assume the role of president for two- or three-year terms. Lack of continuity in leadership style and priorities, fragmenting of loyalty among key executives and managers, and relationship struggles over power and authority seem to be unavoidable using the rotating CEO leadership structure.

The main reason the co-CEO leadership structure fails is that there are too many heads at the top of the company, even with well-defined areas of responsibility for each CEO. The assumption that the co-CEO's are equal in chief executive level responsibility and authority sets up conflict. Many of the same problems associated with the rotating presidency leadership structure apply here and even more powerfully because the confrontations take place daily rather than on a rotating basis.

THE OFFICE OF THE PRESIDENT

A developing new leadership structure that addresses both the necessity of having one head at the top as well as the dilemma of multiple qualified and desirous leaders is the Office of the President model. We have been working to develop and test this leadership structure with clients for several years, and it is very promising. The major difference between the co-CEO and Office of the President models is that the latter provides only one head at the top of the company. The Office of the President, even though occupied by several individuals, provides one, consistent, cohesive, and focused leadership structure just as the traditional hierarchical approach does with the single president or CEO. The focus is on the Office of the President, meaning that it is the one structure, not the one person, that provides leadership for the company.

A good analogy for explaining the model of the Office of the President, as the head of the company, is that of the brain as the "head" of the person. The brain is composed of two hemispheres that have different functions. The right hemisphere is the creative and intuitive side of the brain, while the left hemisphere is the rational and logical side. In addition, each side of the brain controls movement of the opposite side of the body: right brain controls the left side and vice versa. While each side performs different functions and controls opposite sides of the body, we know from brain research that memory and learning is spread throughout the brain in both hemispheres, not stored in a specific location within one of them. The midbrain links the hemispheres together to coordinate and unify thinking, movement, and behavior.

Comparing this simplified brain analogy to the Office of the President, the participants in the office have individual responsibility and authority to carry out the various leadership functions that must take place. They take on specialized functions, yet there is a high level of shared understanding as to the priorities, purpose, values, and protocols that tie them together. The structure provides for the linking together of the functions to bring about coordination of decision making, action, and accountability.

For the Office of the President leadership structure to succeed, a number of essential ingredients must be in place. They fall into four categories:

- roles and responsibilities;
- qualifications and capability;
- Relationship Intelligence; and
- clearly defined long-term goals and accountability.

Roles and responsibilities must be clearly defined and written down in position description format for each of the participants in the Office of the President. This should start with an analysis of all the responsibilities and duties required as if there were a single individual in the position of President/CEO. In other words a detailed job description needs to be written for the Office of the President which includes the following:

- All the functional areas of the company that must have oversight and supervision at the executive leadership level such as sales, marketing, finance, administration, personnel/human resources, production, operations, design and engineering, vendor relations, employee benefit plans, and banking and insurance.
- All of the program areas that must have oversight and supervision at the leadership level such as quality assurance, research and development, and new technology.
- Administration of the Office of the President in terms of coordination of activities, meetings, information flow, etc.

Once all the areas of responsibility have been identified, they can be divided up into specific position profiles for each director of the Office of the President. Note that there will be some responsibilities unique to the Office of the President compared to the single president model. This is because decisions made solely by one person must now be coordinated among several people. Therefore, for example, an element of the position description for the Office of the President that would not appear in that of a single president, is the coordination of the performance reviews of executives reporting to the Office of the President. The list of responsibilities will be divided between two or more individuals who will make up the Office of the President. Each one might be given the title of "Director, Office of the President" in charge of a designated set of responsibilities.

In addition, it is imperative to work out a mechanism among the participants in the Office of the President through which they will judge their individual qualifications and capabilities to assume their set of responsibilities. An objective outside career evaluation for each participant, combined with a facilitated process of understanding, negotiating, and deciding on assignments is the best way to carry this out.

Relationships are the language of family business. Nowhere is this more essential to understand and apply than in the operation of the Office of the President. The primary commitment of all the participants must be to constantly develop their RQ in all the ways we have discussed. *Getting Along in Family Business* should become the instruction manual for running any effective Office of the President. This includes all of the following abilities necessary to produce a high level of relationship skill:

- The ability to bridge inevitable differences with others, and to help them do the same, through respect for alternative ideas and approaches.
- The ability to manage constructively conflicts and false agreements, with and between others, through flexibility and ongoing renegotiation of expectations.
- The ability to plan, and accept appropriate responsibility for, the future through effective and confident management of change.
- The ability to maintain a full and positive sense of personal worth, value, and confidence, while fully participating in close family and other intimate relationships.

We discussed the specific tools for developing these abilities in chapter 4. In addition to Relationship Skill, Relationship Paradigm is an essential factor in the success or failure of the Office of the President leadership structure. Clearly, a negative Relationship Paradigm spells trouble for any relationship because it results in a low level of RQ. A higher level (3 or 4) of RQ is necessary to the success of the Office of the President. We advise against using this leadership structure if RQ is at a Level 1 or 2 unless there is strong commitment by all those involved to a long-term process to improve it. It should also be remembered here that the level of RQ we are referring to is the one that applies to the relationships among all of those who participate in the Office of the President. If, for example, four brothers are involved two of them may have a Level 3 RQ in their relationship while the other two may only have a Level 2 RQ in their relationship. What is important, though, is the relationship among all four of them together. In that relationship their RQ will probably be somewhere between Levels 2 and 3, probably closer to 2.

We have also observed that a successful Office of the President leadership structure is assisted greatly by the presence of an effective outside Board of Directors. This is especially the case when the participants in the Office of the President are all family members and owners. Clarity as to role, function, and accountability within the Office of the President (as well as between it and the other domains within the family business) is very important. The presence of an outside board greatly assists the Office of the President in maintaining and reinforcing clarity in all three arenas.

Clearly defining long-term goals and accountability for accomplishing them requires that the leadership structure provide for strategic planning for the company. Actually, long-range strategic planning is a core requirement of the leadership structure regardless of what model is used: owner-managed, single presidency, or Office of the President. However, a well-developed strategic family business plan is particularly important when priorities and goals depend upon coordination among several individuals and accountability is a high-stakes affair as is the case with the Office of the President.

The **Strategic Family Business Plan** is developed by a Strategic Family Business Planning Team composed of family and nonfamily managers under the leadership of the Office of the President. The president/CEO or Office of the President develops a planning process for the company. Strategic planning is an ongoing endeavor. The outcome of strategic planning is not simply to produce a written document called the Strategic Plan, but to create an environment of persistent attention to the vision, mission, and future of the company, and to have every employee understand their importance in achieving it.

We recommend a three-year planning cycle built on a five-year vision for the company. A complete set of strategic priorities is established every three years and implemented through one-year goals established annually during the three-year cycle. On the third-year anniversary of the plan the five-year vision is updated, so that it becomes a rolling five-year vision, and new three-year strategies are established. Some specifics that should be included in the planning process are as follows (it is noted as to whether each is done annually or every three years):

- Establish a five-year vision statement for the company that incorporates the essential elements of the Family Charter developed by the Family Forum and the expectations of owners as developed by the Shareholders' Council (discussed below). Review and update every three years.
- Carry out a competitor assessment. Review and update annually, completely revise every three years.
- Evaluate company capabilities and weaknesses and environmental threats and opportunities. Review and update annually, completely revise every three years.
- Create, revise, or reaffirm the company's mission statement. Review and update, if necessary, every three years.
- Undertake a portfolio analysis, whether by product line or market segment, that evaluates where the company has the greatest opportunity for growth and diversification based on the mix of company capabilities and product line or market attractiveness. Review and update annually, completely revise every three years.
- Determine three-year strategies to move more than halfway toward achieving the five-year vision by building on strengths, overcoming weaknesses, and seizing opportunities identified in the evaluation of company capabilities, competitor assessment, and portfolio analysis. Revise every three years.
- Establish one-year goals for each strategy (goals for years two and three will be developed in the following two years). Establish new goals annually.
- Develop a detailed implementation plan for each goal that delineates individual tasks in chronological order for completing the goal, the persons involved, resources required, anticipated start and completion dates. Make sure action plans are coordinated and not unrealistic. Establish new implementation plans annually and review and revise quarterly.

- Determine the management coordination mechanisms for evaluating progress on goals and establish guidelines for accountability of persons responsible. Review annually for effectiveness and revise if necessary.

THE MANAGEMENT STRUCTURE

The strategic planning process is implemented through the management structure, the third element in the architecture of family business. A key responsibility of the Board of Directors is to assure that the company has a strong and effective management team structure. This responsibility is usually delegated to the leadership structure of the company to formulate and implement. Typically, the management team structure consists of a number of specific management teams at various levels and in various places throughout the company. The top two or three executive levels often comprise the executive management team. Some of them, in turn, establish management teams with managers and supervisors that report to them. Management teams may be formed, for example in administration and finance, production, quality assurance, human resources, and information technology, to mention a few.

The management team structure is important because it provides the support and channels of implementation needed by the leadership structure to assure that plans are carried out. You recall that we said that managers manage complexity while leaders manage change. The operational complexities of any established family business require coordination and direction. One of the greatest operational problems created when the management structure is not well defined is that the priorities and goals of the company are not in alignment with the company's capabilities and operations. This seems so simple, yet many family businesses fall far short of their potential simply because the hard work that went into developing great strategies gets lost when the functional areas of the company do not have the resources, equipment, focus, direction, or commitment to carry them out. Here is an alignment problem of another kind, but it is not unlike the ones we have discussed before.

The purpose of the management structure is to make sure there is good alignment between goals, priorities, and operations. It does this by establishing and maintaining the three critical criteria of a successful team relationship:

- defined goals;
- clear roles; and
- documented procedures.

Every member of every management team needs to know with absolute clarity what the team is to accomplish. The members also need to know what role they play in this and what is expected of them regarding their role. Additionally, the team needs to have spelled out procedures as to how they will work together on their goals; very mundane things like meeting time-location-duration, documentation and information flow, deadlines, tools and methods to be used, and accountability. It is only when goals, roles, and procedures are clear that the management structure can do its job of managing complexity, not getting bogged down in it.

In summary, the architecture of the business consists of the Board of Directors along with structures for leadership and management. The long-range strategic family business plan provides the focus and direction needed to tie together all of these structures. It also provides the mechanism to represent the needs and interests of the Family Forum, as articulated in its Family Charter, by connecting them into the strategic-planning process of the company. The strategic-planning process also incorporates the financial and societal expectations of the owners as developed by the Shareholders' Council, to which we turn next.

ARCHITECTURE FOR OWNERSHIP

We have now provided voices for the family through the Family Forum and the business through the Board of Directors and its leadership and management structures. We now need to provide the ownership domain with a voice through the structure of the Shareholders' Council. Representing the interests of owners in overseeing the well-being and management of their investment, the members of the Shareholders' Council are all those who own stock in the company. As we have said before in relation to the other structures, in smaller owner-managed family businesses there is no need for a Shareholders' Council unless the owner is for some reason partial to meetings of one person. Even in a partnership of two family members, ownership issues are likely handled in more informal partner meetings over lunch or a cup of coffee.

As the family business becomes multigenerational, ownership typically is dispersed into the hands of multiple owners. A group of owners must now, together, make decisions heretofore made by one or two people. This new generation of owners are siblings and/or cousins who, as a group, must find ways to maintain focus in spite of the growing divergence of loyalty and allegiance in their relationships. A situation where ownership of the family business is shared by a cousin confederacy will exhibit an even greater diversity of interests, needs, and perspectives. Remember, in the evolution of the family business cousins are the first generation who do not all grow up in the same family. This necessitates that a structure be developed that provides a forum for this diverse group of owners to discuss and decide about how they want to conduct their relationship as owners, achieve their financial expectations, and express their values and perspectives as to what their ownership should mean in the larger world.

Ownership issues in every family business constantly overlap with family and business issues, requiring that compromises be made in order to achieve optimum alignment among them. The Shareholders' Council structure provides the mechanism necessary to deal with such interface issues as:

- incorporating family owner values into business strategies and goals;
- integrating owner expectations regarding ROI with company performance;
- deciding about use of profits, for example as distributions versus acquisition versus capital expenditures;
- deciding on the objectives of a family shareholders' agreement and keeping the agreement current;
- coordinating extended family estate planning to avoid problems with future ownership;
- deciding about options related to keeping ownership of the business in the family; and
- educating family owners who have diverse levels of business knowledge about the technical side of business ownership.

Without a *specific* structure through which these issues can be discussed and addressed, they will inevitably be expressed where there is any structure. Family meetings or board meetings thus become the venues for discussing issues and concerns about ownership. In these settings it is likely that information necessary to deal with the issues is unavailable, nonowners are unnecessarily drawn into the discussion, and confusion about who should be discussing these issues, and according to what rules, leads to conflict.

We should also point out that an effective Shareholders' Council, along with the other structures that we recommend in this chapter, is the best way to avoid disgruntled minority owners. In the past, relationships with minority owners were not taken very seriously, and their rights under the law were frequently violated. As a result, closely held company minority owner rights have taken on new meaning as these owners exercise the rights they are entitled to. Such rights include, among other things, access to company records, registration of protest about excessive compensation taken by company executives, and charges that majority owners have breached their fiduciary duty and injured minority owner interests.

SHAREHOLDERS' COUNCIL

Of all the structures discussed in this chapter the Shareholders' Council is perhaps the most simple and easy to establish and operate. Its members are all owners of stock in the business regardless of the percentage of their ownership. The Shareholders' Council typically meets only once a year unless more frequent or special meetings are needed to draft or revise the Shareholders' Agreement, deal with potential sale of the business, discuss a merger or major acquisition, or respond to a crisis. During or in conjunction with an annual shareholders' meeting, the following issues are commonly addressed:

- Review of the company's financial and operational performance for the previous year with reports from management.
- Review of Shareholders' Agreement with consideration of any proposed revisions or amendments.
- Election of directors.
- Consideration of owners' expectations regarding return on investment and decisions about whether to leave profit in the company or take it out.
- Discussion of values and orientation toward ownership and how to coordinate this with the Family Forum and Board of Directors.

The date of the annual meeting of the shareholders is usually set forth in the by-laws of the company, as are protocols for announcements, proxy voting, etc. It is usually a good idea to elect one of the shareholders to serve as the Chair of the Shareholders' Council for the coming year, or perhaps two years. While there may not be anything to do between annual meetings, having a chairperson in place to convene any special meetings and to coordinate and convene the following annual meeting provides orderliness and continuity. It is also essential to have a secretary or recorder to keep accurate minutes of the meeting. Utilizing a trusted executive secretary or assistant for this role works best so that all shareholders can fully participate in the meeting. It is the responsibility of the Chair of the Shareholders' Council to make sure minutes are being recorded either by bringing someone in, or appointing a willing and capable shareholder to the task.

Meetings of the Shareholders' Council need to be called as prescribed in the by-laws of the company. This usually requires written notices a certain number of days prior to the meeting. Provisions should also be in place for calling any special meetings of the Shareholders' Council. All shareholders should be given the opportunity to place items on the agenda for the meeting if time allows. A meeting preparation packet should be sent to each shareholder before every Shareholders' Council meeting. This packet should include a cover letter from the chairperson stating the purpose of the meeting, an agenda for the meeting, and relevant reading materials providing background and perspective on all of the issues that will be discussed. The agenda should specify which items are informational, which are discussion-only, and which will require action at this meeting. The agenda should be approved as the first item of business. This allows the shareholders, as a group, to decide whether to consider special or unusual items placed on the agenda by another shareholder. Last, but not least, the meeting should begin and end on time.

SHAREHOLDERS' AGREEMENT

One of the major responsibilities of the Shareholders' Council is to make sure that a valid, up-to-date, and fully understood Shareholders' Agreement is in force. Creating or revising a Shareholders' Agreement is frequently one of the first tasks of a newly formed Shareholders' Council. Many family business owners think of the agreement between them as only a "buy-sell agreement" specifying restrictions on the transfer of stock. Actually, a well-written Shareholders' Agreement is much more than this. It can also address such issues as:

- What happens in the event a shareholder becomes permanently disabled, gets a divorce, remarries, or wants to cash out?
- What happens if there is a major dispute between four equal owners of a family business with two on each opposing side of the argument; how is a deadlock among owners resolved?
- What kind of protection can be established for senior-generation owners who are concerned their children, who now own majority interest in the company, may make a foolish decision to sell the company?
- How can the company be protected from a "run on the bank"

in the event that several owners decide to exercise a provision for voluntary surrender of their stock, or if several owners die in a short period of time and the company is obligated to redeem the stock from their estates?

- How can the interests of several minority owners be protected if three owners who among them have voting control make a low-ball offer to buy out the minority owners or threaten to squeeze them out by issuing additional stock to be purchased by the majority owners?
- How can the family make sure that ownership of the business remains in the bloodline of the founder if that is their desire?
- What can be done to make sure that a majority owner, or two, who are officers of the corporation, don't siphon off profits in excessive compensation, depriving other owners of a distribution of profits?

These and other such issues can all be addressed in the Shareholders' Agreement. A good Shareholders' Agreement clarifies and specifies how shareholders will manage their relationships with each other in making decisions, resolving conflicts, and setting the direction of the company through its Board of Directors. It addresses more than transfer of their stock.

Ideally, the Shareholders' Agreement is written and in force before ownership goes to multiple owners. Unfortunately, this frequently does not occur and the need for a Shareholders' Agreement, or the need for a good one, doesn't get brought up until there is a problem. Getting five or six shareholders to sign an agreement when there is conflict among them is much more difficult than it would have been if done earlier; it may even become impossible.

Many excellent books have been written on the subject of Shareholders' Agreements[4] and you should consult a legal advisor who specializes in writing them for family businesses. However, the initial step in establishing or revising a Shareholders' Agreement is for the owners to become clear as to their objectives both for themselves personally and for ownership of the company. With these objectives in hand a qualified attorney will have a much easier time drafting the agreement that meets your desires, and it will be much less costly for you. Here are some of the areas you need to be clear about:

- Who will be permitted to own stock; will it be restricted to family members? Do owners have to be actively employed in the business; do they have to be lineal descendants of the founder; etc.?

- What events will trigger involuntary transfer (call); death, disability, termination of employment, divorce, retirement, age, going into a competitive business, etc.?
- Under what conditions will voluntary transfer (put) be permitted?
- Should the company or other shareholders have the right of first refusal for available stock, and should the company (redemptive agreement) or other shareholders (cross purchase agreement) actually be obligated to purchase stock under certain conditions to provide for liquidity to owners?
- How should the company be protected financially if it is obligated to purchase stock from an individual or an estate: an extended pay out period, insurance, etc.?
- How will disputes be resolved other than by majority vote: a clause requiring outside arbitration and the conditions that trigger it?
- Are there any situations in which a super majority (80% majority) vote should be required: selling the business, capital obligations over a certain amount, etc.?
- Can trusts established by and for family members own stock?
- How will the price of stock be determined and will discounts be mandated for minority stock?

- Should the Shareholders' Council have the authority, by majority vote, to block the sale of stock to any potential buyer or transferee?

Again, there are a great many specific provisions that a qualified attorney can advise you about. The greatest fear on the part of most families in business is that they will not think of something that should have been included but inadvertently was left out. Do the best job you can at clarifying your objectives and then make sure that your Shareholders' Agreement is reviewed periodically for completeness according to your situation. Remember, the best time to revise a Shareholders' Agreement is before a problem occurs or relationship problems arise. It is usually just such a problem that causes family business owners to pull their "buy-sell" out, dust it off, and realize in horror that they are trapped by an inadequate agreement.

SHAREHOLDERS' AGREEMENT AND BEYOND

We are indebted to David Juday, Chairman and CEO of IDEAL Industries, and Nancy Juday, Chair of the Family Council and a member of the Board of Directors as well as an attorney, for the valuable information that follows. As we have discussed, the real strength and value of any Shareholders' Agreement lies more in its ability to preserve and strengthen relationships among the owners than in the provisions of the agreement. The agreement reflects the commitments made by family business owners to each other and to their stewardship of the business. David and Nancy, two of the third-generation owners of IDEAL Industries, recognized this fact and spearheaded a project to make sure relationships would be preserved into the fourth generation and beyond. With their leadership, the nineteen second, third- and fourth-generation owners established a voting trust that serves as a companion mechanism to their buy-sell agreement.

In 1997 a change in the tax laws provided the opportunity for IDEAL Industries to elect Subchapter "S" status with the Internal Revenue Service, replacing their existing Subchapter "C" election. Specific changes of importance to IDEAL included the new allowance for a Subchapter S corporation to have seventy-five rather than the previous thirty-five shareholders and for a trust to own stock in the company. There were tax advantages for making the change, but it also required a recapitalization of company stock since preferred stock had been issued under the "C" election. This presented an opportunity to address some shareholder issues that were created by the estate planning done by the first generation and were of increasing concern to David, Nancy, and others. Essentially, two family branches are represented in the ownership of IDEAL Industries. The stock of the company was placed in trusts by the founders with the voting of that stock entrusted to "advisors" of the trusts (trustees) — who were the founders' two daughters and their husbands. As ownership went into the third generation, the potential for proliferation of the number of advisors increased greatly. David and Nancy, though brother and sister, worked very hard to ensure that they represented the entire family. However, they could foresee that the potential existed for problems to develop in the next generation unless the issue of proliferation of advisors was dealt with and the consequences severe. As David says, "The elaborate estate plan established by the founders really drove the successors to a consensus model of decision making." In addition, the provisions for voting control carried the possibility, which no one wanted, that a particular order of death of second-generation family members could arbitrarily place voting control in one, or another group of minority owners. The three problems facing the family were (1) how to preserve the stability of the business and the family by creating a preventive, as opposed to reactive, mechanism for decision making among owners; (2) establish a new structure that would encourage the consensus approach that existed due to the estate planning done by the first generation; and (3) establish a protocol for dispute resolution that would anticipate the possibility of a major breakdown in shareholder relationships as the family became more diverse in membership and interests in future generations.

To address these three concerns the shareholders agreed to establish a voting trust in conjunction with the recapitalization of company stock. While the law only allows one class of stock in an "S" corporation, the shareholders designated one percent as voting common stock and ninety-nine percent as nonvoting common stock. All voting stock was placed in the voting trust, and it is voted by two trustees who are elected by the beneficiaries of the trust. One of the primary reasons behind designating such a large percentage of the stock as nonvoting was to facilitate transfer of stock in individual shareholder estate planning while achieving the purpose of the voting trust at the same time. While the trustees, who serve six-year terms, elect the directors of the company and perform other ownership functions, major corporate decisions such as sale of the company and restructuring of the board are decided by majority vote of the beneficiaries of the trust. In addition, the voting trust contains a very specific provision for dispute resolution between the two trustees. If they are deadlocked on an issue an ad hoc committee composed of the outside directors of the company, the Chair of the Family Council and one additional person selected by the Chair of the Family Council, is formed to work with the trustees in trying to resolve the issue. If this fails, the issue is put before the beneficiaries, who decide it by majority vote. At that point both trustees are required to resign and two new trustees are elected by the beneficiaries. It is assumed that the trustee whose position prevailed would be reelected and the other replaced. The voting trust arrangement provides alternate structure and voice for the ownership domain, an elegant companion agreement to the buy-sell agreement and greatly enhances the preservation and harmony among a diverse group of family business shareholders.

Both David and Nancy make it clear that this did not happen overnight. Nancy says, "The most difficult issue we had to deal with was what to do if an absolutely intractable schism should occur in future generations and provide for a fair and equitable dissolution of the voting trust in the event our ability to agree falls apart." The decision was made that the most fair dissolution would be to put shareholders back into the same equity voting positions they would have been in if the voting trust had never been formed. David says, "It was a heavy investment in the Family Forum process over fourteen years that laid the groundwork for getting this done. You have to deal with family issues first. Then you have to take the time to anticipate what the future may hold and do everything you can to deal with problems before they arise." The important point here is that in family business, the relationship among the owners is more important than the mechanics of how stock is transferred and the solution to the concerns facing IDEAL Industries reinforces the importance of RQ in the health and vitality of those relationships.

Yes, RQ is the technology of relationships in the family business. It takes shape and form through the structures discussed in this chapter. Both dimensions of RQ, Relationship Paradigm and Relationship Skill, form and are formed by the structures in which they reside. The tone, ethos, and operation of the Family Forum, Board of Directors, and Shareholders' Council are all determined by the level of RQ in each group. At the same time, and more importantly, all three structures provide great opportunities to teach and reinforce the principles of RQ in very effective and positive ways. In fact, committing to the process of creating and maintaining these structures in itself builds trust, optimism, and respect — the three ingredients of Relationship Paradigm. Just as IQ remains a concept with no meaningful impact except as it is expressed in the acts and utterances of an individual, and EQ remains a concept with no meaningful impact except as it is expressed through someone's decisions and actions of high integrity and character, so RQ remains a concept with no relevance or impact except as it is expressed through the structures of family business. The architecture of family business turns the principles and practices of RQ, the technology of relationships, into reality.

Notes
1. Personal correspondence.
2. Two excellent references are: Fred Neubauer and Alden G. Lank. *The Family Business*. London: MacMillan Press, 1998; and John Ward. *Creating Effective Boards for Private Enterprise*. San Francisco: Jossey-Bass, 1991.
3. *American Family Business Survey '97* available from Mass Mutual's Family Business Enterprise, 860/987-2031.
4. See Mike Cohn. *Passing the Torch*. New York, McGraw Hill, 1992.

7 Promoting RQ through Stewardship

Successful multigenerational family businesses live by a profound sense that their business is not a personal possession, but rather a trust that has been given to them for safekeeping and for which they have deep caring and respect. The owners of these firms, among the longest lasting and most prominent companies worldwide, view the business more as a responsibility of stewardship than as the privilege of proprietorship. It always seems that in spite of differences, conflict, and even divisions, their stewardship responsibility brings them back to center, back to unity of focus and effort. It tempers proprietary interests that typically revolve around the old viewpoints of "What's in it for me?" or "It's mine and I can do what I want with it." In early October 1997, at the annual conference of the Family Business Network in the Hague, Mr. B. Puech, a fifth-generation owner of the Hermés company, made the following statement in accepting the distinguished Family Business Award from the International Institute of Management Development. Before an international audience of over two hundred family businesses, Mr. Puech confided, "We in the fifth generation of the Hermés do not view ourselves as owners of the company, we are merely taking care of it for our children." What a remarkable and compelling statement of the orientation of stewardship in family business. For families like those who own the Hermés company and who embrace the orientation of stewardship, there is almost a sense of sacred trust akin to that of a parent. As parents we co-create life, but we do not own our children, rather we nurture them into being independent and healthy individuals. For stewardship-oriented business-owning families there is an appreciation of the business as a gift, not one deserved or to which they were entitled, but one which they accept and treasure with respect and gratitude as a family heirloom and legacy. The business and their managers have a clear sense of attachment and personal investment in the company's purpose and values to the extent that their allegiance and loyalty are to the business more than to the founder or owning family. In other words, these families have an answer as to why all of the trouble is worth it, and their answers are bigger than the individual proprietary interests.

Research supports the key role stewardship plays in family business succession. Barbara Dunn determined in her study of ten Scottish family businesses in 1994 that "stewardship of wealth and employees' well-being" and "caring and loyalty to staff and customers" were two of the fourteen "philosophies" these families identified as underlying success.[1] A study by Ivan Lansberg and Joe Astrachan of 109 family businesses on the influences of family relationships on long-term success found that "highly committed families viewed the firm as a continuing legacy in which the family's traditions, identity, and culture are embodied. A distinctive feature of families that are highly committed to their businesses is that the parents convey to their children a sense of excitement about the business and its future. Insuring the long-term viability of the firm is a central concern for these families."[2] Truly it is the principles and practices of stewardship that are central to the long-term success of family enterprise. Throughout this chapter we will elaborate on those principles and practices and discuss how positive Relationship Intelligence promotes an orientation of stewardship; as well as how an orientation of stewardship enhances family relationships by creating a positive and productive paradigm about what it means to be a business-owning family.

STEWARDSHIP VS. PROPRIETORSHIP

While no two families in business are exactly alike in terms of their orientation toward ownership, in every case their actions and attitudes will reflect some combination of the orientation of stewardship and proprietorship. The family that approaches ownership primarily from an orientation of proprietorship views the business as a possession to be exploited and consumed. Exploitation and consumption by individual owners is considered to be the privilege to which they, in exchange for the risks they assume, are entitled. At the extreme, the orientation of proprietorship becomes a very distorted and destructive exploitation of a family business. For example, in some business-owning families, greed and self-interest masquerade as claims of rightful reward and return on investment.

A number of years ago two brothers approached us for help shortly after their father died. There was no written succession plan for this very successful and profitable business. Dad never worked with his sons together, but "individually" over the years, he confided to each that someday this business will be "yours." Unfortunately, leaving the next generation with unclear expectations and vague promises is not an unusual happening. Many times family business owners believe that if their estate planning is completed, if future ownership decisions have been made— that's all that is needed for a smooth transition.

These brothers had never really gotten along in the business. But dad, as is often the case, served as the buffer. Now they needed to tie their minds together, develop a common vision, decide who was in charge of what, how decisions would be made, and so on. One brother was a real risk-taker, saw "millions" of opportunities for growth, and wanted to triple the size of the company in a very short time. The other brother had children who he hoped someday would carry on the legacy handed down to him through owning and managing the business. He hoped someday his kids would manage and own the business. Therefore, he too wanted to grow the company, but not as aggressively as his brother. This partnership was like trying to blend oil and water.

Each of them had fairly good communication skills and excellent knowledge of the business and the market. The real problem was their long-standing negative Relationship Paradigm. There was no trust that either one cared about the other's hopes and expectations. Neither was there trust that the other would not "take over" behind this brother's back. And of course, each felt the business was rightfully his own and that he was to be the one in charge. By the time we were contacted, the self-righteousness that each brother was feeling was rigidly ingrained in his heart and mind.

Our first course of action was to help them create a common vision and reach agreement on each other's roles and responsibilities. That worked well, but when it came time to create an implementation plan, the mistrust and pessimism within their relationship took hold. It became clear that no implementation plan would satisfy both of them because basically each felt, "It's my business and I'll decide." This is an example of what we call extreme proprietorship. Today each is running his own business in competition with the other. The negative Relationship Paradigm, a history of mistrust, pessimism and disrespect, along with inadequate succession planning, was too much of a hurdle to overcome.

The priorities of the orientation of proprietorship, as exemplified in the above example, can be characterized as follows:

- My business exists for my best interests and I expect it to adjust to my needs
- Every day brings a new threat by those wanting to destroy what I have built and worked hard for. I will protect my rights at all costs.
- I intend to take as much as I can out of this business.

PRIORITIES OF SUCCESSFUL BUSINESS-OWNING FAMILIES

Through our consulting and teaching with hundreds of family businesses, we have become convinced that the single most significant force behind unity and alignment within family businesses is the presence of a strong, genuine, and long-standing reliance by owners, family, and business upon a core set of priorities that directs their purpose. Shared priorities or values such as those reflected in an orientation of stewardship provide the glue that keeps relationships intact and protects them from fragmenting along lines of individual self-interest. Expectations and beliefs about ownership are part of the Relationship Paradigm of every business-owning family. They support either a positive or negative Relationship Paradigm depending on whether they engender trust or create mistrust, instill optimism or foster pessimism, promote respect or elicit desrespect. We have identified the following values as representative of those found in successful family businesses:

- They treat the business as an opportunity that has been entrusted to them for its well-being.
- They take to heart versus only giving lip service to their commitment for long-term success, offering quality products and services versus cutting corners to make a fast buck, and attending to the real wants and needs of the customer versus selling them short.
- They feel a genuine sense of love, loyalty, and caring for the well-being of family as a whole and each other individually.
- They live their lives out of a center of gratitude and abundance as opposed to a sense of entitlement and scarcity.

• They recognize they are not islands unto themselves; ask for and utilize outside help and advice appropriately.

• They know the importance of being a relationship-first family business and spend time, money, and energy on opening up communication, they develop a process for sharing information, building consensus, analyzing and solving problems, and creating policies and procedures that keep family and nonfamily employees working together. In short, they understand that relationships are the language of family business and sincerely view them as the "other bottom line" by which they measure success.

Lest you think this implies that things are hopeless if these values are not strongly represented in your family business, we hasten to add that this is not our intent, nor is it true. Given the complexity of family business relationships, it is easy for them to momentarily lose their way on the Relationship Road Map for success. Unless desire and motivation are nonexistent, there is always hope. You may need help seeing the forest as a whole in spite of the overgrown trees. If you are open to doing whatever it takes to get back on track and to investing in creating an orientation of stewardship, you are well on your way to building the foundation for future success and joy in working together.

ACCOUNTABILITY FOSTERS STEWARDSHIP

Accountability is one of the thorniest issues in any family business. It is especially difficult in relationships among multiple family owners, among siblings and cousins who are all equal within the family but not within the business. Siblings and cousins have friction and arguments about accountability more often than about any other family business subject. To whom, or what, are the owners of a family business accountable? You can say "to one another," but history says this doesn't always work even when relationships are good. Some would say, only partly in jest, the Internal Revenue Service. After all, we have all read stories about well-known family business owners jailed for tax fraud. Standards of performance that provide measures of accountability for the employment of family members break down when they relate as owners. What then is the answer of the accountability of owners?

Ownership accountability in family business does not come from the outside; it comes from the inside! It grows out of time-honored family principles based on priorities and values of honesty, fairness, and honoring the family name and legacy. At the deepest level, accountability for family business owners is based on the principles, values, and priorities held by them, and these must be of the highest level. You know when you are carrying out ownership responsibilities in this way because you find integrity and commitment reinforced on a regular basis. This is the pinnacle of responsible family business ownership and when enacted in ownership and management activities, it goes deep into resolving the accountability struggles that otherwise exist. *When what you do in your family business is in congruity with what you believe, and what you believe is centered in the orientation of stewardship, you achieve the most gratifying experience of being a family in business.*

THE SIX PRINCIPLES OF STEWARDSHIP

Developing an orientation of stewardship is an ownership responsibility. It is through leadership provided by the owners that stewardship becomes the benchmark for family members, especially successors, against which to measure their relationship with each other and the business. The difference between an orientation of proprietorship and one of stewardship might best be characterized by the story of the bricklayer and the stone craftsman. It is told that the bricklayer, when asked what he was doing, viewed his work simply as a means to an end and responded, "building a wall." On the other hand, the stone craftsman working on the same wall, but viewing his work through the lens of stewardship, answers the same question, "building a great cathedral that will be the heart of our community for centuries to come."

To help the owners of family businesses initiate and perpetuate an orientation of stewardship, we developed six Principles of Stewardship for family business owners. They are intended to serve as the credo to which owners and family members can subscribe and from which they can take direction. As you will see they are built upon those enduring qualities we have observed in successful family business.

●●●

PRINCIPLES OF STEWARDSHIP IN FAMILY BUSINESS

- Business ownership is not my right but my privilege.
- My business depends on me looking after its best interest, and that means acknowledging when I am part of a problem.
- Every day is a new opportunity for me to do something good for my business; it's up to me whether or not it happens.
- I cannot let discomfort and fear, my own or others', cause me to avoid facing and resolving difficult family and business problems.
- To keep my business healthy, I must remain healthy too, through ongoing personal development in mind, body, and spirit.
- As both an owner and employee, I will not knowingly abuse the privilege of business ownership, nor jeopardize the well-being of the whole for the benefit of any one individual, myself or someone else.

●●●

These Principles of Stewardship represent our paradigm about successful business ownership. They are a powerful set of filters through which owners can view their responsibilities and their relationships. Given the fact that our lives are governed by our beliefs, prejudices, and biases, our paradigms, it is essential that the orientation held toward ownership be one that offers the greatest likelihood of success. The orientation of stewardship is that success paradigm because of its unique power to create and nurture, guide, and challenge the most resilient relationships among family members. The Principles of Stewardship will be meaningless if relegated to the status of "words to live by" and hung on the wall in a gold-edged frame. We encourage you to adapt the principles as a beacon, a lighthouse, to which you orient yourself and from which you evaluate the progress of your journey in family business ownership.

ASSESSING YOUR STEWARDSHIP

We offer you a way to get started on, and continue to build, your orientation of stewardship. The following self-evaluation will help you determine the extent to which you, as an owning family, approach your business ownership and management responsibilities from this perspective. The answers may be obvious, or again they may not. Although not difficult, the process does require honest soul searching. It is our hope that you will use these questions during meetings of owners and family members to challenge and nurture a long-term commitment to ownership as a stewardship responsibility.

QFRs

Principle: Business ownership is not my right but my privilege.

- To what extent do you approach your role as owner with an attitude of humility, gratitude, and responsibility that is apparent to all, as opposed to an attitude of possessiveness, entitlement, and privilege?
- To what extent do family members and employees follow your example and view their relationship with the family business as a responsibility of stewardship rather than the privilege of proprietorship?

Principle: My business depends on me looking after its best interest, and that means acknowledging when I am part of a problem.

- How much do you recognize it, and stand up to be counted, when you contribute to a problem as opposed to avoiding the issue and expecting everyone around you to adjust, thus jeopardizing the best interest of your business?
- How much do family members and employees point fingers of blame rather than embrace honesty and extend arms of reconciliation?

Principle: Every day is a new opportunity for me to do something good for my business; it's up to me whether or not it happens.

- To what extent do you discipline yourself to accomplish every day the one or two things that will have the greatest positive impact on your business as opposed to losing your focus, getting fragmented, and wasting opportunities?
- How much do family members and employees do the same either way?

Principle: I cannot let discomfort and fear, my own or others', cause me to avoid facing and resolving difficult family and business problems.

- Do you put your business at risk by avoiding painful and difficult family and business issues because of your own, or someone else's, fears and discomfort?
- To what extent is avoidance of conflict and growing numbers of false

agreements among family members and employees jeopardizing your company?

Principle: To keep my business healthy, I must remain healthy too, through ongoing personal development in mind, body and spirit.

- How much do you take care of yourself, strive for balance in your life, nurture and live according to your core values and personal mission as opposed to relying on your work and business to be the source of your self-worth and purpose in life?
- To what extent do family relationships and the culture of your business reflect the value of personal well-being, health, and balance in life?

Principle: As both an owner and employee, I will not knowingly abuse the privilege of business ownership, nor jeopardize the well-being of the whole for the benefit of any one individual, myself or someone else.

- To what extent do you take inappropriate advantage of your rights and privileges of ownership because there is no one to question it, and jeopardize the whole for your own or someone else's benefit?
- How much have family members and long-standing employees come to expect special privileges without regard to the impact on the company?

Creating an orientation of stewardship doesn't just happen. It is the result of paying attention to relationships and the core priorities and values that promote responsible, profitable, and successful family business ownership. Stewardship is built each day by how you think, make decisions, and treat each other. It requires a high level of Relationship Intelligence: good communication and negotiation skills and a positive Relationship Paradigm. We have provided you with detailed information about the structures and tools that can be used to foster an orientation of stewardship in your family business. These were laid out in chapters 4 and 6.

Notes
1. Barbara Dunn. "Success Themes in Scottish Family Enterprises." *Family Business Review* VII (1): 21–22.
2. Ivan Lansberg and Joseph Astrachan. "Influence of Family Relationships on Succession Planning and Training. The Importance of Mediating Factors." *Family Business Review* VII (1): 55.

8 Ethical Dilemmas in the Family Business

As you read the title to this chapter you are probably asking yourself, "What in the world does ethics have to do with getting along in family business?" After all, no one in your family or in your business is involved in shady practices, undercover illegal operations, or immoral acts that violate accepted standards of human decency. But before you put the book down or flip to the next chapter, we suggest you read further because there is a particular type of ethical problem that exists in every family business. It is one of the most frequent sources of conflict and disagreement and is faced, not just occasionally, but routinely. It is the flash point when confrontation happens among differing positions, each of which can be claimed as "right" based on values, beliefs, and priorities that are well accepted but which are in opposition.

Most people would diagnose a serious conflict with another person as a clear case of right versus wrong; they're right and the other person is wrong. Very often, when we are called by a family in conflict over business issues, it becomes obvious at the outset that what they want is for us to assume the role of judge and jury. They are looking for us to hear the evidence and pronounce a verdict as to which side is right and which is wrong. In fact, some families in business, like patients looking for the physician who will give them the diagnosis they want, "shop" around for a consultant to find one who agrees with their position. It is much easier to resolve a dispute when one person is right and the other is wrong, when one option is morally or ethically superior to the other. But what happens when the choice is not "right versus wrong" or "good versus evil," but "right versus right," as very often happens in the world of family business.

WHEN IT'S RIGHT VS. RIGHT

Many disputes start out as issues in which both sides have a legitimate reason and justification for their position. Having the skill and understanding to resolve this common family business relationship struggle

175

is a great enhancement to the relationship skill dimension of RQ and is essential to getting along in family business. We suggest you try, right now, an exercise we do with our clients. Before reading any further, fold your arms across your chest. Notice whether your right hand curls over your left arm, or vice versa, or neither. Now, reverse the way your arms are folded. It feels terribly awkward and uncomfortable doesn't it? This is obviously the *wrong* way to fold your arms, right? Of course, there is no right or wrong way of folding arms; one way is just as right as the other. Yet when you have been folding your arms the same way all your life, never giving it a second thought, any other way seems wrong.

Consider the situation confronting Dick Lee and his son Rick. Dick founded Affiliated Steam Equipment Company, a successful distribution business in Alsip, Illinois, in 1958. In 1993, Rick Lee, one of three children and the only one active or interested in the business, had been working in the company for fifteen years. For all practical purposes Rick had been running the company for several years and was ready to take over full ownership of the company. However, at age 81, Dick wasn't ready to turn over control without some assurances. Dick named certain conditions connected with the sale including some continuing income, financial performance criteria, and several perks he had enjoyed. He considered these minimal recognition and reward for forty years of hard work and he would not sell to his son, or anyone else, without them. Dick also wanted to make sure that all three children would be treated equally in his estate plan especially with only one of them, his son, taking over the company.

At age forty-four Rick was not willing to continue building the business unless he had assurance of complete ownership. He could see the handwriting on the wall. He would dedicate his time and energy to building the business only to pay twice by having to buy out the added value from his nonactive siblings. He was not willing to pay his sisters for what he had built, yet he also believed that everybody should be treated fairly in his father's estate plan. As buyer, he felt that a fair sale price was sufficient reward for the seller of any business and that the proceeds would create the liquidity needed to equalize his father's estate. Who was right? Which of these two men had their arms folded correctly?

Most would agree that Dick had every right to expect and deserve a financially secure retirement, including some continued enjoyment of perks he had earned. It is reasonable as well that he wanted his children treated equally in his estate planning. Likewise, Rick had every right to claim the promise of ownership given by his father and for which he had demonstrated his capability. Most would consider it reasonable that Rick expected not to be forced to purchase his own sweat equity from his siblings as a result of his desire to own the company and willingness to pay for it.

Both were right, and this is precisely what makes the situation so difficult. It is the type of dilemma that family businesses confront on a regular basis: a choice not between right and wrong but between two rights, each of which is firmly rooted in values and principles that most of us would uphold as worthy and good. Battles erupt in the halls and conference rooms, and around the dining tables, of family businesses over whether it is right to

- support the individual or the group,
- look long term or short term,
- insist on justice or mercy,
- defend truth or loyalty.

Is it right to continue the employment of a family member executive who clings to her job as a lifeline yet is not performing because of personal problems caused by her child's suicide a year earlier? Or is it right to replace her because her area of responsibility languishes and threatens an entire division?

Is it right to expect that future family member owners will contribute more than other employees in anticipation of their future ownership? Or is it right for family employees to expect the same rewards for their contribution as any other employee?

Is it right for the current generation owners to defend and protect loyal, long-term senior executives who helped build the business? Or is it right for the successors to want their own team of managers in whom they feel more confident and from whom they receive greater support?

ETHICAL DILEMMAS VS. MORAL DECISIONS

At first glance it may seem that these are simply differences of opinion or perspective, and they are, but they are also much more than that. These are examples of ethical dilemmas grounded in deeply held beliefs. Each side of the dilemma is often supported by shared family values. This is what makes such issues so emotional and each side so frequently combative. What we are discussing here is the role of the ethical dilemma in family business, which we distinguish from moral decisions. We define ethical dilemmas like this:

ETHICAL DILEMMA: Points of decision making based on core values that are upheld as right and good but which may be incompatible in certain situations (e.g., being truthful versus loyal).

Compare the ethical dilemma to its cousin, the moral decision. While strongly emotional, moral decisions are much easier to resolve. In a moral decision you only have to choose between right and wrong. Compare the definition of ethical dilemma to that of the moral decision.

MORAL DECISION: Points of decision making based on law, truth, or commonly accepted moral principles that, for the majority of people, clearly delineate right from wrong.

Is it against the law? Will the action taken cause a response of moral repugnance or disgust? How would you feel if your action was made public knowledge? These are the tests of moral decisions and it is easy to decipher right from wrong.

For example, is it right or wrong to hide financial perks provided tax free only to family members in violation of the law? Is it right or wrong to withhold important corporate information from minority shareholders to protect and advance self interest? Is it right to expose employees to unsafe and demeaning working conditions to satisfy the financial needs of owners, or dispose of toxic waste into the environment? The answers are clear as to what is right and wrong regardless of how strong the emotion. Moral decisions are based on values and beliefs inherent in the law, generally accepted values, and commonly held moral principles.

BUILDING EMPATHY THROUGH ACTIVE LISTENING

The first line of prevention against ethical dilemmas running amuck is to identify them properly as early as possible and reverse the downhill slide while there is still openness, flexibility, and desire to find a mutually beneficial resolution still exist. One method has been tried and proven in achieving this first, and perhaps most important, goal. It is the tool of active listening that we described in chapter 4. You will recall that active listening means that you repeat, in your own words, what you believe the other person is saying to you before you give your response. Applied to an ethical dilemma such as that between Dick and Rick, it might go something like this:

Dick: I can't understand how you can oppose my requests for continued income and seem so unconcerned about my desire to treat you and your sisters all equally. I've worked hard all these years to provide for my family and that includes me. I have no reason to sell you this business and take less than I could get if I were to sell it to someone else. And as long as I'm financially dependent on the success of the company I think I deserve some performance safeguards from you just like I've always expected from myself.

Rick: I can't understand how you can be so unconcerned about the impact of your demands on the business and, yes, I do believe it's important that you treat all of us equally in your estate but my efforts in building this company should be in my estate plan, not yours.

Dick: This isn't going to get us anywhere. We both think we're right. Let me try to understand your position, Rick (an active listening response). You want to make sure the business can support my financial requirements without putting undue strain on you and the business. You don't think it's right for you to be generating your sister's inheritance . . . that's up to me and them. Is that right?

Rick: Yes, it is.

Dick: Would you please try to put in your words what you hear from me?

Rick: Well, I guess you're wanting to make sure that the lifestyle you've worked hard for doesn't go downhill just because you sell the business to me; and that the business doesn't go south once I'm in full control. I also know that you have to provide equally for all three of us and I have no problem with that, in fact that's how I want to treat my kids. Did I get it?

Dick: Yes you did. Can we agree that both of us are right . . . that you don't want to do me or your sisters in, and I don't want to make it impossible for you to have what you deserve . . . that we both want what's right for both our family and our business?

Rick: I can buy into that!

Why does active listening work? It works because ignoring and misinterpreting what the other person is really saying fuels an adversarial posture. Active listening, i.e., listening for the purpose of understanding, breaks down polarization and builds trust. Active listening supported by an attitude of respect, mutual care, and concern is the foundation for solving ethical dilemmas. Such a conversation, however, becomes increasingly difficult as time passes. Have it as early as possible.

RAISING THE RIGHT QUESTIONS

Ethical dilemmas are not new to our era. Since final and clear-cut answers to ethical dilemmas can never be found, our ancestors came up with three questions that can help guide us, even today. We have added a fourth to the list. Usually one, or a combination of the four, provides the guidance and direction needed to get to a resolution.

Question 1: What is best for the most people involved? This requires us to do what Steven Covey admonishes in *Seven Habits of Highly Effective People*[1] and that is to "begin with the end in mind." It pushes us to look at what the consequences would be should our position or intentions be fully achieved. If Dick, because of his demands, jeopardizes the health of the business, what would that achieve? If Rick because of his counterdemands winds up losing his chance to grow the business even further, what would that achieve?

Question 2: Would you want your action to become the standard for everyone else? Suppose you keep your distressed, non-performing child in a key position because she needs the income and, even more importantly, a place to go to work everyday to keep from sitting at home and getting more depressed. Is that the standard by which every employee should be evaluated? If you refuse to sign the buy/sell agreement because you want freedom to do whatever you wish, without consideration of your co-owners, with your one-third ownership, is that the standard by which you want all shareholders to be governed?

Question 3: Do unto others as you would have them do unto you. Simply put, are you dealing with others the way you want them to deal with you if the situation were reversed?

Question 4: If you view ownership of your family business primarily as the responsibility of stewardship, are you being a good steward? As we wrote in the previous chapter, stewardship means that what you own belongs to you for safe keeping and responsible development. Parents who seek to "own" their children end up destroying their relationship with them. Family business owners who seek to use the business and family solely for their own purposes end up destroying their relationship with both. Being a responsible steward means putting what is entrusted to you first, and yourself second.

BUILDING BRIDGES TO SUPPORT DECISIONS

Why is all this so particularly important to family businesses? First, ethical dilemmas are a significant and unrecognized source of misalignment among the needs and demands of family, business management, and ownership, the three domains of every family business. In one way or another, as we discussed in chapter 3, the vast majority of difficulties in family business can be attributed to such misalignment, more so than to the faults and foibles of any individual. Resolving ethical dilemmas is essential to helping family, business, and ownership work together by building bridges between their very different measures of success and the values and principles that underlie them.

Second, the importance of finding ways to manage ethical dilemmas grows geometrically as the family business moves into the sibling and cousin stages of development. The further the family evolves away from the founding generation, the greater the diversity of values, principles, and priorities and the more fertile the soil for growth of ethical dilemmas.

As Dick Lee and Rick Lee gained this knowledge and came back to the drawing table, they resolved their differences. Today, Rick is the sole owner of a successful and growing business. Dick enjoys consulting to the company, spending winter in Florida, and having time with his grandchildren. Perhaps, though, the most powerful result is the one Rick mentioned at a meeting of family businesses as he patted his father on the arm and said, "The best thing is, I got my Dad back!"

DIAGNOSIS IS HALF THE CURE

As individuals, both Dick and Rick experienced many long-term, successful relationships. But with each other and in particular over the issues of succession planning, buying, and selling the business, their relationship over time became polarized. A symptom of the polarization was how they framed the issue: right versus wrong. From there it turned into a no-win situation.

We were able to quickly see that each of them individually had good Relationship Skill tools for solving problems, adapting to change, carrying out joint tasks with others, and having fun. Each of them had also experienced in the past a fair amount of trust, respect, and optimism in their relationship. All of these facts made for a positive diagnosis.

Our initial work was to reframe the problem they brought to us. They defined the problem as their need to complete the succession plan and we suggested that their greatest need was to rebuild their relationship with each other.

They had each worked with an accountant and dad with an estate planner to come up with ways to sell the business. This process continued to drive the wedge even deeper in their relationship, not because there was anything technically wrong with the plans, but because they were trying to solve the wrong problem. We have seen situations like this many times. This is what has convinced us of the importance of having a relationship-first family business.

After reframing the problem, we helped them work on some new communication and negotiation skills, develop a deeper appreciation and understanding of the changes that had harmed their relationship, and restore a positive Relationship Paradigm. The latter involved helping them deal with their expectations and prejudices with each other by rebuilding trust, optimism, and respect. This took place by following the steps of LSi's Relationship Roadmap (chapter 4). Sharing information, confirming expectations, and using active listening skills — all tools we have spoken about in *Getting Along In Family Business* — were essential to "getting them back to zero." Once this was done, we helped them work on redefining roles and responsibilities for the transition of ownership and leadership. We then sent them back to their accountants and estate planners.

About three weeks later Rick called and sounded as if he was set back in his original discouragement that nothing would really change. He asked if we thought he should deliver an ultimatum. We encouraged him to hold on, to continue using the listening and negotiation skills, and to remember ultimately that he wanted more out of this than just owning a business. He *wanted a good relationship* with his dad. Rick appreciated that reminder, and we discussed the importance of his taking time to be with his dad outside of dealing with reaching a buy-sell arrangement. This was a critical time for him to reinforce his love, loyalty, and care and vice versa. Rick took that advice.

Two months later, eighteen months after we started working with them, Rick called. He sounded overjoyed and even amazed that he and his dad had arrived at a mutually agreeable arrangement for Rick to buy the company. Rick's new partner would now be the bank. What we find so rewarding in our work with family businesses is the positive residual effect on family relationships that come from resolving business problems. We hear stories years later about how *good* family relationships have been. The newfound trust, optimism, and respect has usually extended out to include other family members in the business and outside the business. This is the result of improving Relationship Intelligence. Once you overcome the barriers in one relationship, it helps you deal with the negative Relationship Paradigm that exists in other relationships; and it gives you the enhanced skills to do so.

Note
1. Stephen R. Covey. *The Seven Habits of Highly Effective People.* New York: Simon & Schuster, 1989.

9 Leadership in the Family Business

Leadership in a family business is like no other kind of leadership in the world! Like the leader of any business the leader of a family business must be strong, visionary, creative, focused, and expertly knowledgeable about the company and its industry. Leaders must also be able to translate vision and strategy into action by inspiring and motivating people. Family business leaders must be able to do all of this and more. In addition to shouldering the demands of leading the business, the family business leader also carries the weight of leading the family in the business, and doing both simultaneously. The leader of a family business usually feels not only the need for a degree in business but one in family psychology as well.

There's a specific reason for having a chapter on leadership in a book about getting along in family business. One of the most important responsibilities of any family business leader is to provide direction for the complex network of relationships within and among the three domains. *Leadership is generally defined as the process of influencing others toward the accomplishment of a common goal.* Given this definition, the leader of a family business must be able to understand and promote Relationship Intelligence within the family and throughout the company. The tools and methods discussed in chapter 4 provide not just the technology of relationship management but the technology of family business leadership as well.

Few family business leaders, regardless of what family generation they are in, approach the challenge of leadership with a full understanding of the diverse expectations placed on them, especially the ones family members may have of them. Even the brightest and most talented leaders, in terms of traditional leadership skills, can be totally naïve when it comes to the relationship aspect of the mantle of family business leadership. As one second-generation family busi-

183

ness CEO said to us, "I agreed to be the leader of the business, not the leader of the family. Every time I turn around someone is expecting me to take charge of family matters like my father did. This is expecting too much, I am not the papa of this whole family!"

WHAT MAKES IT SO DIFFERENT

Eight years ago, Tom Reiser joined the publishing business that his father had purchased twenty-five years earlier and subsequently developed into a full-service publishing house. Coming into the family business, Tom joined his two sisters, Carol and Fran, who had been with the company twelve and nine years, respectively. Carol, who was the company's leader in sales, and Fran, who had distinguished herself in management of one of the company's divisions, were well respected and liked by all the employees. Tom was recruited as the "heir apparent," by his father, who was anticipating retirement in a few years and felt the company should continue to be headed by a male CEO. Tom was employed at the time as a V.P. of finance in a Fortune 1000 company and an active military reserve officer. Publicly Carol and Fran accepted their father's decision, because they had confidence in Tom's abilities, but privately they resented being "outplaced" simply because of their gender. Rounding out the picture, dad convinced Tom to bring Tim, the youngest of the children, into the business three years earlier and "give him a chance to make a success of his life." All four of the siblings, Tom being the oldest, were within six years age difference. Dad anticipated transferring ownership of the business equally to his four children if they could get along and worked hard to make the business a success.

Problems erupted when Tom, very skilled in financial management with demonstrated leadership ability as a military officer, got in over his head when it came to leading the family business. His father, a gentle, nondirective, and soft-spoken entrepreneur, was loved by all. Tom, an outspoken, opinionated, and directive leader turned the company around from marginal to profitable performance. In fact, Tom was respected and appreciated by his father and siblings for his success in managing the business. Unfortunately, Tom had also managed to forge a conflicted relationship with his father, whom he publicly criticized for being a lousy manager; with his sisters, whom he chastised for not knowing what they wanted in life; and with his younger brother for being "a nice guy but completely incompetent." Father's plans to gift ownership to his children and have them work together under Tom's leadership were all placed on hold. No one was sure the business should stay in the family, and if it did whether the next generation had any hope of being able to work together.

Obviously, this family's level of Relationship Intelligence was not well enough developed for them to succeed. Their Relationship Paradigm was more negative than positive. Getting to know the family, we could see how the roots of the negative Relationship Paradigm reached back into the history of the family. There had never been a strong family bond among them even as the children were growing up. Instead, a kind of emotional distance among them was growing into mistrust, disrespect, and a rising feeling of pessimism. In addition, they had never developed some of the most basic tools of Relationship Skill for creating understanding, managing change, and negotiating differences. Tom, to his surprise and chagrin, found that he was prepared to lead the business but not to lead the family in the business. In fact, he had no desire to lead the family and resented having to, as he put it, "coddle" family members. Like many who are in positions of leadership in family businesses, Tom had no idea what he was signing onto when he said "yes" to his father's invitation. This deficit would prove fatal to his ability to lead the family in the business. It would necessitate one of two alternatives neither of which was positive for the parents: If they were to continue family ownership of the business, a choice would have to be made between having Tom alone or the other children manage it. Making it work together, while an option for the other three siblings, was not an option for Tom, who made it clear he would fire his brother and probably his sisters. None of the other three was capable or interested in being the CEO of the company. The other alternative, which they eventually chose, was to sell the company to a third party. The hope and desire to continue the business in the family hinged on one factor: leadership. The family could not overcome Tom's lack of interest or motivation to provide leadership for his siblings and parents in improving their Relationship Intelligence, and thus his ability to lead.

LEADERSHIP IS A RELATIONSHIP-FIRST ROLE

As you can probably surmise, the special challenges of family business leadership are directly linked to the multiple domains of influence and interest represented by the domains of family, business, and ownership. Leadership of a family business requires the ability to manage these multiple challenges, which are all linked together by relationships. You recall how relationships are the glue that not only provides cohesiveness within each of the three domains but also ties them together with each other as they interface and interact. Success in leading a family business is as much, the management of relationships as it is the management of tasks. While you could make the case that this is true of leadership in general, a very special challenge faces family business leaders, who must not only deal with the present, but also with the paradigms and emotions that come out of the history of being family.

In family business, people wear so many different hats as family members, employees, managers, and shareholders, that it's sometimes hard to keep track of them. Any one person can, and typically does, wear hats in several, if not in all, of the domains. It is obvious that dealing with family members is different from dealing with employees. The issues you face as co-owners are different from those you face in a manager-employee relationship on the job. Leadership in this morass of overlapping and competing interests and concerns relies on rules that can get very fuzzy. Figuring out the best way to proceed can become murky. The leader of a family business can feel like the game show contestant prompted to choose between "doors number 1, number 2, or number 3" hoping by chance to pick the right one yet knowing the odds of doing so aren't that great.

Added to the demands brought on by the inherent complexity of family business is the fact that many family business leaders are "home grown." They learned leadership by watching more senior family members, observing the good and the bad, what worked and what didn't, and then deciding either to emulate them or vowing never to be like them. Even those who have successful previous middle-level management experience outside the family business may never have had the opportunity to be mentored in leadership. In lower and middle-level management positions, leadership often focuses on tasks, on getting things done, on implementing a plan. There can be little, if any, emphasis on the management or leadership of relationships unless perhaps you've worked in human resources, the area to which people issues are often relegated.

The place where Tom, and other family business leaders make their first mistake is in assuming that their only responsibility is leading a business according to business rules. Leading the business is only one part of the job. To understand what a family business leader does we have to go back to what a family business is. To review, a family business is a business in which business and family relationships both impact the other. Further, a family business is always made up of the relationships among the three overlapping domains of family, business, and ownership. Success in a family business is the direct result of how well, or poorly, these three domains are aligned with one another. Whether in definition, description, or operation, relationships are at the heart of family business. You can't understand leadership of the family business without recognizing that relationships are at the heart of the leader's role.

MANAGING INTERFACE ISSUES

In actuality the designation of "CEO" for the leader of a family business means two things: Chief Executive Officer and Chief Emotional Officer. This is where the unprepared family business leader can run headlong into unexpected demands and problems. For the person who thinks of the job of leadership as focused only within the business domain, and thus related to efficiency, effectiveness, and profitability, the intrusion of family issues will be a shock. When, on the other hand, the family business leader understands that the job also entails balancing these realities of business with the intricacies of family relationships, shock is replaced by preparedness to face the challenges involved.

On a day-to-day basis family business leaders are impacted by the murky areas where rules get confusing as they encounter the three areas of overlap between (1) family and business, (2) business and ownership, and (3) family and ownership.

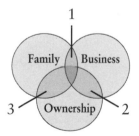

As we have said, compromises are always necessitated by each of the three domains in order to accommodate the alignment of their divergent needs. Compromise is the process of creating the best possible fit and synergy between the domains at any given point in time. Remember also that flexibility in relationships is a crucial element in accomplishing the ongoing adjustments that must be made to maintain the optimal alignment. Here are some of the more typical overlap issues and decision points in which a family business leader can get caught up. Some of them, especially in the family and ownership overlap area, may seem inappropriate or unusual concerns for a business leader until you recall that leading a family business is like no other kind of leadership in the world.

●●

Where family and business overlap . . .
- supervision and accountability of family employees;
- educating family members about the business;
- setting of compensation and benefits for family employees;
- managing financial practices and performance; and
- balancing business needs and family expectations.

Where business and ownership overlap . . .
- long-range planning that reflects family owner values with business strategies and goals;
- overseeing the integration of owner expectations regarding ROI with company performance; and
- balancing decisions about use of profits, for example as distributions versus acquisition versus capital expenditures.

Where family and ownership overlap . . .
- the impact of decisions made about the objectives of a family shareholders' agreement;
- coordination of extended family estate planning to avoid problems with future ownership;
- decisions about options related to keeping the business in the family; and
- education of family members about the meaning and value of business ownership.

●●

STYLES OF LEADERSHIP

Leadership is the process of influencing others toward accomplishing a common goal. In family business the most challenging goal is to build and sustain the best possible alignment between family, business, and ownership. As you know there are many different styles of influencing others. The way in which the family business leader influences others is a key ingredient to the leader's ability to succeed. Often referred to as leadership style, many different ways of categorizing the leader's approach to influencing others have been developed.

Leadership styles vary widely and there have been many different schemes proposed by authorities on leadership for categorizing them.[1] One scheme contrasts a laissez-faire leadership style with an authoritarian style. In the former the leader allows maximum freedom, holding very loose reins on followers. In the latter the leader is very directive, demanding that people follow orders. Other schemes contrast what might be called visionary leaders with those who are more pragmatic and utilitarian in style.

Push and Pull Leaders

A common thread running through many of the different schemes is that they are all based on a similar polarity of style difference, what we call the *push style* on one end and the *pull style* on the other. Push leaders are directive and driving while pull leaders are participative and engaging. Push leaders are usually charismatic and lead by personal charm and magnetism. They are sometimes referred to as "benevolent dictators." Pull leaders, on the other hand, blend into the group, working hard to build consensus and group commitment. They are sometimes referred to as "coaches" or "cheerleaders."

LEADERSHIP STYLE CHARACTERISTICS

Push Style "Benevolent Dictator"	Pull Style "Coach" or "Cheerleader"
• Directive	• Participative
• Relies on personal magnetism	• Values agreement and cooperation above all
• Best in crisis or start-up situations	
• Danger is high reliance on one person	• Danger is slow and cumbersome decision-making and action
• Builds RQ through strong personal commitment and charisma	• Builds RQ through fostering consensus and acceptance

Push leaders utilize their high level of personal magnetism to inspire and challenge. Typically determined and directive in the way they approach others, push leaders work best in crisis or start-up situations. Pull leaders, on the other hand, value agreement and cooperation above all else, relying on their ability to build unified commitment. Relying on delegation and group process, pull leadership works best in situations where there is a common goal, a high level of trust, clearly defined roles and responsibilities, and ongoing good communication.

Push leadership can be compared to the hub of an old fashioned wagon wheel. At the center of everything the push leader ties together the spokes of the wheel, the people involved, focusing effort and productivity to the center and redirecting stability and cohesiveness to the outside fringes. Most founders of family businesses are push style leaders who are often elevated to something approaching sainthood by the people they have hired, helped, and inspired. The good news is that people join together and produce. The bad news is that they join together primarily because of the leader. Without the leader there is no unity, momentum, nor productivity.

Pull leadership, on the other hand, can be compared to the rim of the wheel. The rim connects the spokes at their most diverse points to equalize the distribution of the load and to link the strengths, as well as minimize individual weaknesses of the individual spokes. The pull leader provides a cohesive force to facilitate a group effort and prevent fragmentation among strong-willed and independent people. Many second-generation family business leaders, following a push style founder, are drawn to the pull style of leadership. It is especially attractive as an alternative leadership style for managing sibling and cousin relationships. It also makes a statement, or so it is hoped, that this new generation is different, more egalitarian and able to share power and control. The good news is that that this style can lead to a more professionalized company with greater depth of leadership talent. The bad news is that productivity can suffer, fragmentation among family members can set in, and decision making can grind to a halt, all in the service of reaching consensus.

LEADERSHIP STYLE AND RQ

It might seem that pull leaders are more suited to and effective at building Relationship Intelligence because of their consensus-building style. This is, however, not necessarily the case. Pull leaders can, in fact, stifle the growth and development of RQ by minimizing conflicts and individual differences or by failing to provide sufficient direction toward the learning of tools for building Relationship Skill. Push leaders, on the other hand can effectively use their charismatic and directive style to lead the family into redefining a more positive Relationship Paradigm or improving Relationship Skill. Needless to say, it is the rare family business leader that has a pure push or pull style. More commonly, leadership style is a mixture of the two even though there is usually a preference for one style or the other.

The greatest flaw in both the push or pull style of leadership is that they each create a strong dependency by the organization on the leader. If either the hub (push style of leadership) or the rim (pull style of leadership) goes away, the spokes are left without the force that joined them together. Even with all of the consensus building and participation characteristic of the pull style of leadership, there is still a significant dependence on the person.

While both push and pull leadership styles create dependency on the leader, they also create a parallel kind of dependency of the leader on the followers. Both push and pull leaders are dependent for their success on the group they are leading. In part, this is as it should be since no leader is ultimately any more effective than the extent to which others follow and participate. However, it is also true that both the push and pull leaders in a family business can be whipsawed by those who either reject their direction outright or refuse to buy in, or even simply know how to push the leaders' emotional and psychological buttons. Because the primary focus of leaders with these leadership styles is on getting others to follow or comply, they can easily be hamstrung by powerful, strong-willed family members who exert more push or more pull.

QFRs

- Describe the three most significant alignment issues (among family, business, and ownership) that are facing you today.

- What are the five most important lessons about leadership you learned from watching and observing others and how have they affected your leadership today?

- Do you consider yourself primarily a push or pull style of leader?

- Based on the characteristics of push and pull leadership styles, what are the pluses and minuses of your style given the alignment issues you identified above.

CENTERED LEADERSHIP

Because relationships are at the heart of the family business leadership challenge, an alternative style of leadership is needed. It is, in fact, a style of leadership that doesn't even occur on the continuum of push or pull styles. It is a style of leadership that focuses as much, if not more, on how the leader manages herself or himself as it does on man aging others. It focuses on the leader as the catalyst of well-defined, properly structured, and clearly directed relationships, and that is exactly what the family business leader needs to accomplish.

We call this the Centered Family Business Leadership style. Whenever an object is tilted off its center of gravity, it is unstable and its equilibrium is vulnerable to further imbalance, even collapse. The easiest way to experience this is to stand with your feet spread apart the width of your shoulders with your head directly above your hips. In this position it is difficult for another person to push you enough to cause you to move because you are positioned in your center of gravity; you are centered. Try leaning forward or backward; another person can easily cause you to move with much less force because you are not centered.

Carry this metaphor over into how you feel as you provide leadership within your family business. There are likely times when you feel off balance, vulnerable to being pushed this way and that, psychologically and emotionally unstable in the face of the pressures. We often compare leadership in the family business to juggling. The next time you watch a juggler notice how important it is that they are always physically positioned in their center of gravity. They may move from one side of the stage to the other, spin and turn in their act, but they always quickly return to their center of gravity. Juggling the complexities and demands of family business leadership means you must constantly seek to be centered no matter how often you move from one issue to the next or how much you have to spin and turn while keeping all the balls in the air.

George is the sixty-one-year-old second-generation president of his family's $40 million manufacturing company. In addition to inheriting the role, he also inherited a bunch of family employees, several of whom are in top executive positions in the company. He grew up with a charismatic father who founded the business in 1946. George tries very hard to balance his leadership style between the push and pull extremes. He has a degree in engineering and is the only college graduate in the family.

George's father was an alcoholic who told George that the business would always take care of him. He even told George on many occasions that he wouldn't be able to get a real job because he had little marketable ability. When George was appointed president, the scuttlebutt around the company said it was because he is the oldest son and in Polish families that's the way things are done.

George knows what tasks need to be done to get product out the door. He is generally good at getting people to do the work either by directing them or by getting them into teams to come up with solutions everyone buys into. In other words, he is able to strike a largely effective balance between push and pull styles of leadership. But George still has a big problem.

George's problems emerge when stress, pressure, and anxiety build up in the relationships among the family members, those in the business and those who are owners, but are not working in the company. Recent decision points that have turned into major disruptions include: (1) his brother-in-law who is V.P. of marketing refused to cooperate with the controller's directives, approved by George, as to which expenses are allowable and which are not: (2) a major customer threatened to pull all its business because of quality problems—an area for which his brother is responsible and who responds by defending his record; and (3) his younger sister, who is board chair, began to take unilateral action to establish a deferred compensation program for family executives without apparent concern for the financial impact on the company.

In all of these situations, George went ballistic, reacting to each one as a personal attack on his position as president. It would be an understatement to say that he lost his center of leadership balance. In the face of being shoved and coerced he became dictatorial and abusive in ways reminiscent of his father. It was George's inability to carry out a centered style of family business leader that caused everything to come unwound in dealing with fairly routine management and supervisory tasks such as employee accountability and discipline, problem resolution and governance decision making. Confronting all three overlap areas of family and business, family and ownership, and business and ownership, George succumbed to the kinds of pressures that are typical in family business.

The ability to lead a family business successfully, which also means to succeed in developing Relationship Intelligence within the family and business, hinges on Centered Family Business Leader ship. Our two examples of Tom and George in this chapter both illustrate how vital this is.

UNDERSTANDING AND IMPROVING CENTERED FAMILY BUSINESS LEADERSHIP

The central and required elements of Centered Family Business Leadership were first identified by a pioneer in the field of family systems psychology, Dr. Murray Bowen.[2] Bowen, a psychiatrist by training, studied factors related to long-term success of family relationships. He identified two factors related to healthy interactions in families that are also directly relevant to leadership in the family business. One of these he called "self-differentiation," and the other is a process he called "triangulation" that takes place in all relationships.

Self-differentiation is a kind of emotional maturity understood from and interpreted through the perspective of family relationships. To what extent are you able to be fully your own person, with your own unique ideas, desires, feelings, and preferences while also fully participating in your family? Does your family's lack of tolerance, acceptance, and recognition of you mean that you have to check who you really are at the door of family gatherings? Does it cause you to constantly question yourself? Do you feel that you have to be constantly on guard to protect yourself either from being abandoned or consumed by your family? Those who have never established the ability to relate to their families both as fully independent yet emotionally interconnected people tend to have great difficulty maintaining healthy and satisfying long-term relationships. They have a difficult if not impossible time defining their own lives and charting their own destinies. They always measure themselves against someone else's yardstick rather than their own. They are, therefore, extremely vulnerable to what others think of them and what responses they get from the group they are in. They develop a highly sophisticated and powerful relationship radar system that picks up signals as to what others are thinking and feeling. They are washed back and forth with the ebb and flow of reactions and perceptions of other people.

On the other hand, when you have a much higher level of what Bowen calls self-differentiation, you feel comfortable, confident, and capable with who you are because who you are has been, and continues to be, affirmed, understood, and valued by your family. You're able to maintain and enjoy relationships because your self-esteem and emotional well-being do not depend on how others relate to you. At the same time you are able to have long-term satisfying relationships simply because your self-acceptance makes you more enjoyable to be around. Others can count on your being straight and open with them without reactivity and unreasonable demands on the relationship.

Now, how does this apply to leadership in the family business? Centered Family Business Leaders inevitably have a high level of self-differentiation. Centered Family Business Leadership comes from a person who, more often than not, is able to fully and confidently center herself or himself within their business-owning family and with others as well. Tom and George both struggled with their own problems of self-differentiation in their families. They did so, however, in different ways, and their stories illustrate the two extreme ways a low level of self-differentiation affects family business leaders. Tom's approach was to cut himself off from his family by creating emotional and relationship barriers between himself and family members. His decision to fire his siblings, if he were given the authority to do so, was driven by his need to cut himself off from family members in the face of emotional pressures. George, on the other hand, allowed himself to be taken advantage of, and for granted, because he shrank away from confronting difficult and justifiable issues in a straightforward way with his siblings. When he responded with emotional outbursts or withdrawal it only served to convince both family and nonfamily employees that George was too unpredictable and unreliable to effectively lead the business.

CHARACTERISTICS OF CENTERED FAMILY BUSINESS LEADERS

There are three characteristics of Centered Family Business Leadership.

1. The Centered Family Business Leader takes a defined and nonreactive position on matters of importance, especially with strongly charged emotional issues. This means that the Centered Family Business Leader assesses and understands all aspects of an issue, evaluates the options that are available, is clear about what he or she wants in relation to it, and with a balance of emotion and reasoning comes to a position on what is best for the business and family. In addition, and this is important, none of this is done in reaction to, or against others. Centered Family Business Leaders know where they stand, and they can justify their position without being defensive. Perhaps the acid test of Centered Family Business Leadership is when the leader establishes a position on an issue that is the same position taken by a family opposition coalition. When you can say, "Even though we have been on opposite sides of things and have had more than our share of arguments, I agree that your position is the right one and I will fully and confidently support it," you have achieved the finest form of a defined and nonreactive position.

2. The Centered Family Business Leader maintains a nonanxious and calming presence especially, and most importantly, in the midst of emotional and relationship turmoil. The tuning fork trap, when the leader picks up and begins to vibrate with the same emotional and psychological tone and intensity of the group, is one of the surest 1be able to absorb and contain, rather than resonate and reverberate, with the stress and anxiety that others are going through. It is the ability to balance emotional responsiveness with reasoned objectivity. One of the classic examples of this characteristic of leadership was Captain John Lovell's radio call from Apollo 13 to NASA Mission Control as his space craft was reeling after being hit by an unknown object and was losing life support systems quickly. With calm and resolve he said, "Houston, we have a problem here!" When there's trouble on the horizon or disaster in the wings, a group needs a leader who can face a crisis with assurance, confidence, and resolve.

3. **The leader stays connected.** Of all three characteristics of Centered Family Business Leadership, this is perhaps the most difficult to carry out. Remaining connected means that the leader continues to pursue and solicit contact and communication with all those involved even in the midst of intense divisiveness and emotional pain. In our earlier example, this was very difficult for George to do. He disconnected from his family members both physically, by leaving for days at a time, and psychologically, by tuning them out and avoiding them. Staying connected means you keep reaching out especially when you feel least like doing so because you know that when your relationship with others is broken, it is impossible to lead them. One of the great sayings attributed to the marriage encounter movement is that "Love is not a feeling, it is a decision." Simply put, in marriage you sometimes decide to act in loving ways even though you don't feel loving. Similarly, staying connected as the leader of your family business when relationships are difficult is not based on a feeling or emotional reaction, but on the decision to do it for the sake of the relationships.

These then are the three cardinal characteristics of Centered Family Business Leadership. All three are essential and work in tandem with each other. They characterize the leader who is able to stay connected with everyone involved, especially the obnoxious ones, maintain a personal presence of confidence, calm, and resolve, while presenting ideas and solutions without reactivity. Is this magic, does it avoid resistance and sabotage, and does it always guarantee success? Of course not! But when you're centered in these ways, it's a lot more difficult for someone to push you off balance and it's a lot easier for you to lead others into new and higher levels of Relationship Intelligence at the same time.

TRIANGULATION

By now, we hope you're convinced that relationships are truly the language of family business, and that it's this language that makes leadership in a family business so unique and challenging. Managing the stress, tension, and anxiety in those relationships is one of the major challenges faced by family business leaders. The fact is that there is always stress and anxiety brought on by business pressures and family dynamics. Freedom from dealing with relationship dynamics is never an option for the leader of a family business; the only option is doing it well or poorly. Doing it well requires understanding some basic elements of relationship dynamics and how to keep them from becoming mired in destructive patterns. This is where knowledge about the process of triangulation is very useful because it is a good way to understand that it is one of the most basic of all patterns in human relationships.

Jack, Richard, and Karl are the second-generation owners and managers of a distribution company started by their father. Jack joined the business right out of college fifteen years ago, followed two years later by Richard. Karl came into the business ten years ago. Their father appointed Jack president when Karl joined the company only to remove him and give the job to Richard three years later. Over the years there have been many confrontations among the brothers over employee issues, compensation, different styles of managing, and a host of other subjects. Focusing on finding a solution to the specific problem they were having often worked for that problem but almost invariably caused a problem someplace else. For example, when they solved a compensation conflict between Jack and Karl by agreeing to pay themselves equal bonuses at year end, Richard got into an argument with Karl over Richard's contention that he should get more because he brought in 80 percent of the sales.

While they couldn't see it, even a casual outside observer could detect the triangulation going on among these three. Over a span of three years, each one had at one time or another, been in the uncomfortable outside position in relation to the other two, who would be getting along just fine. Someone was always the black sheep, the troublemaker, the irritant for the other two. Not only this, but whoever was outside would draw employees into the problem, innocently enough, either by seeking allies or creating hassles with employees who reported to one of the other brothers. Employees caught on to this pattern as well and often used the triangulation between the brothers to their own advantage, like the time a manager previously denied a raise by Jack, got it from Richard who at the time was on the outside.

How Triangles Work

Relationship triangles work like this: When a relationship between two people enters a stressful period, one of these two people pulls a third person into the relationship to form a triangle among the three of them, thus the term *triangulation*. Why do they do this? The answer lies in the fact that the stress and strain of the troubled relationship between the original two people becomes increasingly uncomfortable. Perhaps they try to find relief from the discomfort by working it out or avoiding each other, but the stress continues to build. By bringing a third person into the tangle between them, they relieve the pressure they have been under by establishing a new focus in the third person. This is why we form triangles, to make us more comfortable and reduce the stress between us. Examples abound as to how this happens in family businesses. A spouse and mother is drawn into an increasingly stressful and conflicted relationship between a father and son in business together. The new CFO is quickly pulled into the middle of a battle between the CEO and board chair. The successor in a family business is sucked into an intense battle between his mother and his uncle, the two owners of the company, over a shareholders' agreement dispute. The president of a third-generation family business is expected to take sides between his parents and siblings, on one side, and his cousins and their parents, on the other, over issues of compensation.

Family business leaders are extremely vulnerable to the destructive power of triangulation given the powerful combination of the intersecting dynamics of the family, business, and ownership domains and the leader's position of influence. Family business leaders can easily get triangled between

- a family member and a nonfamily manager;
- two family members, one active in the business and one not;
- two other family employees;
- a spouse and a child who are both in the business; and
- two family members of different generations.

One of the most frequent places family business leaders encounter destructive triangulation is when it comes to holding family employees accountable for performance. Holding employees accountable is difficult enough for any of us, but when the employee is a family member and their performance is subpar, the stress and anxiety in the relationship can become intense. It's at this point that either the family member supervisor or the family employee triangles in a third person, often the CEO. In this triangulated alliance it is either the supervisor trying to build a case against the underperforming family employee or the family employee trying to get the family member supervisor to back off.

Triangles are as inevitable as the stress in family relationships that cause them. What is important is knowing when you're getting stuck in a negative one. There are four symptoms that will tell you when you are in a triangle you need to deal with.

1. You are taking on too much responsibility for the other two people and for what is going on in the relationship between them. The classic example of this is the enabling spouse going overboard making excuses to a third party for the actions of the irresponsible alcoholic, but there are many less obvious ways this happens. Trying repeatedly to convince others in the business to find a position in which an unmotivated family member can succeed, ignoring a problem so as not to make the other person feel bad if you brought it up, making excuses for someone's failures, and trying to resolve a problem that's entirely between two other people, are all common examples of how you can get involved in an overresponsibility triangle trap.

2. You are stuck in repeating negative relationship cycles. Do you find that the same problems and conflicts keep coming up over and over again in a particular relationship? A common and very destructive relationship cycle in family business is one in which three people repeat a pattern in which they exchange the roles of victim, persecutor, and rescuer. As problems and conflict heat up, one person assumes the role of being taken advantage of by the problems (victim), another the role of being angry and attacking (persecutor), and the third the role of taking care of everybody and making everything O.K. (rescuer). Roles shift as the "victim" gets fed up and becomes a "persecutor," the "persecutor" feels guilty for overreaction and blaming and becomes a "rescuer," and the "rescuer," seeing no progress, reaches rope's end and becomes a "persecutor." The shift in roles has no particular sequence but takes place when one member of the triangle changes roles. To keep things balanced, so to speak, the other two persons shift roles in response, but someone is always a "persecutor," someone else a "victim" and a third person a "rescuer." And it goes on and on ad infinitum. It's a particular and common form of triangulated relationships that looks like this:

Victim

PROBLEM

Persecutor   Rescuer

3. **You are unable to make decisions.** The third symptom is related to the first two. When a relationship is truly stuck and immobilized in a triangle, it is very difficult to make an effective decision because it seems that no matter what you decide, it will be wrong. Jack, Richard, and Karl found it virtually impossible to make decisions about routine operational matters, not to mention long-range strategic issues because one of them was always either isolating himself or throwing hand grenades while the other two were afraid of upsetting the precarious truce they had between them. We talked about false agreement in chapter 3 and it is a major problem here. Because relationships can become so fragile and frightening when the cycles of a negative triangle get established, it is safe and easy just to avoid rocking the boat by being agreeable even when you have no intention of following through.

The Cure Is in Centered Family Business Leadership

The antidote to these symptoms of negative triangulation is Centered Family Business Leadership. The push style of leadership is extremely vulnerable to destructive triangles because it seeks the solution through forcing a resolution. The pull style of leadership is also highly vulnerable because it seeks a solution through consensus and agreement. The push leader's directive and inspirational style, and the pull leader's collaborative and delegation style can keep both stuck in either taking too much responsibility or being seduced by false agreement. When the Centered Family Business Leader, on the other hand, takes a defined and nonreactive position, provides a nonanxious presence and stays connected, the triangulation is attacked at its very core. When the cause is dealt with, the symptoms of taking on too much responsibility, repeating negative cycles, being unable to make decisions, and false agreement fade as a result.

Centered Family Business Leadership is an important component in building RQ in your family business. Because the Centered Family Business Leader possesses emotional maturity and the ability to effectively handle the relationship complexity of family business, he or she is in the best position to challenge and redefine a negative Relationship Paradigm and to generate interest and willingness to build a better toolbox of Relationship Paradigm. The Centered Family Business Leader is the ombudsman for positive change and the catalyst for relationship renewal.

Notes
1. There are many excellent books on the leadership style.
2. Read more about Dr. Bowen's work in a superb collection of papers presented at the Georgetown Family Center Conference on Organizations in 1995 and published as *The Emotional Side of Organizations: Applications of Bowen Theory*, ed. Comella, Bader, Ball, Wiseman, and Sagar. Washington D.C.: Georgetown Family Center, 1996.

RQ and Working with Family Businesses

INTRODUCTION

Understanding and using the principles and practices of RQ explained in this book are as relevant and important to the relationship between a professional advisor/consultant and a family business client as they are to family business relationships themselves. Collaborative relationships among professional advisors as they serve family businesses is also a place where RQ has direct impact. This chapter is divided into two parts: part I—The Family Business Advisory Relationship addresses how RQ impacts the relationship of the advisor with a family business client. In part II—The Role of the Family Business Advisor, we focus on the role of the family business advisor/consultant as a relationship change agent; the lessons that RQ teaches us about it; and effective interprofessional collaboration when working with family businesses.

Part I of this chapter will certainly be of interest to family businesses and their advisors alike. The level of Relationship Intelligence in the relationship between an advisor and a family business has everything to do with being able to accomplish whatever task is at hand, whether that has to do with deciding on the terms of an estate plan, getting family owners to agree on a buy-sell agreement, or reaching agreement on mission and goals through the strategic planning process. Since relationships are the language of family business, paying attention to the quality of the family business advisory relationship is essential. In part this means achieving the true purpose of communication, creating understanding, within the advisory relationship. Such understanding is the backbone for developing trust, mutual respect, and optimism in the family business advisory relationship.

Part II of this chapter, dealing with interprofessional collab-

203

oration, will be of special interest to all family business advisors/consultants whether their approach is mainly advisory or process oriented. At the same time, it will help those in family businesses become more aware of what they should expect from their advisors. They will learn to recognize how reaching even a technical solution means attending to relationships. The complex needs of family business are best addressed by advisors/consultants from different areas of expertise, working collaboratively with each other on behalf of the client. In far too many instances the collaborative effort is handled poorly. What should be an enhancement of professional services for the family business becomes a burden because their advisors/consultants are unable or unwilling to work out their collaborative relationship.

PART I The Family Business Advisory Relationship

The family business advisory relationship is formed when the business-owning family establishes an important and influential affiliation with the advisor(s) or consultant(s). This may sound like a strange way to describe the client-advisor/consultant relationship. Many of us, business-owning families and advisors/consultants alike, are accustomed to thinking about our relationship as more of a one-way street the success of which is defined by what the professional does for the client. Looked at as a give-and-take relationship, however, the success of the family business advisory relationship is defined by how well it functions as the mechanism for achieving the combined needs of all the participants: family members, business managers, owners, and advisors/consultants. In this sense the relationship is defined by what the client and the advisor/consultant do with each other.

The family business advisory relationship operates according to the same fundamental principles that govern any relationship. The success or failure of the family business advisory relationship is determined by its level of RQ. To be sure, there are those situations which only directly involve a professional and constituents from one of the three domains and it remains this way for the duration of the relationship. These kinds of engagements, to differentiate them from the family business advisory relationship, can more accurately be described as family advisory, business advisory, or owner advisory relationships. Such engagements are usually fairly short in duration and narrow in focus, and require circumscribed contact among the participants. To illustrate, a family advisory relationship might be for family therapy to deal with a troubled parent/teenager relationship, a business advisory relationship to deal with a production process problem, or an owner advisory relationship to deal with revising the shareholders' agreement. However, in a long-term professional relationship, even one that begins very focused in only one domain, and especially those in which the client's needs are less well-defined and circumscribed, there is another and more intricate level of involvement that quickly develops. In these situations the family business advisory relationship will inevitably expand to involve all four constituent groups: family, business, ownership, and the advisor(s)/consultant(s).

An insurance agent once remarked that after he had negotiated for a year with the owner of a family business about a large life insurance policy to fund the estate plan, the owner's children started calling him. They voiced their concerns about their father's intentions in the estate plan. When the father, who had a history of conflict with his children, got wind of the phone calls he abruptly ended the relationship with the insurance agent a week before he would have signed the contract. Family conflict found its way into this advisory relationship that only seemed to involve the owner. Likewise, most business attorneys can recall the frustration and complexity of trying to draft or revise a shareholders' agreement while constantly being buffeted by family conflict. The family business advisory relationship almost always becomes entangled because of one of the two distinguishing characteristics of family businesses: the complexity of the competing and overlapping family business domains, and their respective measures of success. Some family business advisory relationships have a history that is decades long, and in this the relationship even shares the other distinguishing characteristic of family business relationships; a long history.

A family business advisory relationship is formed for the purpose of either solving or preventing problems; problems are at the heart of the relationship. In this sense, the measure of success is the extent to which an existing problem is solved or problems that are anticipated are prevented. There is no other reason for initiating and sustaining a family business advisory relationship. This fact makes this relationship extraordinarily vulnerable to the dynamics of family business because problems rarely are contained in only one of the domains. For example, the problem is lack of productivity and profitability; the measure of success is in the business domain; and the recommendation from the advisor/consultant is to terminate a nonproductive family employee or reduce inflated family member salaries. The family business advisory relationship is fulfilling its purpose but in doing so is caught cross-grain between business and family. Or consider the problem of long-standing and chronic family disharmony that is negatively affecting the company. The solution involves getting into open and confrontational discussions about deep interpersonal wounds. The family business advisory relationship is fulfilling its purpose of strengthening family ties but in so doing risks, at least temporarily, reducing the productivity and effectiveness of family executives at a time when the business is suffering already due to the family conflict. The measure of success in the family business advisory relationship, problem solving and prevention, gets caught between the divergent needs and interests of the three domains of family.

This is why RQ is of such great importance to the family business advisory relationship. Maintaining equilibrium, efficiency, and effectiveness requires the highest level of Relationship Intelligence possible. It is simply a fact that a negative Relationship Paradigm and a low level of Relationship Skill will undermine the ability of the family business advisory relationship to fulfill its purpose: problem solving and prevention. There is a parallel here with the impact of RQ in family business relationships. A family business may have great technical capability and knowledge about its products and services. A low level of RQ does not diminish the company's knowledge and technical capabilities, but it does make it difficult or impossible to utilize them in efficient, effective, and profitable ways. Similarly, a consultant or advisor may be very capable and knowledgeable in an area important to the family business needs. A low level of RQ does not diminish that knowledge and capability, but it does make it difficult or impossible to put it into action. Without trust, optimism, and respect, the three relationship dilemmas that must be dealt with in any relationship, and at least basic tools of Relationship Skill, no family business advisory relationship will survive.

RQ AND THE FAMILY BUSINESS ADVISORY RELATIONSHIP

As we have said, the family business advisory relationship is subject to all of the principles and practices of Relationship Intelligence. The ability of this relationship to fulfill its purpose of problem solving and prevention depends on how successfully a positive Relationship Paradigm and high level of Relationship Skill develop. The level of RQ that exists in any given family business advisory relationship depends on four situational factors:

1. the length and history of the relationship;
2. the prior experience of the family business with professional relationships, especially those involving advisors or consultants from the same discipline as the current one;
3. the advisor's/consultant's prior experiences with family businesses similar to this one; and
4. the extent of the investment made to strengthen the Relationship Paradigm and the Relationship Skill dimensions of RQ in the relationship.

RELATIONSHIP PARADIGM IN THE ADVISORY RELATIONSHIP

The Relationship Paradigm that exists within a family business advisory relationship depends on how the three relationship dilemmas have been resolved. You will recall that these are:

- trust versus mistrust;
- optimism versus pessimism; and
- respect versus disrespect.

The four situational factors indicated above will have a direct impact on how easy or difficult it is to deal with the three relationship dilemmas. Trust, optimism, and respect, or their opposites, will build on the extent to which the participants in the relationship have had experience together that creates an atmosphere of reliability, openness, honesty, capability, and trustworthiness. How long this takes depends on many factors, including the baggage about such relationships that the parties bring, and the extent of the investment they are willing to make in building their RQ together. If, for example, the family business has an attitude that all lawyers are con artists, the lawyer has the attitude that all family businesses are hopelessly encumbered by family problems, and together they make no effort to develop a well-structured and planned advisory relationship, you can imagine how unsuccessful and unsatisfactory that relationship will be! There are times when tragedies like this happen, not so much by intent but by neglect. The family business advisory relationship is frequently taken for granted, or worse yet, the participants make the fatal assumption that the quality of the relationship, other than being courteous and pleasant, is largely irrelevant to the success of the work being done.

RELATIONSHIP SKILL IN THE ADVISORY RELATIONSHIP

The level of Relationship Skill that exists within the family business advisory relationship is built on two pillars: tools and structure. Every family business advisory relationship depends on the creation of genuine mutual understanding through good communication, clarity of expectations and management of change, conflict resolution, and bridging of differences. The professional should set an example of this and provide leadership and encouragement within the relationship in attending to the development of Relationship Skill tools.

Along with the application of the right Relationship Skill tools, the family business advisory relationship depends upon solid and well-articulated structures. By structures we refer to the meetings and mechanisms through which the relationship works and is linked to other important relationship domains within the family business. As for meetings they need to be well planned and held in settings conducive to the work being done. Mechanisms such as record keeping and reporting, accountability, and fee payment need to be clearly defined and understood. A plan for implementing the consulting engagement needs to be spelled out in writing with responsibilities and completion dates assigned.

Combining the right tools with the right structures helps develop and maintain the Relationship Skill dimension of RQ in the family business advisory relationship. At the same time, being intentional and conscientious about establishing trust, optimism, and respect forms the basis of a positive Relationship Paradigm. Together, the two dimensions of RQ provide the vehicle by which professional expertise gets successfully delivered, understood, and implemented. A family business advisory relationship suffering from a low level of RQ must either be improved or ended for the sake of all those involved.

ASSESSING THE LEVEL OF RQ IN THE FAMILY BUSINESS ADVISORY RELATIONSHIP

The RQ model is useful in identifying the initial characteristics of a family business advisory relationship and how it needs to develop if it is to fulfill its purpose. It is rare that a family business and an advisor/consultant will initiate a family business advisory relationship at Level 1—low Relationship Skill and a negative Relationship Paradigm. Essentially, such a relationship would have to overcome huge obstacles related to lack of trust, optimism, and respect with little or no skill to do so. This, for example, might be a family business advisory relationship involving a family business in severe interpersonal and financial crisis that believes all advisors and consultants sell snake oil, being brought together, by their attorney or bank, with an advisor who sees no hope or possibility for this group of malcontents. From the outset, there is poor communication, unclear expectations, and lack of planning. It sounds awful, but some people try to struggle against all odds to make such situations work. It is likely that the family business itself requires drastic measures as a result of its long-standing low level of RQ and the impact on the company. The best a family business advisory relationship could expect would probably be one which focuses on the positive side of getting this family out of being in business together with the least amount of continuing damage to the business and the family.

A brother and sister, equal owners in a successful third-generation family business, were finally pressured by their outside board members to get professional help in dealing with the severe and relentless conflict between them. The first time we met with them and the two outside directors, it was obvious they wanted nothing to do with us. They were insolent and rude. Nevertheless, they needed help badly and agreed to a second meeting. We moved ahead to meet a third time for a two-day intensive family business retreat, focused on getting their issues on the table in a structured setting in an effort to resolve them by using the Relationship Skill tools we taught and coached them in using. Three days after the two-day meeting, which went somewhat better than expected, given how bad things were, the brother called and said he was canceling the remainder of the contract with LSi and refused to pay the balance of our agreed-upon professional fee. A year later they were in litigation and lost the business over two years to bankruptcy.

This unfortunate situation taught us an important and sobering lesson. There are some family businesses we, as consultants, cannot help regardless of how eager and persistent we are. In this situation, obviously a Level 1 RQ family business, we tried to push ahead against the odds, but the truth was that trust, optimism, and respect were never established in the family business advisory relationship which likewise became stuck at Level 1. This does not mean that family businesses with a Level 1 RQ cannot be helped if the client and the advisor/consultant can establish a Level 2 family business advisory relationship. In this situation the client was unwilling to work toward establishing trust, optimism, and respect;

and truthfully, after being fired neither were we. Obviously, the tools we taught them during the meeting did not stick. In fact, the acid test as to whether a Level 1 RQ family business can move to Level 2 RQ, is the extent to which they are able to continue utilizing and practicing the new skills they have been taught. When these new skills quickly evaporate in favor of the old destructive patterns, in spite of repeated reinforcement by the advisor/consultant, there will be no forward movement.

Typically, family business advisory relationships begin at either Level 2 or Level 3 of RQ. Just as they never get off the ground if they start at Level 1, they rarely begin at Level 4. Repeated positive interaction and investment over time are required to build the high levels of trust, optimism, and respect and to develop the depth of Relationship Skill tools characteristic of a Level 4 relationship. Clearly, every family business advisory relationship aspires to a Level 4 of RQ. It is here that the relationship enjoys the necessary efficiency and effectiveness that allows it to truly fulfill its purpose of problem solving and prevention, with the emphasis on prevention. To get there a number of specific methods and tools can be used to strengthen both Relationship Paradigm and Relationship Skill in the family business advisory relationship.

To build Relationship Paradigm—trust, optimism, and respect:
- establish guidelines for fulfillment of responsibilities and expectations;
- openly communicate about concerns and problems;
- know where you're going and have no surprises;
- express appreciation and confidence; and
- abide by the code of conduct appropriate to a professional relationship—confidentiality, doing what's in the best interest of the group, and avoiding or disclosing conflicts of interest.

To build Relationship Skill:
- learn how to communicate, especially listening, to achieve understanding;
- establish a process for review and renegotiation of expectations and renewal of commitments;
- incorporate the resources needed to address First-Order and Second-Order Change as discussed later in this chapter; and
- develop and follow an advisory/consultation plan.

When You Begin at Level 2 . . .

The family business advisory relationship that begins at Level 2 is sustained in its early stages by its better-than-average level of Relationship Skill. Because of this the relationship has a sufficiently good level of communication and understanding, ability to bridge differences and renegotiate expectations as things change, and spell out and implement a plan for accomplishing its goals. A higher level of Relationship Skill is important to offset the more negative-than-average Relationship Paradigm that is operative. Most likely the relationship formed either from outside pressure, as described in Level 1, or because of a crisis that has to be resolved, and the advisor/consultant has the needed technical ability to help. The higher level of Relationship Skill often masks the negative Relationship Paradigm as everyone in the group focuses attention on solving the problem or crisis that is threatening the family business. In this sense the negative Relationship Paradigm and its destructive effects are ignored and its influence underestimated.

Unless, however there is movement toward a positive change in the Relationship Paradigm, when the problem is solved or crisis averted, this family business advisory relationship will deteriorate quickly. The Relationship Skill, while strong enough to fulfill the initial purpose of the relationship, is not strong enough to overcome the negative Relationship Paradigm. The family business may engage a different advisor/consultant each time a crisis or problem erupts, in a series of disjointed project engagements. While this may seem acceptable, the real downside is that there is likely no attempt to solve the deeper causes of the crises and problems. What may be the solution to one problem may cause other problems due to lack of attending to the big picture.

When You Begin at Level 3 . . .

The family business advisory relationship that begins at Level 3 is usually described by those involved as a "great fit" which means there is a strong positive, enthusiastic, and hopeful climate in the relationship. Using the language of RQ, even at a very early stage, there is a significant degree of trust, optimism, and respect which, of course, are the hallmarks of a positive Relationship Paradigm. A positive relationship like this so early in the family business advisory relationship is likely due to the reputation and presentation of the advisor(s)/consultant(s) and the desirability of the client. For instance, a well-known and prestigious family business contacts a prominent and highly respected advisor. Although they have never met, each knows the reputation of the other and because of that knowledge there is initial, and latent, trust, optimism, and respect present in the relationship. Whether the relationship is formed to solve an existing problem or to anticipate and prevent future problems from occurring, it is essential that all those involved begin to direct effort toward improving Relationship Skill almost immediately. Lack of Relationship Skill will sour even the most promising Level 3 RQ family business advisory relationship. Participants in the relationship will struggle only so long with lack of good communication, persistent faulty understanding and confusing expectations, and lack of structure and follow through.

To keep the positive Relationship Paradigm from deteriorating, the group will need to establish a high level of sophistication in their communication tools (not just the transmission of information characteristic of Level 2 but the creation of true understanding); improve their ability to negotiate and renegotiate expectations and commitments; clearly delineate roles, responsibilities, and accountability; and work on the ability to openly discuss differences and disputes, and resolve them. When we describe the level of skill needed as "a high level of sophistication" we specifically mean skill at the level of dealing with the complexity of the overlapping and interfacing dynamics among the three domains of family, business, and ownership. This is a major factor that differentiates the Level 3 from the Level 2 family business advisory relationship. In the latter, the relationship has the Relationship Skill needed for resolving and preventing one-domain problems, but it is probably not adequate for dealing with the true complexity of family business.

PART II The Role of the Family Business Advisor

As we have said, the measure of success for the family business advisory relationship is the solving and prevention of problems. The role of the advisor/consultant in that relationship is to facilitate the changes necessary to achieve this purpose of problem solving and prevention. Regardless of the professional's basic education and training, whether in a technical or process-based profession, the work cannot be done unless the advisor/consultant is able to facilitate a positive change in the client's thinking, actions, or intentions. We covered the basic dynamics of change in chapter 4, including the formula for motivation and Lewin's three stages of change. Now we need to go one step beyond these basics and look at the fact that the family business advisor/consultant is called upon to facilitate two types of change.

FIRST-ORDER AND SECOND-ORDER CHANGE

There are two types of change in human relationships; one changes behavior; the other changes perception.[1] The first type of change is known as First-Order Change and represents a change in behavior or situation, but no comparable change in the perspectives of those involved. First-Order Change can generally be easily observed by others. Changes to the Relationship Skill dimension of RQ are First-Order changes. They are changes in behavior such as learning to listen, implementing methods for resolving conflicts, taking action to clarify expectations, and renewing commitments or creating a plan and sticking to it. First-Order Change, however, does not mean that our beliefs, prejudices, or perspective have necessarily changed at the same time. For example, having a baby requires a change in the behavior of the mother and father, but becoming parents is an inner change affecting how they define who they are. When we had our daughter, our behaviors and schedule changed drastically, but it took a while before it fully "sank in" that we were parents, a new and very profound definition of who we were as people. Graduation from college or graduate school changes your situation; you are no longer a student. It takes an inner redefinition, though, for you to think of yourself as a professional ready for the tremendous responsibilities of a career.

It is rare, as we will discuss later, that changes in behavior alone are sufficient to change our perspective or beliefs. Often a business family learns the techniques of communication and may perform them mechanically, but they still don't trust or respect each other. Or it's clear in a family business that goes through the motions of strategic planning, yet resists the planning facilitator at every turn, that the people involved still believe planning is an exercise in futility because they view themselves as having no alternative other than to react to daily crises. Thus, there is a second type of change, known as Second-Order Change, that alters our beliefs and prejudices, how we perceive and define our situation, how we view ourselves and our relationships. Some people grow into adulthood and still think of themselves as children, as dependent and unable to manage their own lives. Other people, still short of achieving their chronological maturity, think of themselves as adults, independent and quite able to manage most aspects of their lives. Growing up is a combination of aging (First-Order Change) and maturity (Second-Order Change), and one does not necessarily correlate with the other.

It is obvious from some of our examples that both types of change also apply to groups and relationships. The work of the family business advisor is to facilitate change of both types. The leadership role of advisor/consultant within the family business advisory relationship means focusing on teaching the family members skills for new ways of behaving along with helping them change the way they perceive their relationship as a family business. The approach to achieving the former is instructional and intellectual while the approach to achieving the latter is therapeutic and emotional. Facilitation of First-Order Change requires a knowledge of the skill or behavior that is desired and how to implement or practice it. Facilitation of Second-Order Change requires a knowledge of the internal dynamics of emotional and interpersonal process and how to help a group of people migrate from their current destructive, but familiar, relationship into a more positive but totally unknown and unfamiliar relationship. Assisting someone with First-Order Change is like feeding them a meal; they are satisfied. Facilitating Second-Order Change is like teaching them to fish; they are self-sufficient.

The nature of these two types of change is such that there are times when a change of one type provokes a change of the other type. We refer to this as the *spontaneous interactive change effect*. It is spontaneous in that it is unanticipated and unplanned. We mention it because consultants are sometimes perplexed when they are, for example, teaching new relationship skills and find that the group suddenly moves to a new way of defining their relationship. The spontaneous interactive change effect only happens when there is a considerable amount of readiness and motivation on the part of the family business to embrace a new way of interacting with each other, and it is usually a phenomenon that affects individuals more than groups. An example of a First-Order Change invoking a Second-Order Change is when a serious accident or a serious change in health causes the person to completely redefine his priorities and perspective. An example of a Second-Order Change invoking a First-Order Change occurs when an individual, through a process of serious self-evaluation, personal or family counseling, or even religious experience, evolves into a new self-definition and new perspective on her world, and her outward behavior and actions evidence the fact that she is different on the inside.

Helping a family business improve their level of RQ requires change of both types. The complexity and deep history that exist within family businesses make it unlikely that a spontaneous interactive effect will take place; as we said, it is more an individual phenomenon. What is more likely is that efforts to change behavior, for example, new ways of communicating or problem solving, will deteriorate unless there is a commensurate change in the way the group defines its relationships. Similarly, improving how family members perceive and define their relationships, their Relationship Paradigm, does not mean they automatically have the skills to implement it regardless of how much they want to. The ruts of old relationship patterns, from years of operating by the old Relationship Paradigm, get carved deep. Without new tools of Relationship Skill to support the desired new Relationship Paradigm, any family business will be drawn right back into the old ruts.

Since the work of family business advisors/consultants deals with both kinds of change they must be prepared and qualified to facilitate both. If they are not, it is important to stick with their area of professional expertise and bring in another professional who can address the other. Process-oriented consultants, trained in such fields as psychology, family therapy, and organization development, typically focus on Second-Order Change, viewing their role as first to help clients redefine their situation by creating new beliefs, perspectives, and prejudices. The process used is often decidedly therapeutic, beginning with a diagnosis that leads to a plan of intervention that results not just in a reduction in symptoms, but removal of the cause. The intended end result is a healthy and harmonious family business. Extremists from this professional perspective view being directive, instructional, and intellectual as intrusive, short-sighted, and interfering with the client's right to their own process of self-discovery and choice.

Advisory-oriented consultants, trained in such fields as law, accounting, banking, and insurance, typically view their role primarily as that of providing specific advice and counsel, using their expert understanding of the technical body of knowledge in their discipline, to direct and instruct their clients toward the outcome of choice. The process used is typically factual, analytical, prescriptive, and directive. Extremists from this professional perspective view concerns about redefining the relationships as insufferably tedious and dangerously inefficient.

It is important not to see the two approaches, process and advisory, as mutually exclusive but as two ends of a spectrum. Individual professionals will fall somewhere on that continuum depending on their education, professional socialization, experience, and personal preferences. Some will view themselves as equally prepared and qualified to facilitate both types of change while others will think of themselves as more toward one end or the other. Someone fully capable in both arenas will have education, training, experience, and credentials in both; as would be the case, for example, of a licensed attorney who also has a license in psychology. There is a model for this in that many tax and estate lawyers are licensed attorneys as well as certified public accountants.

Most professionals who work with family businesses have added some additional training and experience to their profession of origin. For example, a family business attorney in addition to expert knowledge in preparing estate planning documents (advisory), may also have developed the skills to facilitate discussion and resolution of an ongoing and heated family dispute that is in the way of getting objectives clear and documents signed. Or, a family business psychologist, in addition to expert knowledge in resolving severe interpersonal conflict by working with whole family groups, may also have developed the knowledge to offer information about options for ownership transfer and estate tax minimization during a family business retreat. The important point for the integrity of the family business advisory relationship is that the advisor/consultant is not offering advice or facilitating a process for which he or she is not qualified. With that said, it is also important that professionals working with family businesses continually develop skills in both areas commensurate with their interest, capability, and willingness to invest in doing so.

RQ AND THE TWO TYPES OF CHANGE

The ability of the family business advisors to facilitate both types of change is very important to helping family businesses improve their RQ. You will recall the RQ matrix as four quadrants representing the four levels of Relationship Intelligence.

Positive change in RQ follows a predictable path that parallels the four levels. Growth in Relationship Intelligence moves sequentially from Level 1, through Levels 2 and 3, into Level 4. Depending on which level a family business is currently in, this allows both the advisor/consultant and the family business to determine which level they can progress into next. The change pattern for RQ looks like an inverted Z when superimposed on the RQ matrix, as is seen on the following page.

RELATIONSHIP INTELLIGENCE MATRIX

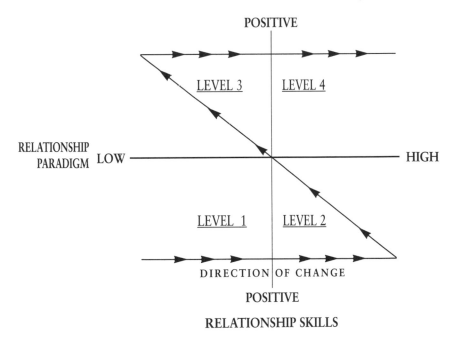

POSITIVE

LEVEL 3
Positive Relationship
Paradigm

Low Relationship Skill

LEVEL 4
Positive Relationship
Paradigm

High Relationship Skill

RELATIONSHIP
PARADIGM   LOW ─────────────────────────── HIGH

LEVEL 1
Negative Relationship
Paradigm

Low Relationship Skill

LEVEL 2
Negative Relationship
Paradigm

High Relationship Skill

NEGATIVE

RELATIONSHIP SKILLS

PATH OF CHANGE IN RQ

POSITIVE

LEVEL 3   LEVEL 4

RELATIONSHIP
PARADIGM   LOW ─────────────────────────── HIGH

LEVEL 1   LEVEL 2

DIRECTION OF CHANGE

POSITIVE

RELATIONSHIP SKILLS

With very few exceptions, it is not possible to move from Level 1 to Level 3 or from Level 2 to Level 4. The reason for this is the interactive effect between Relationship Skill and Relationship Paradigm. Recall the formula for motivation that we described in chapter 4: Vp x ESp = M, or perceived Value times perceived Expectancy of Success equals Motivation. We value something to the extent that it is important and desired. We expect success in achieving it to the extent that we have confidence in being able to accomplish the thing that is important and desired. Motivation will be high only if the end to be achieved is important and valuable, and there is confidence among those involved that they can successfully reach the end.

Unless there is a major crisis or other Relationship Paradigm altering event, those in a Level 1 family business relationship will not only be unable to see the value of working on a new Relationship Paradigm; they will not believe in the possibility of achieving it. As they learn new tools of Relationship Skill, they gain increased expectancy of success which, in turn, increases the motivation to move ahead and ultimately, when they move into Level 2 RQ, to work on improving their Relationship Paradigm as well. It is working to improve Relationship Skill that makes it possible to move from Level 1 to Level 2 RQ. Our first step with business-owning families who are beginning at a Level 1 RQ and have the motivation to move into Level 2, is to work with them in developing Relationship Skill. This starts with active listening and a process of renegotiating expectations. The success in Relationship Skill can help the family business group to experience success and hopefully to be more motivated and to feel more positive about each other. The family business able to experience new understanding and appreciation of each other's perspective through better communication, or have new success in being able to resolve conflicts and manage issues, will have glimpsed above the negative paradigm "box" in which they have put their relationship and see that there are alternatives. This creates the energy and motivation to commit to the hard work of redefining and restructuring the attitudes, beliefs, and prejudices, that is, in moving from Level 2 to Level 3 by developing a more positive Relationship Paradigm.

Did you notice on the Relationship Intelligence matrix an apparent regression in relationship skill as a family business relationship moves from a Level 2 RQ to a Level 3 RQ? The explanation for this seeming paradox is fairly simple. At Level 2 RQ, the tools of Relationship Skill that have been developed are within the context of a negative Relationship Paradigm. As the family business group builds a more positive Relationship Paradigm the demands on their Relationship Skill tools increase greatly. We are not saying that they lose the Relationship Skill acquired at Level 2, but, those skills are not adequate to sustain an increasingly positive Relationship Paradigm and the increased expectations and possibilities this creates. It would be very difficult or impossible, for example, for a Level 2 RQ family business group to fully establish the process of relationship renewal as defined in LSi's Relationship Roadmap, or to fully implement the issue management process described in chapter 4. Likewise, such a family business would encounter many barriers to developing the structures for each of the domains as described in chapter 6. This is because the negative Relationship Paradigm in Level 2 RQ will undermine these efforts while the rapidly improving positive Relationship Paradigm of a Level 3 RQ will make people expect, want, and need these things. As Level 3 develops through the work done in redefining the relationship and developing a positive Relationship Paradigm these latter tools of Relationship Skill (see chapter 4) and the relationship structures (see chapter 6) must be developed. In this sense the increased level of Relationship Skill needed to support the improvements in Relationship Paradigm at Level 3 RQ, results in the apparent lowering of Relationship Skill.

This process might be more easily grasped by understanding change from a different context. A middle-class family will typically have a different paradigm about money than a wealthy family. The middle-class family may be used to spending just about all of their income on expenses, with perhaps a little left over for fun and relaxation. For them, money may be something they don't have enough of. The wealthy family, being used to plenty of expendable income, has developed the knowledge and skill of planning and saving. For them money is something they have plenty of. The level of income of each family in some respect affects how they perceive the world, themselves, and what opportunities are available to them. What happens when our middle-class family wins the lottery or receives a large inheritance? They may experience a dramatic shift in how they view themselves and their situation. Their lifestyle changes drastically but unless they learn new skills for managing money and for being wealthy, they may soon lose it all. Many horror stories are told of promising athletes who at a very young age go from virtual poverty to great wealth only to lose it to gambling, drugs, and unrestrained spending. The point is the same: old skills of coping and managing life are no longer adequate when we achieve a dramatically more positive view of life. New skills are demanded and must be established to prevent regression back to where we started.

Without continued improvement to the higher and more resilient tools and structures of relationship skill there is danger, even likelihood, that the family business's old Relationship Paradigm will creep back in over time. Frustration and antagonism generated by the inability to interact and function at the level of sophistication needed will dissipate the trust, optimism, and respect the family members have worked so hard to build. Hopefully, though, Relationship Skill will grow as required and the family business will move to a Level 4 RQ where the positive Relationship Paradigm is perfected and sustained by a high level of Relationship Skill.

During the transition of the family business from a Level 2 RQ to a Level 3 RQ, the task of the family business advisory relationship is critical and can be tricky. If the emphasis continues on skill development without blending in, when the family is ready, the crucial work of improving Relationship Paradigm, the window of opportunity to do so may be lost. The glimpse of hope, the anticipation of a new perspective, the perceived value of moving ahead, can be lost when the pace of skill development slows and stops because it cannot proceed further without improvement in Relationship Paradigm. On the other hand, premature work on improving Relationship Paradigm without some of the basic tools in place to provide the mechanisms needed for improving it will keep the family stuck in an endless cycle of processing why and how their relationships are so awful. Their attempts to move to a new and more positive perspective on their relationship becomes mired down because they do not have the knowledge and tools needed to implement it.

The timing of intervention strategy happens best when the family business advisory relationship has a well-developed plan of implementation. Such planning is one of the tools of Relationship Skill that is inherent in a high RQ family business advisory relationship. This tool, along with the other tools discussed, is fundamental in the work between advisors/consultants and family businesses. They are not simply tools that advisors/consultants teach family businesses to use. The successful family business advisory relationship is a rich blend of professional expertise along with openness from the family business, but it only works when RQ provides the catalyst to unleash the potential that exists in the ingredients.

RQ AND INTERPROFESSIONAL COLLABORATION

The other area of professional practice for which Relationship Intelligence has importance is interprofessional collaboration. As we said at the beginning of this chapter, collaboration among a variety of types of professionals representing different areas of expertise is essential to serving the overall needs of family businesses. It is also a fact that each profession brings its own professional culture, as we will discuss later, and bridging those cultural differences is an immense challenge. Establishing a collegial professional relationship with a high level of RQ means dealing with Relationship Paradigm and Relationship Skill in a specialized context. Having a high level of RQ in a professional relationship among a group from the same professional discipline, while no piece of cake, is easier than it is with a multiprofessional group. When the participants all share the same professional language and culture, it can be easier to resolve issues related to trust, optimism, and respect. Attempts at interprofessional collaboration plagued by a low level of RQ will be frustrating, threatening, and discouraging.

DEFINING COLLABORATION

What is successful interdisciplinary collaboration when it comes to working with family businesses? The model typically portrayed is that in which one of the professionals involved serves to coordinate the consulting process. As needs are identified that are outside that individual advisor's/consultant's expertise, additional professionals are brought in to address them. The attorney will bring in the psychologist or organizational development consultant to deal with the interpersonal and management relationship issues. The accountant will bring in the attorney to draft the legal documents. The insurance professional will bring in the accountant or attorney to formalize the buy-sell agreement. The psychologist or organization development consultant will bring in the financial planning professional to establish the owner's retirement financial requirements. This type of interprofessional collaboration is the most simple and basic kind used to respond to the multiplicity of family business needs and the one most frequently practiced.

Unfortunately, in spite of how important it is, very little research and study has been done on the subject of interprofessional collaboration in work with family businesses. However, there are some relevant and interesting things to be learned from work that has been done on strategic alliances. In many ways, interprofessional collaboration can be viewed as a form of strategic alliance.

Interestingly, strategic alliances and interprofessional collaborative relationships in serving family businesses are motivated by very similar factors. The ones generally identified include delivering value-added services, gaining competitive advantage, and addressing a more complex market. Further, it is important to note that studies of alliances show that those between two weak partners, between competitors, and between a weak and a strong partner never succeed long term. Alliances between two strong partners who become increasingly competitive over time succeed in their initial objectives but often end up with the sale of one partner to the other. The only type of alliance that seems to work, long term, is one between two strong and complementary equals.

These findings about strategic alliances are illuminating in discussing interprofessional collaboration for several reasons, all of which are directly related to the principles of Relationship Intelligence. Let us paint a picture as to why the principles and practices of RQ are so essential to interprofessional collaboration. For one thing, the differentiation of services among the professional disciplines that serve family businesses has become confusing and ill-defined. Legal firms are doing family counseling, mediation, and tax planning. Accounting firms are doing general business consulting, personnel consulting, business valuations, and family business consulting. Banks are selling insurance and offering investment advisory services. Insurance companies are doing business, financial, retirement, and tax planning. Financial planners and business consultants are selling insurance. Such a situation creates an environment ripe for the development of severe problems in the relationships among and between the professional advisors. Why is this so?

When professional boundaries become unclear and historically protected professional territories are transgressed, the Relationship Paradigm operative in the collaborative relationship is strongly tilted toward mistrust, pessimism, and disrespect. The possibility of creating a relationship between two strong and complementary equals, which the studies say is the only successful kind, is very difficult. When similar conditions related to confusion over boundaries, roles, and functions, as are found in today's professional relationships, exist in any relationship, whether marriage, family, friendship, business, or social, they are destructive. In younger families when parents behave like children and children take on the roles of parents, in business when roles and responsibilities are unclear and confusing, and in friendships when one person's success is viewed as a threat to the other, problems are brewing. The same is true for professionals and their work together. The stronger and deeper we try to build the collaborative relationship, the more important boundaries, role, and function become.

Along with the confusion over professional boundaries is the fact, mentioned earlier in this chapter, that every family business professional comes from a profession of origin, each with its own unique and deeply imbedded norms, practices, and values. Professional training provides not only the "tools of the trade" but a "professional society" that prescribes how members are to view the world, understand it, and be successful in it. We come from such different professional cultures, because of professional socialization, that we have very different customs that dictate how we conduct relationships between ourselves and our clients. For some, the individual is the client (e.g., the business owner), while for others it is the group, (e.g., the family in the family business). Some professions focus more on rationality and logic while others see the really important stuff in feelings and intuition. These differences in professional culture create huge barriers that get in the way of collaboration as they fuel the incongruence between professional practices that relate to everything from professional ethics to billing practices.

Along with the blurring of professional boundaries and our different professional cultures making collaboration difficult, we must add the differences in the language that professionals use. The uninitiated among us (whether lawyers, accountants, psychologists, or business management consultants) don't even understand what the others are talking about when it comes to talking about family business issues. Family psychologists talk about the circumplex model and repetitive nonproductive sequences in family systems; lawyers talk about GRITS and GRATS and NIMCRUTS; and accountants use codes that refer to multiple pages in the tax law like 2036c and 2073, not to be confused with 2703. Learning a foreign language is easy compared to this! There are many barriers to overcome and this is precisely why RQ is so essential to making interprofessional collaboration work; it is, after all, just one more example of a situation in which the quality and durability of the relationship makes or breaks success. The truth is that success in interprofessional collaboration requires the bridging of cultural barriers, and all that goes along with that, more than it does simply learning how to imitate each other's knowledge and skills. The dilemmas of interprofessional collaboration are, first and foremost, a cultural and not an educational problem.

Turning once more to insights from studies of strategic alliances, Rosabeth Moss Kantor, writing about what makes strategic alliances work, approaches the subject from the relationship perspective. In fact, she compares business alliances to marriage and has a list of criteria she considers essential to success. She calls them the "Eight I's That Create Successful We's" and they parallel the principles of RQ that we have described.[2]

- **INDIVIDUAL EXCELLENCE:** Both partners are strong, have something of value to contribute, and have positive progressive motives.
- **IMPORTANCE:** The partnership fits major long-term strategic objectives of the partners that make them want to work at it.
- **INTERDEPENDENCE:** The partners need each other because of complementary skills and assets, they cannot accomplish separately what they can do together.
- **INVESTMENT:** The partners invest in each other to demonstrate their stakes in the partnership by putting financial and other resources into the relationship.
- **INFORMATION:** Open communication is fostered with information necessary to the relationship shared on a regular basis, including their objectives and goals, technical information, and concerns over problem areas or changing situations.
- **INTEGRATION:** The partners develop linkages and shared ways of doing things to make the collaboration go smoothly, they are both teachers and learners.
- **INSTITUTIONALIZATION:** The partnership is given formal status with clear responsibilities and decision processes.
- **INTEGRITY:** The partners relate to each other in ways that engender trust, mutual respect, and appreciation among them.

Not only are these central to the formation of a strategic alliance, they are also critical elements to the development of a truly interdisciplinary collaborative relationship. Successful interprofessional collaboration takes long-term repeated interaction between the same people. Unless trust, optimism, and respect have the time to develop, the relationship will not succeed long term and none of these will develop without a singular focused commitment to the relationship. A collaborative relationship is a two-way street: to get something you have to give something.

THE CONTINUUM OF COLLABORATION

In an effort to clarify our thinking about interprofessional collaboration, we created the chart on the following page, the Continuum of Collaboration in Professional Services. There are several important assumptions that went into the creation of the chart.

1. First and foremost there is not one form, but multiple forms of interprofessional collaboration.
2. The continuum from left to right involves an increasing depth and intensity in the collaborative relationship with greater demands on those involved.
3. There are pros and cons for both professionals and their clients in each type of collaborative relationship identified.
4. Different types of collaboration are more or less important to family businesses with different concerns.
5. As the level of collaboration increases, the probability of it occurring decreases.

SIX STYLES OF INTERPROFESSIONAL COLLABORATION

Moving from left to right on the continuum six styles of interprofessional collaboration are identified. Each style involves a progressively greater intensity of collaboration between the professionals, greater complexity of client needs and requires increasingly greater effort to implement. All six styles should be differentiated from professional alliances that are formed simply for the purpose of marketing and business development. While these are a legitimate and valuable type of professional relationship they do not represent a true form of interprofessional collaboration as we think of it. The distinction is easy to make: marketing alliances are designed to serve the needs of the professionals, while collaborative professional relationships, as we are describing them, are designed to serve the needs of the family business client.

Typical:

SIMPLE REFERRAL—A client need is identified that is outside the scope of the delivering professional's ability, and the client is referred to the appropriate professional resource.

CONTINUUM OF COLLABORATION IN PROFESSIONAL SERVICES

TYPICAL		OCCASIONAL		RARE	
Simple Referral	Cross-disciplinary Consultation	Referral and Coordination	Cross-disciplinary Collaboration	Multidisciplinary Collaboration	Interdisciplinary Collaboration
PROS	**CONS**	**PROS**	**CONS**	**PROS**	**CONS**
Easy to manage	Highly vulnerable to interface issues between the domains	Attention is given to coordination of professional services	Significant vulnerability to interface issues between the domains	High level of coordination of professional services	Requires considerable time and effort to manage
Connects professional expertise to specific family business needs	Little, if any, coordination of professional services	Greater likelihood that underlying issues will be identified	Differences between professional cultures become more of an issue	Fully addresses interface issues between the domains	May be more costly
Provides maximum freedom for family business and professional	Underlying issues can go unidentified by primary professional	Fosters collegiality and learning among professionals	Requires time and effort to manage	Underlying issues easily identified	Differences between professional cultures have to be resolved

TYPE OF CLIENTS SERVED

SINGLE FOCUS	SEQUENTIAL FOCUS	MULTIPLE IMMEDIATE FOCUS

INCREASING INTENSITY OF COLLABORATION
DECREASING LIKELIHOOD OF OCCURRING →

CROSS-DISCIPLINARY CONSULTATION—The delivering professional identifies a client need, or a barrier to continued work with the client, and consults with another appropriate professional as to methods for addressing the need or removing the barrier. This is sometimes combined with Simple Referral or is followed by Referral and Coordination.

- **Pros:** Collaboration in these styles of professional relationships is easy to manage given the fact that there is no coordination between the professionals other than arranging the referral or the consultation meeting or phone call. For family business issues that are single focused on a specific matter or within a single domain, these forms of collaboration function well to connect specific professional expertise to the need of the family business. In addition, there is maximum flexibility for both the family business and the advisor/consultant in the selection and extent of involvement with the other professional(s).
- **Cons:** There is virtually no coordination of the various professional services. With Simple Referral it is up to the family business to figure out how to fit various pieces of advice together. With Cross-disciplinary Consultation all of the information flows through the primary advisor/consultant, which means it can be distorted or modified by that person's own biases and prejudices. Perhaps the most significant downside to these styles of collaboration is that they have significant exposure to being drawn into and subverted by the needs and interests of the other domains. What may appear to be a single-focus issue rarely is in family business. As we have said, many advisors/consultants enter the family business in one domain only to find themselves pulled into all three. Along with this is the possibility that an important issue residing in one of the other domains and perhaps having significant influence on the issue at hand may go undetected by the primary professional involved.

Occasional:

REFERRAL AND COORDINATION—A client need is identified that is outside the scope of the delivering professional's ability, the client is referred to the appropriate professional resource, and the two professionals informally coordinate their work with the client.

CROSS-DISCIPLINARY COLLABORATION—A client need, or barrier to continued work, is identified that is outside the scope of the delivering professional's ability and (an) appropriate collaborative professional(s) (is) are brought in, on an "as needed" basis, to work directly with the delivering professional and the client to address the need or barrier. This comes close to what is often referred to as a joint venture.

- **Pros:** As we move up the continuum into the middle area with its two styles of collaboration, it is obvious that more attention is being given to the coordination of professional services. Even though the coordination is informal or more ad hoc in nature, there is much greater focus on tying the various aspects of the advice or consultation together. Because of this there is also greater likelihood that underlying issues from multiple domains that may be affecting the problem(s) at hand are being observed and identified because of the direct involvement of more than one professional discipline. Even though it could be considered more a benefit for the professionals involved, the fact that these styles of collaboration promote collegiality and learning among them is actually a genuine benefit for the family business as well. These styles of collaboration work well when the problems identified by the family business can be resolved in a sequential manner. For example, the first problem that needs to be resolved is family conflict, which can then be followed by getting the shareholders' agreement executed, allowing the company to move forward with the long-range planning it has needed to do for some time. It works less well when issues all require attention simultaneously; for example, neither strategic planning nor the shareholders' agreement can wait on the other to get done.
- **Cons:** There is still a significant degree of possibility that the work of the primary professional will be disrupted because of interface issues between the domains. The amount of coordination and ongoing attention between the professionals to the big picture within the family business is very minimal. Along with this is the fact that the professionals involved have most likely not resolved how to deal with the different professional cultures and approaches from which they come. Because there is a greater intensity of contact among them, these differences can become increasingly divisive or confusing. Dealing with these issues, along with the greater depth of collaboration, requires

more time and effort on the part of the professionals involved which, though it has certain benefits as mentioned above, takes away from other important activities.

Rare:

MULTIDISCIPLINARY COLLABORATION—Professionals from complementary professions work together on a regular and ongoing basis, identifying themselves as a team providing a collaborative service approach, with clear distinctions between professionals in terms of expertise and areas addressed. This comes close to what is often thought of as a strategic alliance. From the perspective of professional culture these relationships can be thought of as multilingual, meaning the various advisors and consultants involved can speak each other's professional language, as discussed above.

INTERDISCIPLINARY COLLABORATION—This level of intensity has probably not been achieved yet; at least we haven't heard of it. In it, professionals from different professional orientations have developed a common thought process regarding service to family business clients through their ongoing accommodation to each other's approach. The "delivering professional" is the team, and individual's variations in serving clients have to do with specific technical skills, professional licensing, personal preference, or a decision by the team. This comes close to what is often thought of as a merger, and there is likely some form of formal organization and collective charging of fees.

- **Pros:** At the most intensive level of collaboration there is a high degree of coordination among the professional services involved. In most situations the team of professionals become involved with the family business from the outset ensuring that the needs and issues from all of the three domains are being scrutinized and identified. For this reason these approaches can identify and address, in a coordinated fashion, the interface issues growing out of problems that exist within each of the three domains. The team easily and confidently works on the interface issues that arise out of the overlaps between the domains and it is unlikely that there will be an underlying and unidentified problem in one of the domains.
- **Cons:** Either of these styles of professional coordination requires a tremendous amount of time and effort to manage. The fact

is that another level of relationship system, the advisory/ consultation relationship has been added to those of the family business itself and the family business advisory relationship. This means that the differences in professional culture and approach have to be addressed and resolved, which is a huge challenge. In a real sense both styles can be compared to learning a foreign language. In the first, Multidisciplinary Collaboration, while you can speak and understand in the foreign language, you still translate everything into your native tongue. In the latter, Interdisciplinary Collaboration, you actually think in the two languages at once with no internal translation necessary. This requires a huge commitment that few, if any, have chosen to make at this point.

SORTING IT OUT FOR YOURSELF

The continuum of collaboration should not imply that the right hand of the continuum is better or more ideal than the left hand. Every professional who works with family businesses needs to decide what style of collaboration best fits him or her, recognizing the pros and cons of each. Advisors and consultants vary in their desire and interest in collaborating with other professionals. Family businesses with relatively simple concerns can likely be handled by a Simple Referral or Cross-disciplinary Consultation approach. In more complicated situations requiring the direct and sequential, or simultaneous, involvement of several professionals, the best collaborative approaches would be further to the right on the continuum, referral and coordination or cross-disciplinary. Sequential situations are characterized by family businesses in which there is a current major and unavoidable issue that affects either the family, business, or ownership. Not that there aren't other significant issues that must be resolved at some point, but they can be delayed and dealt with as next steps. You might, for example, encounter a situation in which family members are in conflict and there is no succession plan, but the business is struggling just to stay open. Until the deteriorating business condition is fixed, no one has the energy to tackle the other issues and, in fact, if the business closes the other issues will be largely academic.

When there are multiple and immediate issues the best approach will be either Multidisciplinary or Interdisciplinary Collaboration. These are best by far in situations where problems affecting family, business, and ownership (or all of them together) cannot be delayed. Such a situation could be encountered in which severe family conflict leads to the likelihood that two key family executives will leave the company, which is itself struggling financially and operationally from the years of family conflict. A way needs to be found to rejoin these family executives lest the business situation deteriorate even further, while at the same time, developing a strategy to regenerate the business now and get the company back on its feet. Neither problem area can wait for the other to be solved.

As a professional relationship moves toward the right side of the Continuum of Collaboration in Professional Services, the importance of RQ becomes more and more pronounced. The greater the intensity and depth of the collaborative relationship the greater the effect of Relationship Paradigm and Relationship Skill. A positive Relationship Paradigm depends on how the relationship issues of trust, optimism, and respect are addressed. Relationship Skill, grounded in the tools of good communication, management of differences and conflict, planning and implementation, is strengthened by clarity of roles, responsibilities, expectations and functions, and provides the operational structures needed.

Last, or perhaps more accurately first, you need to decide what style(s) of collaborative relationship(s) meet your clients' needs and your professional practice needs, and fits with your personal needs and aspirations. You can do several specific things to help decide what style of collaborative relationship suits a situation best. At the same time each step will help you in the development of the highest level of RQ possible as you go about forming and developing your choice. There are two phases to the process of deciding what you should do about interprofessional collaboration.

PHASE ONE—SORTING IT OUT

Here is where you begin the homework you need to do to figure out where you want to go.

- **Define the vision for your practice.** Just as we recommend that family businesses develop a picture of where they want to be five years from now, we recommend the same thing for you. What do you hope your professional practice will look like in five years, and what role will interprofessional collaboration play in it? What kinds of clients will you be serving, from what locations, with what revenue expectations? What competitive position do you want to have in your marketplace?

- **Define the scope of services you provide now and will provide in the future.** What range of services do you need, and want, to provide in order to achieve your five-year vision and beyond? Will your services be an extension of what you are doing now or will they be diverse? How much integration and collaboration with other professionals will be required to get your services to market?
- **Define the type of client(s) served now and in the future.** Do you currently seek and serve clients with a broad or narrow set of needs? Will that be the same or different in the future? What opportunities and obstacles will you encounter in the future when it comes to interprofessional collaboration and serving your clients?

PHASE TWO—MAKING IT WORK

Once the homework is done, you should have clarity about your preferences, needs, and motivation related to interprofessional collaboration. Now it's time to sit down and talk to your professional colleagues to exchange information and clarify expectations, as we described in chapter 4 when discussing LSi's Relationship Roadmap.

- **Openly discuss with the others in your potential or existing collaborative relationship both your and their expectations, intentions, and desires.** Through this process you must all be able to answer the age-old question, "What's in it for me?" In all forms of collaboration, and especially in the more intensive types, you also have to answer the question, "Do I like these people, do we share common enough perspectives and values, and do I believe we can resolve issues of trust, optimism, and respect?"
- **Make the investment.** A high RQ collaborative relationship between professionals never happens without considerable effort, commitment, and investment. In the more intensive styles of collaboration, one of the main issues that has to be resolved is the extent to which the members of the group are willing to contribute money, time, and proprietary information in building the relationship. If this is not dealt with it can, and will, undermine the trust, optimism, and respect essential to an ongoing positive Relationship Paradigm even in simple referral collaboration.
- **Institutionalize the relationship.** When you and others arrive at a commitment to proceed, it is important to establish the structures to support the relationship. This is a key component

in the Relationship Skill dimension of RQ in any collaborative relationship. You will need, for example, tools for resolving differences and conflicts, planning and accountability, reporting and coordination, and managing operational activities such as fees, files, and staff. The type of structures required will obviously be quite different at each end of the Continuum of Collaboration, but no matter how simple or complicated, they must be developed.

POSTSCRIPT: THE REBIRTH OF FAMILY BUSINESS!

Working with family businesses as a professional advisor or consultant is exciting and rewarding. At the same time it is usually an adventure that takes you places you've never been before, some of which you never want to revisit. Interest of professionals in working with family businesses has not always been as intense as it is today. As recently as ten or fifteen years ago family businesses did not think of themselves as having unique needs and conditions that took them beyond other types of businesses. Family businesses did not self-identify as family businesses, referring to themselves instead by their industry type, then by their location and size and only as an afterthought by their type of ownership, that is, "family owned." Not long ago if an aspiring member of a business-owning family was enrolled in an MBA program at one of the prestigious Eastern universities he or she would be so self-conscious and embarrassed about being from a family business that the fact would be hidden. For many years in business circles the term "family business" implied small, ingrown, backward, and loaded with family turmoil—not a real positive image.

This, too, was frequently the image-by-association of professionals who worked with family businesses. The accountant was considered the Patriarch's green eyeshade confidant who's biggest job was to keep the mouth shut about where the money was and went. The attorney who worked with family businesses was often viewed by colleagues as not able to succeed in the really high-profile and lucrative branches of law and so retreated to the safety of general counsel to the family business. Advisors and consultants from other fields such as management, organizational development, banking, operations, and human resources who worked with family businesses likewise often felt second fiddle to their colleagues who touted their big-firm experience. It was not uncommon to get an incredulous chuckle when describing a family business client to a consulting colleague from a big firm who would say, "I don't know how you can stand working with such narrow and difficult clients!"

What a difference a decade makes! Today, there are educational programs specifically for family businesses at these same prestigious universities, and Big Five consulting firms have their own family business consulting divisions. Not only have family businesses become aware of just how vital they are to the economies of every nonsocialist nation in the world, they now readily and proudly identify themselves as family businesses in their slogans and advertising campaigns. Along with recognizing that they do have a unique and special blend of needs, they now expect the professionals who serve them to understand and handle that blend. It is our bias that doing so requires more than merely repackaging standard services that are provided to any and all businesses and calling them "Family Business Accounting," "family business management" "family business legal specialists," "family business banking." The enlightened family business purchaser of professional services expects and deserves more.

Up to this time professional services to family businesses have, by and large, been built on the framework of the individual professions in which we advisors and consultants were originally trained. Now referred to as the "profession of origin," family business advisors and consultants come largely from one of four basic professional disciplines: law, financial services, the behavioral sciences, and the management sciences. Practitioners from the first two, law and finance, often referred to as the "technical" or "hard" disciplines, augment their traditional advisory consulting with group process and family systems knowledge and skills borrowed from the behavioral and management disciplines. Similarly, practitioners from the behavioral (psychology, family therapy, organizational development, and psychiatry) and management (management practice and organizational change) disciplines augment their process consulting with technical knowledge and skills borrowed from the advisory disciplines. Thus, lawyers and accountants learn how to teach communication skills and run family meetings. Psychologists, family therapists, organizational development consultants, and management specialists learn the language of the tax code, estate planning, and family limited partnerships.

No matter what discipline you have been trained in, advising and consulting with family businesses requires knowledge about and understanding of relationship dynamics, including how they evolve and change. Like it or not, when you deal with a family business, your client is a relationship even when it doesn't appear that way, or you don't intend it to happen, or your professional ethics prohibit it. This reality is especially difficult for advisors traditionally trained in the legal and financial services fields. Interestingly, professionals from the technical disciplines who invite and enjoy the relationship aspect of their work with clients are the ones most drawn to working with family businesses. We find that our seminars with CPAs, attorneys, and insurance professionals are filled with people eager and excited to develop a deeper understanding of how to work with client relationships. As one attorney put it, "This is the magic that makes the mundane more enjoyable." An insurance professional commented to us several years after attending one of our seminars, "Understanding what goes on in the relationships in family business makes it possible for me now to see behind the curtain. It was all there before, I just didn't know it."

Even more important than the fact that understanding family business relationships makes work more enjoyable and meaningful for the professional, is that it is an essential component of success or failure. The dynamics of family business (meaning the constant interactions that take place among the three domains) are an awesome and powerful force. Entering the family business to provide advice and counsel means having to engage with that force at one time or another. When the dynamics of the family business are positive and constructive, that force can be a great resource to you in your work. On the other hand, when the dynamics are negative and destructive, that force can make it impossible for even the most skilled advisor to be effective.

The fact is that you are an agent of change regardless of your profession of origin. The ultimate value of any advisor's or consultant's work is the extent to which it results in a positive change in the client's situation. Nothing is more unsatisfying professionally than to give your best effort only to have it stonewalled or dismissed. Even more important, as a trusted advisor/consultant to family businesses, you are the steward not only of your professional expertise but of relationships entrusted to you because they are troubled, broken, and confused. This means you are a steward of RQ, primarily within your family business advisory relationship but through it in the teaching and coaching of your family business clients about the true meaning of stewardship in their relationships as well. Yes, working with family businesses is exciting and rewarding; it's also a calling that requires and deserves the very best we can give.

Notes
1. P. Watzlawick, J. Weakland, and R. Fisch. *Change: Principles of Problem Formation and Problem Resolution.* New York: W.W. Norton, 1974.
2. Rosabeth Moss Kantor. "Collaborative Advantage: The Art of Alliances" *Harvard Business Review*, July/August 1994.

Index